A History of Anthropological Thought

With all good wishes
for 1982

Edmund

Also by Sir Edward Evans-Pritchard

WITCHCRAFT, ORACLES AND MAGIC AMONG THE AZANDE
(*Clarendon Press, Oxford, 1937*)

THE POLITICAL SYSTEM OF THE ANUAK OF THE ANGLO-EGYPTIAN SUDAN
(*Percy Lund, Humphries & Co, for the L.S.E., 1940*)

(co-editor with M. Fortes) AFRICAN POLITICAL SYSTEMS
(*Oxford University Press for International Africa Institute, 1940*)

THE NUER
(*Clarendon Press, Oxford, 1940*)

THE SANUSI OF CYRENAICA
(*Clarendon Press, Oxford, 1949*)

SOCIAL ANTHROPOLOGY
(*Cohen and West, London, 1951*)

KINSHIP AND MARRIAGE AMONG THE NUER
(*Clarendon Press, Oxford, 1951*)

ESSAYS IN SOCIAL ANTHROPOLOGY
(*Faber and Faber, London, 1962*)

THEORIES OF PRIMITIVE RELIGION
(*Clarendon Press, Oxford, 1965*)

THE POSITION OF WOMEN IN PRIMITIVE SOCIETIES
AND OTHER ESSAYS IN SOCIAL ANTHROPOLOGY
(*Faber and Faber, London, 1965*)

THE AZANDE TRICKSTER
(*Clarendon Press, Oxford, 1967*)

THE AZANDE: HISTORY AND POLITICAL INSTITUTIONS
(*Clarendon Press, Oxford, 1971*)

MAN AND WOMAN AMONG THE AZANDE
(*Faber and Faber, London, 1974*)

A History of
Anthropological Thought

SIR EDWARD EVANS-PRITCHARD

edited by André Singer

with an introduction by Ernest Gellner

FABER AND FABER
LONDON : BOSTON

First published in 1981
by Faber and Faber Limited
3 Queen Square London WC1N 3AU
Printed in The United States of America by
Hadden Craftsmen, Inc.

Evans-Pritchard, Sir Edward
A history of anthropological thought.
1.   Anthropology-History
I.   Title
301   GN17
ISBN 0–571–11712–0

Contents

Preface

Professor Sir Edward Evans-Pritchard was writing *A History of An-thropological Thought* when he died in September 1973. He was bas-ing much of the work on a series of lectures given over twenty years to students at the Institute of Social Anthropology at Oxford. These lectures were being revised and updated to form a collection of essays about those thinkers whose influence he felt had played the greatest role in the moulding of British social anthropology as it was when he took over the chair at Oxford in 1952. The first five essays were originally published in the *Journal of the Anthropological Society of Oxford,* a policy he intended to continue with each essay before publishing them together as a collection. He was anxious that this work survive him, and it was his request that, in the event of his death, I complete it for publication.

There can be few prospects more daunting than taking over the work of a great scholar. In editing the rest of the essays I have had to take material from many sources, but all of it was written by himself. Despite the considerable volume of his publications, it is surprising how little of his available work is devoted to the promi-nent figures of the social sciences. He held very definite and well-considered views about the development of social anthropology, some of which have been published in one form or another else-where. I have also drawn on his unpublished notes and lectures. The collection is therefore not as he would have presented it. Al-though the writings were already in existence, the selection and presentation are mine and must differ from the form they would have taken under Evans-Pritchard's hand. Regrettably many of his thoughts on important figures were never committed to paper, and their omission from this book produces an imbalance which he would have rectified. I suspect, for example, that he would have omitted some of the essays I have presented here, and I am certain he would have included essays on the remaining members of the *Année Sociologique* group as well as on Fustel de Coulanges and Spencer. Some anthropologists, whom I feel sure he considered important and would have included in his final version, but on whom he left insufficient material for full chapters, I have inserted in an appendix entitled "Notes and Comments." Others, such as Morgan, Lowie, or Marx have been omitted altogether rather than be represented by sketchy and misleading paragraphs.

But for some of the anthropologists there was too much material. In *Theories of Primitive Religion*, Evans-Pritchard gives considerable coverage to Durkheim's ideas on sociological theories of religion as expounded in *Les formes élémentaires de la vie religieuse*, but he also had far more detailed and revised material amongst his notes including the draft of a paper that he had given informally at a seminar held by Steven Lukes at Balliol College, Oxford. The chapter in this book on Durkheim (chapter 14) is based largely on that paper, with an introduction taken from his notes. I am sure it would have been revised had Evans-Pritchard had access to Lukes's own definitive work on Durkheim (*Emile Durkheim*, 1973), but nonetheless it remains Evans-Pritchard's last unpublished serious essay and goes considerably further in its ethnological criticism than anything he wrote earlier. In it, he criticizes Durkheim severely for his work on religion, despite his own great admiration for the more general contribution that Durkheim and his followers made toward the development of social anthropology in this country. Indeed, in his easy on Robert Hertz (chapter 15), Evans-Pritchard appears to contradict this indictment of Durkheim by writing, "I am convinced that no field study of totemism has excelled Durkheim's analysis." But Evans-Pritchard wrote this at least twenty-five years previously, and perhaps his later analysis of Durkheim reflects a more critical retrospective look at the discipline as a whole.

In all his writings, and especially in his notes, Evans-Pritchard was frequently critical and often caustic. I have included many such comments since they give a truer picture of the way in which he saw his predecessors. His remarks also provide obvious clues to the way he formulated his own anthropological ideology, although he might upon reflection have presented them in a less trenchant form had he completed this manuscript. While, for example, he was able to write of Max Müller that he was "a linguist of quite exceptional ability, one of the leading Sanskritists of his time, and in general a man of great erudition; and he has been unjustly de-cried," he also noted that Müller was "so verbose and so imprecise that it is often difficult to know what he is driving at, even what his sentences mean. He was a sententious deist of the worst possible Victorian-cum-Lutheran sort." About Pareto he was even more damning. He wrote that "Pareto's theories are pretentious. Behind a great show of impartiality and scientific method we discover pla-giarist, populizer, polemicist and metaphysician. His writings are always witty and his criticisms of philosophers are often sound, though seldom original. It cannot be said that he has contributed much to sociology. Indeed he seems to have been little acquainted with its aims and methods. However, let it be said in Pareto's fa-vour that his treatise is so bad that it exposes, and thereby enables us to see more clearly, fallacies hidden with greater skill by other metaphysicians masquerading as scientists."

But Evans-Pritchard could also be generous and complimen-tary, in particular when writing about the *Année Sociologique* group, whom he admits were the most influential in the formation of his own thinking; or about a less influential scholar but a personal friend, Franz Steiner. Overall, however, he did not plan to produce a book about personalities, but about ideas. In his original course of lectures at Oxford, the foundation for this book, he stated the following: "For at least 250 years people have been asserting that social phenomena can and should be studied as natural phenom-ena, using the same methods as those which had proved so suc-cessful in the physical and organic sciences, though of course with different techniques. Laws would then be established which would have the generality of those of the laboratory sciences. Such laws would have to be significant as well as valid. There could then be an applied science of man. The attempts were first made in the form of qualitative generalizations, then of quantitative ones, mostly, explicitly, or implicitly, on a universal scale. To attain the ends sought only one method could be employed, the comparative method. It had not yielded the results hoped for.

"But if no high level of generalization has been attained or per-haps can be obtained, we have in the process of seeking for regular-ities learnt much about social institutions, especially those of prim-itive man. Almost all the basic assumptions of Victorian writers about primitive institutions have been blown sky-high. Much of this mining was done by Crawley, and in the light of his field re-search by Malinowski. The impact of fieldwork study on theoretical propositions was crucial. But there was also much positive advance attained in and by the negative criticism of earlier theories—in learning what they were not, we learnt also something of what the institutions of primitive man could be.

"A considerable advance was made even in the pre-fieldwork period when research was aimed not at the discovery of laws of universal validity, of inevitable succession or development, but was restricted to enquiry into particular problems in societies of the same historical culture or of the same structural type. When the era of fieldwork came about, it became possible to test those theoretical propositions which had any heuristic value.

"But where do we go from here? The body of general theory which could alone make facts significant seems to be lacking. It was at one time provided by the idea of social evolution and for a short time by a rather vague and functionalist theory. Are we then faced with mere empiricism, an endless collection of facts which can, in the absence of a theoretical framework, scarcely be related to each other—which is more or less the state of affairs in historical studies? This may be so, but it is no use spinning theory merely for the sake of it, when the known facts do not support it. One can also say that if in the light of our increased knowledge it is difficult to formulate any high-level generalizations, at least we know much more about the nature of the phenomena investigated, which implies a more rigorous typology or classification, which in its turn implies some sort of hypothesis or theory. Whether we can get much further than this remains to be seen. All that can be said at present is that here and there we make small advances: we understand better the interrelation of social activities."

Part of Evans-Pritchard's contribution to those advances was his analysis of the work and thoughts of authors selected for their significance, theoretical or historical, to the development of anthropological thought. "What I shall be trying to expound is a history of certain fundamental ideas as exhibited in a succession of classics. The problem is where to begin, since speculation about the nature of social institutions goes back to the earliest phases of literary thought. White is quite wrong in supposing that speculation about human affairs came after those about the nature of the physical universe. Aristotle and Plato are obvious choices, but the distance is too great and the trail too tortuous and dim; and we should never get too near the present. Then I think of Ibn Khaldun, of Vico, of Bacon, of Montaigne, of Bodin, of Boussuet, of Hobbes and Locke. But no. I have sometimes started with Machiavelli—but again, no. We will start with Montesquieu, who can justly be regarded as the founder of modern sociology." That is how he envisaged this book.

Acknowledgment is due to the Leverhulme Trust for financial support given to Professor Evans-Pritchard during the time he was preparing this volume.

The task of preparing these essays for publication was considerably lightened by the assistance and encouragement of Godfrey Leinhardt and Lynette Singer, to whom I express my thanks. I am also grateful to Mandy Budd, Phillippa Pia, and Stephen Segaller for their help in typing the various drafts of the manuscript.

Many of the texts recorded here have appeared elsewhere, often in the vernacular as well as in translation, and I make acknowledgment to the editors of *The Journal of the Anthropological Society, Man, The Times* (London), and *The Times Literary Supplement.* I am also most grateful to the following publishers: Cohen and West, Athlone Press, the Clarendon Press, Oxford, Allen & Unwin, The University of Chicago Press, and Faber and Faber.

ANDRÉ SINGER

August 1980

BIOGRAPHICAL NOTE

André Singer was a student and friend of Professor Sir Edward Evans-Pritchard during the later years of his life. He was his research assistant from 1971, and it was Evans-Pritchard's wish that Dr Singer complete this book for publication should he himself be unable to do so.

Dr Singer is currently the Producer of Granada Television's anthropological film series *Disappearing World,* and was joint editor of *Zande Themes: Essays presented to Sir Edward Evans-Pritchard* (Blackwells, 1973). He is author of *The Pathans of Pakistan* (Time-Life Books, 1981) and was principal consultant for *World Atlas of Man* (Marshall Cavendish, 1979).

Introduction

Edward Evans-Pritchard was one of the most distinguished and influential anthropologists of his generation: some would say, *the* most distinguished and influential. The present volume contains his vision of the past of his own discipline—the past living in the present one should say. When reading it, a number of general points become clear—about anthropology, and about E-P, as he was affectionately known in the trade.

The two interconnected points which emerge about E-P are that he does not write primarily as a historian, nor even as a historian of ideas, but is engaged in a living debate; and secondly, that there simply is no Evans-Pritchardian *position*, let alone dogma. This second trait is unusual among men of great influence in a social science. Generally speaking, the reason why they attain great influence is precisely because they articulate some overall vision, some focal idea or intellectual organizing principle, in a novel (or seemingly so), powerful, and well-orchestrated manner. This vision then seems to illuminate a whole field and others can fruitfully apply it—until such time as it becomes stale and there is more pay-off in denying than in affirming that idea. To say that such men ride in on the backs of a powerful paradigm is not necessarily to denigrate them: it is valuable that this should be done, and we are all in their debt. But it is not the only way, and it was not E-P's way.

No doubt E-P will always be associated with certain themes, such as his "segmentary" interpretation of Nuer and Bedouin politics, his account of the socioconceptual mechanics of Azande magic, or the rationality of Nuer religion. Yet the renown or influence of those interpretations does not hinge on any total originality of the central ideas employed (nor would he have claimed this); rather, it hinged jointly on the ideas and the impressive quality of the fieldwork and argumentation which sustained them, not to mention the elegant quality of the prose which expressed them.

I used to suppose that Evans-Pritchard had improved on Durkheim's notion of segmentation by adding the vertical dimension to it: in "segmentary" societies, it is not merely the adjoining coordinate segments, at the same level of size, which resemble each other—but larger units also resemble their own segments, and they resemble their subsegments, and so on. In fact, Durkheim was perfectly familiar with this vertical pattern (through knowing about North African societies), although he failed to appreciate its full importance. He thought it was merely a more developed variant of standard or lateral segmentation. He did not quite see that unless segmentation was both lateral *and* vertical, it could not be credited with solving the problem of the maintenance of order in societies largely devoid of political (and other) specialization and division of labor. E-P effectively completed this supremely important argument.

Two topics are very pervasive and conspicuous in modern thought in general, in the attempts of contemporary man to understand himself and his own situation: rationality and the state, our orderly thought and our orderly society. Rule-bound thought and a rule-bound polity, the overcoming of anarchy in ideas and in institutions: are they connected? At least once, in Hegel, the claim was made that reason and the state are intimately linked. On the left, naturally, it is reason and *revolution,* the inversion of the present evil order, which are seen as bound together: it is revolution, the new antilegitimacy, which is seen as the march of God on earth. As we see ourselves so closely identified with reason and with political order, present or latent, it is also natural to look at the savage for enlightenment about the state of ignorance which prevailed when both reason and order were lacking, and as the clue to the acquisition or loss of legitimacy. It is precisely in these two areas, the location of order in seeming prestate anarchy, and of reason in seeming unreason, that E-P's central achievements are to be found. He did not leave any very profound mark on the ideas of economic anthropology: in the Malinowskian school, one has to look to others, such as Raymond Firth, for that. The problems on which he left a really profound mark are those of the lack of centralized order, among the Nuer, and those of the lack of reason, among the Azande. The apparent anarchy of the Nuer and the use of magical notions among the Azande are equally repugnant to the modern mind: it was left to E-P to highlight the cunning of reason among the Nuer and the Azande, the manner in which seeming anarchy deviously served a hidden order, and the way in which magic had its reasons of which the mind knows nothing. The significance of the present survey by E-P of the anthropological past, of essays on various ancestors, written or conceived at widely different points of his career and development, is that it highlights his own view of the relationship of his work to the development of the discipline.

What kind of figure, what kind of relationship to the anthropological tradition *does* emerge? Not that of a prophet, but rather an intellectually restless, ever-questing, sceptical Hamlet. E-P had lived through a revolution, the Malinowskian replacement of evolutionism by functionalism, and the institutionalization of a certain style of fieldwork fused with ideas partly borrowed from French sociology, a revolution which had so completely transformed social anthropology in Britain and in its anthropological empire—an empire which has survived the political one, which it was sometimes accused of serving, and on which the sun still does not set—and he had played a crucial role in it. But—and this emerges very clearly from the present volume—he was by no means an uncritical, or wholly committed participant in it. He, the superb practitioner of the kind of fieldwork and analysis which it commended, was not, as far as that revolution and its doctrines went, an unqualified True Believer. He appreciated in detail the problems and difficulties which had led up to that revolution, which made it appear necessary, and he knew the force of the considerations which justified it, but he had his doubts, for he was also acutely sensitive to its weaknesses and deficiencies.

The present volume or collection of essays on the history of anthropological ideas will no doubt be outstandingly useful to students and others seeking a lucid, incisive introduction to the subject in general. This was the purpose originally served by the lectures on which these essays are based. Evidently they satisfied that need admirably, and they will continue to do so. They will be slightly, and perhaps rather beneficially, dated: the more recent currents of opinion, whether *structuraliste,* revival-Marxist, or the exemplars of various forms of subjectivism and neo-idealism, which have made their impact since these lectures were conceived or given, are not discussed. Mary Douglas's study of Evans-Pritchard (*Evans-Pritchard,* Fontana, 1980), for instance, treats him as a precursor of the rather subjectivist, "humanistic," hermeneutics-obsessed trends of recent decades. I very much doubt whether such an interpretation can do him justice; he had far too much sense of political and external reality to be drawn to their cloud-cuckoo-lands where you invent your world by your concepts. I wonder whether it is not much better to see him in relation to his ancestors (as evident in this volume) than to these questionably legitimate and collateral descendants.

The absence of these trends in the volume may not be altogether a loss: current fashions, in anthropology as elsewhere, are sometimes ephemeral. But whatever their merits—and their merits may vary a great deal from case to case—they can speak on their own behalf, and they have ample opportunity for doing so, and they receive an attentive hearing. By contrast, those older tributaries to the great flow of anthropological current of ideas which preoccupied Evans-Pritchard are now at risk; they may be unjustly ignored and they do not, all of them, have adequate expositors or searching critics. They are at risk, they may be buried in a stratum of thought quickly covered up by the accumulating strata of subsequent generations. The dead are not always treated with respect, for they cannot answer back, *parfois c'est les morts qui ont toujours tort,* for they have no votes to cast, and their feelings need not be considered. Evans-Pritchard argues with them as equals, without condescension or undue familiarity, neither dismissing them because the issues they faced have by now been supposedly settled, nor embalming their ideas in undue reverence. It is fair to say that he applied the same standards to them as he would have done to a contemporary—which is not to say that he forgot the context in which they wrote, or the fact that this context often differed from his own or ours. All this will help ensure that these lectures will go on serving the purpose for which they were originally designed.

Yet, valuable though they will be when so used, this is not the most important or the deepest relevance they have. Their main interest is that they display the ongoing dialogue with the past of a man who had taken part in an intellectual revolution, and had indeed played an important role in it, but was not wholly convinced of its merits, nor given to the illusion that his was the last word. He had lived through it and had known the *ancien régime* as a living thing, he knew both its successes and its weaknesses. He did not wish to revive it, certainly; but he was not intoxicated by the new order, much as he had done for it. Perhaps there are men like that in political revolutions too, men whose inner voice provides a comparative commentary and who indulge in a sustained dialogue with the past, and no doubt such reflections, if recorded, are well worth having. He never rejected the revolution but he was not starry-eyed about it.

Such a dialogue with the past by someone for whom that past is still alive, warts and all, has quite a different quality from the reflections of those who only learned about the past after it had been buried. Such men either repudiate it too easily, without too much concern with detail and with an exaggerated estimate of the achievements of the revolution, or, later, they may romanticize the past and reconstruct their own version of it. None of this was true of him; and it is this distinctive angle which gives these essays their special flavor and their ultimate interest.

What was this revolution in which he had taken part? It seems to me to have been a genuine and important one, going to the very roots of anthropology as a distinct discipline. Let us approach it indirectly. In logic, there is no good justification for a distinction between sociology and social anthropology: is there one law for one part of humanity, and another for the rest? Lévi-Strauss rightly derided Jean-Paul Sartre for implicitly supposing something of the kind. But the boundaries of sciences, like those of states, are not generally born of logical considerations, and often rightly defy them. The two subjects were born of different preoccupations. Sociology came into being because men were struck by the contrast between an old aristocratic-agrarian-military social order and a commercial-industrial-bourgeois one which seemed to be replacing it, and they sought the meaning of this transition and its place in human history at large. Anthropology as a distinct subject was born later and was, it seems to me, the inevitable consequence of a number of very pervasive nineteenth-century themes: the evolutionism inspired by Darwin and by the then conspicuous facts of European history, jointly with the incorporation of very alien peoples in the accessible world. Evolutionism—in a broad sense which incorporates both biologically and the historically inspired brands, and both continuity and jump-stressing visions of upward development—was more than a mere theory: it was a philosophy, a theodicy, a moral vision, a surrogate for religion. It saw in evolution and progress the key notions in which human life was to be interpreted, and human suffering justified; these notions did not merely explain, they conferred moral meaning and order on the world. Given such a vision, it was quite inevitable that archaic, "primitive" people would acquire a very special interest, no longer as curiosities, but as evidence about our own crucial evolutionary past. Anthropology in effect came into being as the time machine science.

The Malinowskian revolution was precisely, in its essence, the definitive break with the time machine approach. The underlying intuition—let the dead bury their dead—was powerful and coherent, even if the same cannot always be claimed for its accompanying methodological and substantive rationale. Edmund Leach has argued, contrary to this picture, that Malinowski was and remained an evolutionist (*Current Anthropology,* vol. 7, no. 5, pp. 560–76). No doubt he was: he did not revert to Aristotle or to the Old Testament. But what was being repudiated was not a naturalistic and evolutionary account of the emergence of man and human society (let alone the view that some such account must be true, whether or not we know *which one*), but rather its *relevance* to our understanding of how concrete societies really "function." A question was being rephrased. It was not the truth, but the relevance of evolution which was denied.

The reasoning which supported this conclusion contained a mixture of deeply felt considerations which were both substantive and methodological. The Time Machine approach in anthropology had the curious effect of seeing societies as bundles of survivals: though the investigator looked at a tribal people as evidence of our past, the profoundly diachronic perspective somehow led him to explain their own peculiarities in turn in terms of another more distant past, further back still. (That further past could only be reconstructed by means of a theory whose empirical basis then turned out to be the reconstruction deduced from the theory itself—a blatantly circular procedure. But how did he know about it? Had he any evidence concerning that other past?) And was there much evidence of the savages' *present*, come to that, given that he relied on travelers' tales rather than going and seeing for himself? Institutions are constrained by the context of other institutions, not by their own and isolated history, and travelers' tales tend to ignore context and concentrate on spicy titbits.

The whole "survivals" approach is a bit paradoxical. An institution is assumed to have developed and persisted at period 1 because, at that time, it served an essential function—the institution, or a degenerate form of it, is however observed in period 2 when it appears to be pointless and illogical—its presence during period

2 is explained as a *survival* from period 1. The tacit premise employed for the reconstruction of the social order of period 1 is functionalist, for it assumes that the order in question was a reasonably tight system, containing such elements as were required to serve its needs and help it survive. (Otherwise, were it a loose system permitting the coexistence of any set of institutions, reconstruction from the limited data provided by "survivals" would be impossible, for *anything* might have coexisted with the fragments which we also possess.) Similarly, the identification of a contemporary custom as a "survival" is only possible if the rest of the culture is seen as functional and mutually constraining, so that the "survival" can stick out as something exceptional and requiring a special explanation. But at the same time, the sheer existence of survivals, in this sense, presupposes that functionalism is not entirely true after all, that the nature of social behavior in one sphere is not altogether constrained by needs and the customs obtaining in other spheres of the same society, so that incongruous survivals are possible, after all. So it looks as if the practitioner of reconstructions of evolutionary stages by means of survivals, incoherently and arbitrarily uses contrary assumptions at diverse points in his argument. I have stated this argument in the abstract: the great interest of E-P's critical comments on his predecessors is that he notes this kind of error in the concrete detail and at the same time retains a sense for the merit of the enterprise.

The new doctrine contained a mixture of substantive and methodological claims. There was the objection to "speculative history" on the ground that it invented history without evidence, and the not quite identical charge that such reconstruction was circular; there was the opposed positive "functionalist" view that synchronic, or lateral constraints by other, simultaneously operative institutions, are more important than diachronic constraints reaching out from the past, or more strongly, that diachronic constraints are absent altogether; and there was the related but once again not identical doctrine that societies are normally in a kind of stable equilibrium. This view is related to the preceding one in various subtle ways: unless there is equilibrium, it is difficult to give "functional" accounts of institutions, for these amount to showing how persistence of a society is furthered by each institution and hence such stability must be assumed to exist if the specification of the factors furthering it are to be the very paradigms of explanation. Conversely, and paradoxically, the denial of the relevance of the past events leads to the attribution of a kind of null hypothesis status to the assumption that the past was similar to the present, and hence the view that stability does indeed prevail.

So, in practice, the revolution was simultaneously substantive and methodological. It led to a "functional" view of society (a view it in fact inherited from conservative political philosophy, though some erroneously credited it with inventing the view, and for this it was later accused of being a lackey of imperialism), and to a revaluation of the relationship between evidence and theory, and to a new kind of theory. The new anthropologists reached this by way of doubts about the general outlook of their evolutionist predecessors.

Generally speaking there are (at least) two paths to doubt. One is inspired by the leap from data to theory. The distance separating the two is great, and thus makes the jump perilous. This is the Empiricist way to doubt. On the whole, modern science has faced this problem with a surprised bewilderment at how lucky we have been: our data do not really establish our theories, yet how strangely successful is our theoretical enterprise! Philosophers then try to explain how we come to be so lucky.

The case of anthropology is rather exceptional. Its revolution set out to explain not past success but past failure, and to set it right. The old background theory or paradigm (namely evolutionism) seems sound in itself, yet the specific theories which, jointly with data, it inspires, appear so often to go wrong. E-P persistently lists the various errors committed, even though he does do it with sympathy. The anthropological revolution was haunted by a sense of error, and diagnosed as the consequence of the original sin of speculative reconstruction. This can usefully be broken up into the two subsins of unchecked speculation, and of invoking the past to explain the present (argument from survivals). These two sins are logically independent even if they were committed jointly, and indeed also jointly denounced. The new method of sustained fieldwork and functionalist explanation avoided both: data were gathered by contact and immersion, and the present was explained by the present.

But there is also another path to doubt, and this is the idealist one. It invokes (though not by name) the Principle of Internal Relations, which says that everything is what it is by virtue of its relations to all other things, so that you cannot know any one thing unless you know the lot. Human societies are particularly favorite objects of this view. But how can you know *the lot?* You can't. This is the idealist way to scepticism. Functionalism countered this problem too: the fieldworker, totally immersed in a small community, saw it in the round and as a whole, and by showing the contribution of each part to the maintenance of the whole, thereby explained the perpetuation of the whole. (This assumes that the whole *is indeed preserved*—in other words is stable, so that under the proclaimed agnosticism about the undocumented past, there lies hidden a strong assumption about its stability.) Thus holistic fieldwork and "interdependence" explanations jointly overcome the idealist grounds for doubt. Fieldwork immersion and abstention from speculation about the past give us both reliable data *and* contact with a solid totality, it was felt.

So the revolution simultaneously cured the empiricist inference-guilt *and* catered to the idealist sense of something far more interfused. A simple solution for empiricist doubt in anthropology would be to say: but *all* science is essentially guesswork. That doesn't invalidate it, as long as, once the guess is formulated, it is perpetually *checked* against facts. But this easy solution, inspired by Popperian views of science, will not work, in so far as it won't obviate the need for arduous prolonged fieldwork, if indeed facts are profoundly intertwined with each other in any one society, and hence it takes a long, long time to extract them. So, even if their hypothetical "guesswork" quality is no longer held against our accounts of social practices, their fusion with context *still* creates a problem: we have great trouble in extracting and insulating them sufficiently so as to be able to use them to test theories. In any case, when anthropologists objected to *guessing* and used the term pejoratively, they were objecting not to theory as such (which they may or may not have recognized as essentially hypothetical) but to the substantiation of theory by data which were themselves guesswork, and moreover were invented in the image of the theory which they were to test. Testimony out of context is useless. The interconnectedness of institutions also makes it very hard to be sure about the kind of units which really count as the evidence for a given theory, for the truth of a given *guess.** The errors committed by the erstwhile time machine had led anthropologists to their sense of inference-guilt; the nature of their subject-matter—intimate societies—

---

* For a critical examination of this revolution from a position which firmly repudiates the idea of guessing as Original Sin, see Ian Jarvie, *Revolution in Anthropology,* Routledge, 1964.

led them to a sense of interconnectedness and an aversion to abstracting-from-context.

The overall situation is full of ironies. A true and important background idea (evolution) inspired faulty method and much error; an untrue or at best half-true theory (pervasive stability, irrelevance of the past, harmonious interdependence, and mutual support of institutions) led to valuable, accurate, and illuminating research. The explanation of the paradox is perhaps not difficult. Abstract patterns of evolutionary direction are only connected with the year-to-year or generation-to-generation life of communities by so many intervening steps that, for most practical purposes, it is better to disregard them altogether. Their impact on specific local changes cannot simply be assumed, but requires specific evidence on each occasion. By contrast, the functionalist vision, however untrue in the long run and in the abstract, does greatly sharpen the observer's eye for the way in which diverse coexisting institutions set limits for each other and form some kind of more or less persisting unity. If you start your observations with functionalism as a baseline, it is not too hard to put in the corrections later, as you proceed; but if you begin with some stratospheric evolutionary scheme, it is less likely that you will ever get it right.

E-P had an acute sense of all this, and this book tells the story of all the sins which led up to the revolution and made it seem necessary, and to constitute a great *épuration*. Yet he was also worried about where this would lead. It could lead to a natural history of societies, a scientific comparative sociology, which would erect a body of generalizations on the basis of the functionalist accounts of individual communities. Or, at the other extreme, it could lead to a cult of social idiosyncrasy, with each society legitimately contained with its own, collectively private system of meaning. E-P never reached this latter extreme position, though his work (bowdlerized for the purpose) has been most unfairly invoked for this argument: and it is surely perverse to treat him as a precursor of such a position. *His* feet at any rate remained firmly on the ground. Rather, he moved to a compromise position, including a more critical use of history and a restricted use of the comparative method.*
It is true that he moved; what is untrue was that the direction of

* Adam Kuper, *New Society*, 17 April 1980. See also Kuper's *Anthropologists and Anthropology. The British School 1922–1972*, Allen Lane, 1973, Penguin, 1978.

the movement was firm and dogmatic. He remained sensitive to the powerful considerations underlying the various rival positions. The worries about adequate evidence, about the relationship of ethnographic data to general theory, the limits on useful comparison, the extent to which institutions constrain each other—it is all these concerns that haunt his summaries of the views of his predecessors. It is worth looking in some detail at some of the examples.

Montesquieu is praised, but twice reprimanded for propounding "logical constructions unsupported, or inadequately supported, by facts." This brings out one of the strands of the anthropological revolution in which Evans-Pritchard took part: its guilt-ridden conscientiousness about data, its high standards of documentation, which were both used to damn predecessors and to haunt the consciences of the practitioners. Speculative history was, as stated, the Original Sin of anthropology: and the new functionalist anthropologists felt threatened by the possibility that they too were damned, and, just as the Calvinist entrepreneurs allegedly went on to accumulate capital so as to prove to themselves that they were saved, these anthropologists accumulated superb field data in a singular attempt to prove that they were redeemed—and the world benefited from their *Angst.*

The problem of data-and-theory is in fact more complex than may at first appear. Inadequate documentation covers diverse and logically rather disparate sins: inferring or reconstructing the past where data (notably documents) are absent; using the alleged past to explain the present; accepting second-hand reports; and accepting reports of institutions *out of context.* (The sin of being second-hand and being out of context are not at all identical and either can be committed without the other.) The requirement of context is a kind of obverse of the repudiation of explanations by-past-condition; if synchronic constraints alone explain, the past cannot do so, and vice versa. But this leads to problems. If synchronic constraints explain *and* the present is stable ("functional"), how is change possible? If the present is not stable, how can present constraints explain anything, for in the absence of stability we do not know whether they do constrain effectively.

Yet this fastidiousness about data, with its diverse and not fully coherent roots, slides over, if one is not careful, into a much more general problem, that of the adequacy of *any* data (however rich, contextually assembled, and first hand) as the support of *any* theory; in other words into the problem of science as such. After all,

Evans-Pritchard knew that Montesquieu used *some* data; and he also knew that even the best contemporary fieldworker does not and cannot have *all* data, and incidentally that he must presuppose some theory in "contextualizing" information and this theory must be speculative in some measure, and moreover even the best fieldwork contains some second-hand elements, for no one can check the reports of all his informants. So, allowing for all that, did Montesquieu differ *in principle* from a modern anthropologist, or only in his specific performance, limited as it was by available information? The official answer of the anthropological tribe, which Evans-Pritchard does not here repudiate, is the former; but I think he felt uneasy about it, and there are ample signs of this in the rest of the volume.

Philosophically speaking, the paradox of the anthropological revolution and its view of its own method was this: its acute distrust of inference (especially to the unobserved and undocumented past) impelled it towards a kind of "I am a camera" cult of direct observation, akin perhaps to what is now called phenomenology, a telling-it-like-what-it-is blow-by-blow, an intimate fidelity to reality, a theory of knowledge-by-total-immersion, a total and intimate confrontation with a solid reality; but its equally strong sense of the interdependence of social institutions, of the organic unity of social life ("functionalism"), led it to credit genuine understanding only to contextual interpretation, not to mere inert and atomized observation. But contextual interpretation is *interpretation!*

The cult of fieldwork was justified by both these background notions: its point was that you should *see* what really happened rather than reconstruct it, and also that you should see, feel, the social *context*. So it is as if some ultraempiricism, distrustful of all inference from data to unobservables, was fused with some ultra-Hegelian position, invoking the Principle of Internal Relations to show that nothing can be understood, or nothing can be even perceived or exist, apart from its relationships to other parts of the whole to which it belongs. The Principle of Internal Relations insists that our relations to other things are parts of us; hence knowledge of any one thing presupposes the knowledge of all the things to which it is related; hence any real knowledge is knowledge of the totality, and all partial knowledge is distrusted. Such a fusion of viewpoints may be curious, but it did seem to occur, and I don't think this was even the only occasion in the history of thought when it occurred. But jointly, the two considerations inhibited theorizing. The respect for Context inhibited comparison, the embargo on speculation inhibited the formulation of ideas which would have been tested by comparison. Two quite incommensurate grounds for suspicion coexisted within this vision.

The next author discussed, Lord Kames, does not greatly impress Evans-Pritchard, yet he inspires him with a very similar expression of evidence-guilt, or is it theory-guilt? "[Kames] . . . laid down a very sound directive for anthropologists to follow: that one should never draw general conclusions from particular facts. Dominated by empirical fieldwork many English-speaking anthropologists have forgotten this advice, which is different from saying that we should not try to see the general in the particular."

The remark is interesting. The curious charge against "many English-speaking anthropologists" suggests that the prohibitions or taboos which their revolution imposed on them, did not inhibit theorizing as such, but did inhibit comparison or the use of evidence wider than that of one field study. There is of course the question of how one identifies the general correctly in the particular, without relying on the particular alone.

Ferguson is next, and E-P thinks highly of him. He too is seen as a protosceptic, repudiating mere conjecture. He is quoted so as to show that he had more to say on just *how* we can see the general in the particular, and he is shown to have anticipated crucial later anthropological doctrines. Like his contemporary Adam Smith, he saw the importance of the division of labor, and his interpretation of its significance had about it at least as much of Durkheim as of Smith: the interdependence it engenders is an important source of a society's internal cohesion. Concerning war and conflict, Ferguson was a good protofunctionalist, anticipating the doctrine of "balanced opposition," of the beneficial consequences of rivalry on the internal solidarity of the rival groups. John Millar is praised as highly, and again, for his recommendations about how to proceed as much as for his substantive doctrines.

Condorcet strikes relatively few sparks off Evans-Pritchard. But one is tempted to speculate about the profound nature of the resonance of Comte. Comte, as he observes, was ever a paradox—republican royalist, aristocratic proletarian, Catholic freethinker; and a man of powerful, tempestuous passions. As for his patron, teacher, and inspirer, Saint-Simon, Evans-Pritchard averts his gaze with a shudder: "Heaven forbid," he says, "that we should enter into the tangled relationship of the two men." One wonders whether Evans-Pritchard smiled to himself when he wrote this sketch of Comte. His own profound paradoxes and powerful passions, the contrasts and counterpoints of his life and attitudes, still await, and certainly deserve, their biographer. And heaven forbid (and if heaven does not, my prudence will) that I should enter into the tangled relationship between him and Malinowski, the senior guiding spirit of the anthropological revolution. Suffice it to say that according to rumor, when Malinowski died, Evans-Pritchard confessed himself to be heartbroken and observed that to be deprived of the object of so passionate a hatred was to face an empty life. But while it is too soon perhaps (and in any case I am not competent) to record the personal story, the purely intellectual involvement with the issues which led up to that revolution, and which it brought forth, can be indicated. Comte also provides Evans-Pritchard with one of the opportunities to spell out clearly his own doubt about the Malinowskian revolution: "We must be clear in our minds . . . what Comte . . . and indeed also the anthropologists of the nineteenth century in general, understood by the sort of history they thought worth pursuing, for their perspective has been largely lost, possibly to the detriment of our subject (social anthropology), which may have to some extent abandoned thereby what gave it its bearing and its consistency."

So we see him, on the one hand, persistently harping on the failure of our ancestors to live up to methodological principles which they often perceived, which we in turn hope to serve better, and which contained unresolved internal difficulties; on the other hand, we see in this passage an undisguised expression of the feeling that something central may have been lost the very moment when method was made more rigorous. And yet he also promptly noted Comte's unashamed, brazen unilinealism, so extreme that it is content to observe but one civilization. It seems neither the past, nor comparison with other civilizations or cultures, can be eschewed without loss. And here there was a methodological revolution which could lead to eschewing both. Its sensitive, guilt-ridden fastidiousness about unsubstantiated speculation and inference led it to restrict itself to solid field data; its sensitivity to the Principle of Internal Relations (under the new name of functional interdependence) led it to suppose that it had in any case no need of those inferred, speculative data which it had also prescribed. So, rather conveniently, that which was forbidden was also not desired. (Yet at the same time, one also has the uneasy feeling that a fully rounded-off picture of any society, however small and intimate, requires some inferred, nonobserved data; and when one comes to larger and more complex societies, this uneasy feeling turns into a certainty.) Nonetheless, Evans-Pritchard went along with this revolution, not with a light heart, but at any rate practiced with brilliance the style of research and analysis which it had engendered and legitimated.

McLennan was perhaps the paradigm of the kind of anthropologist repudiated by the functionalist revolution. He upheld explicitly the notion of unilineal evolution, and favored the method of inferring to the past from "survivals." But it is interesting to note the respect with which Evans-Pritchard examines his arguments. They are dismissed, when they are dismissed, on grounds of specific errors of fact or logic; they are not dismissed generically, on principle, as infected with some pervasive evolutionary sin. Though Darwin is mentioned as the source of a confusion in McLennan and his contemporaries, it is not the overall pursuit of an evolutionary scheme, but the more specific underrating of the role of the family in primitive society which is cited as the key error.

Yet he does deplore McLennan's influence on his next author, Robertson Smith. Here he notes with favor that Robertson Smith's attempts at historical reconstruction were made in connection with cultures both similar and generically related; in later life, Evans-Pritchard did indeed incline to the view that the comparative method was effective when deployed within the limits of such cultural similarity. He notes the success of evolutionary-comparative reconstruction in law, mythology, and philosophy. So why should it not work here? Once again, he concludes that Robertson Smith's central ideas about the religion of the Semites fail not in principle but through factual errors: the basic method, aim, and *Fragestellung* are not misguided, and if Robertson Smith erred, it was in a task which in principle could be carried out successfully and completed. He cites Malinowski and Radcliffe-Brown as thinkers who held that Robertson Smith used a legitimate tool (the comparative method) for an illegitimate end (historical, causal, diachronic laws, when it would have been in order to use the same method in pursuit of functional laws of interdependence). It is clear that Evans-Pritchard held both tool and aim to be legitimate: the fault lay only in execution. And yet, one feels that he also sensed that the manner in which these faults had been committed, led to that revolution, whose adverse judgment on the past he refrained from fully endorsing.

Though Evans-Pritchard is sympathetically sensitive to the basis of the evolutionist orientation of his nineteenth-century authors, he does not comment on the manner in which Henry Maine constituted an interesting exception—though this fact is highlighted by some of his own quotations from Maine. Maine's vision of human history was rather of the characteristically twentieth-century, "Gatekeeper" kind: "The stationary condition of the human race is the rule, the progressive the exception"; in other words, we understand how we came to be where we are, not by considering a universal single path inexorably leading here (along which some segments of humanity supposedly move faster than others), but rather, by considering those fortuitous or providential exceptions which from time to time allowed some society to find a way through a wall which, for most of mankind, remained impassable. Maine, once again, is praised by E-P for practicing the comparative method, but doing so with restraint: his famous generalization about the passage from contract to status, and his belief in a starting point with *patria potestas,* apply to one cultural tradition only. Maine himself said that the movement of *progressive* societies exemplified this powerful trend—and as we have seen, he considered progress to be the exception, not the norm. Evans-Pritchard joins Sir Frederick Pollock in defending Maine from the criticism based on the fact that agnatic societies of the Roman type are by no means universal: no matter, but within that tradition, Maine seems to have been not too far from the truth. Evans-Pritchard notes, with a side glance at contemporary trade unions, that the victory of contract over status has not been complete. He does not go further, to consider the possibility that modern society may now exemplify a trend actually contrary to Maine's principle—*from* contract *to* status.

In connection with Tylor, Evans-Pritchard resumes some of the debate with McLennan, but in a manner which highlights the connection between specific error (all that he attributes to McLennan) and the use of an approach which is misguided *in principle*. He notes with favor Tylor's attempts to bring quantitative rigor into his pursuit of "adhesions" (synchronic clusters of social traits) such as, for instance, between matrilocal residence and ceremonial avoidance by the husband of his wife's relatives. But what of negative instances, e.g., patrilocality *and* avoidance by a husband of his wife's parents? Tylor invoked the famous notion of *survivals* so as to explain this away. By the time one may appeal both to synchronic affinity of customs, *and* to survival from an unsubstantiated previous stage in an alleged evolutionary sequence, the game becomes too easy.

E-P also invokes the awkwardness of comparing supposedly similar institutions, drawn from otherwise disparate cultural contexts. So, when torn between pursuing synchronic fit (functionalism), intersocial comparison, and placing in evolutionary sequence, his warmth towards elements of this sequence seems to diminish in the order in which I have listed them. Yet his increasing scepticism as we follow this sequence does not lead either to complete repudiation or to loss of sympathy, and always hinges in large part on whether or not evidence is available. (The trouble with the whole debate was of course that two issues were never emphatically separated: the contingent absence of evidence for diachronic stages and the logical irrelevance of the past as such—which would hold whether or not evidence happens to be available.)

Evans-Pritchard is especially warm about Lévy-Bruhl, in deliberate defiance of what he considered an unduly harsh assessment of him by English-speaking anthropologists. This is interesting in the author of *Nuer Religion* who had evidently delighted in saving the Nuer from attributions of irrationality or "pre-logical mentality." Lévy-Bruhl is praised for his freedom from individualism, psychologism, and historical speculation: the prelogical mentality does not occur as a result of an individual's erroneous reasoning (as in Frazer and Tylor), but because of a shared collective style of thought which the individual acquires by learning (rather than working out for himself), and whose nature is to be understood from itself, rather than through speculatively established antecedents. Lévy-Bruhl needs correction and toning down rather than outright rejection, Evans-Pritchard suggests; and there is a certain complementarity between him and Pareto, both of whom allow Evans-Pritchard to pursue his fascination with rationality.

E-P finds the complementarity of Lévy-Bruhl and Pareto amusing: "Lévy-Bruhl has written several volumes to prove that savages are pre-logical. . . . Pareto has written several volumes to prove that Europeans are non-logical." But Pareto was, unwittingly, a practitioner of sound method: he was a fieldworker, for he wrote about societies he knew, namely his own Europe and its ancestral predecessors, whose writers could speak in their own voice and be properly understood. "He was in a sense a field-worker," though alas Hesiod and Plato cannot be crossexamined, so it seems he was but a deficient fieldworker, for the informants were dead. Nevertheless, the restriction of comparisons within a single cultural tradition, as usual pleases Evans-Pritchard.

If Evans-Pritchard goes out of his way to defend Lévy-Bruhl, Frazer, "the best-known name in anthropology," provokes him into sustained and effective criticism. Methodologically his sins are multiple—"suffering from the influence of current psychological and evolutionary theories," he also used the comparative method badly: he used a vast and uneven mass of data, torn from context and often unreliable. Thus the persistent motif of the requirement of well-checked, contextually bound elements, only linked in comparison when within range of each other, makes its reappearance. His most telling criticism takes the following line: Frazer's account of the savage, magic-addicted mind is that it works in terms of certain principles of association (contiguity, resemblance) which in fact are seldom valid. But Frazer cannot answer the question of why the savage does this some of the time, but by no means all the time. Frazer could perhaps reply in terms of his doctrine of the permanent intertwining of the three threads of magic, religion, and science: for he did not deny that a little science was everpresent. And if the thread of science was already so powerful even at the savage state, we have no explanation of why it dominated some areas, but some only. If only Frazer had incorporated the situational context, E-P sighs. He might have added that Frazer's official theory (as distinct from others which can be detected as implicit in *The Golden Bough*) makes both primitive man (and all other men for that matter) far too much of an intellectual, concerned only with cognition. This error of course goes hand in hand with ignoring the context of magical belief. Incidentally, he seems to me in error when he stresses the influence of contemporary psychological theories on Frazer: Frazer's psychology may have been confirmed by contemporaries, but basically it derives from the eighteenth-century doctrines of Hume. Frazer married Hume's psychology to the mass of ethnographic material available to him. He asked not "What would I think were I savage," but rather, "Given that the savage is an intellectual and Hume's psychology is correct, how did the savage reach the conclusions which all these varied reports attribute to him?"

But it is perhaps the subsequent chapter on Durkheim, which is the most severe, with the possible exception of the one on Malinowski. Durkheim was apparently guilty of many sins, including taking over from Robertson Smith his errors about early Semitic religion, his mysterious belief in the possibility of establishing positive conclusions from a single well-explored case, "an evolutionary fanatic" who wished to explain social phenomena in terms of pseudohistorical origins (here again, it is not clear whether the *pseudo* or the *historical* is the worse sin, whether Evans-Pritchard is objecting to inadequate evidence, or to the "genetic fallacy" of explaining institutions in terms of the past, irrespective of whether the evidence is adequate or not); the overstressing of the sacred/profane opposition, which Evans-Pritchard says he himself never found of any use in the field; an implicit unilinealism, evident in the assumption that simple societies must be alike; an overrating of the impact of crowd activity in ritual; psychologism (an interesting charge, given Durkheim's own proclaimed antipsychologism); and a selective, opportunist use of the comparative method.

This is not the place to try to evaluate these multiple charges. But it is a pity Evans-Pritchard did not pair off Durkheim and Frazer, in the way in which he did amusingly juxtapose Lévy-Bruhl and Pareto. Frazer was rightly criticized (not quite in these words) for supposing that the savage was always doing the same kind of thing, namely acquiring knowledge about the world, presumably with a view to manipulating it. He did not consider the contrast between diverse intellectual operations, such as those accompanying a ritual and those which are simply technical. Durkheim did *precisely* this: he was preoccupied by the separation between the compulsiveness of some ideas and the contingency of others. The equation of rationality with conceptual compulsion, and its explanation in terms of social ritual, is highly suggestive, irrespective of the soundness of Durkheim's methodological program notes accompanying it, so to speak, or of his use of ethnography. Evans-Pritchard might have placed Durkheim alongside Lévy-Bruhl and Pareto, noting that one of them thinks that the savage is prelogical, the second that we are nonlogical, and the third, that we are *all* of us compulsively rational, and rational just because we are ritually compulsive.

Yet E-P's feelings about Durkheim were not without ambivalence. He was capable of a warmer appreciation of him than one would suppose if one looked only at his chapter on Durkheim. The subsequent chapter on Hertz gives credit to Durkheim for having enabled his students, such as Hertz and Mauss, to deploy the synchronic, integrative, total approach, which led to the better quality ethnographic data which were now available being used sensibly, without excessive diversion of effort into speculative genetic, historical schemata. They no longer had "to fight philosophy and psychology for *Lebensraum;* that battle had been won." So E-P concedes that Durkheim's battle had been worth fighting. E-P goes on to make a most interesting remark about this great battle for the soul of anthropology (between Context and Evolution): the crucial date had been 1864, when Fustel de Coulanges published his great work. It was he and Montesquieu and Tocqueville who apparently were the knights fighting for the good cause, against Saint-Simon and Comte; and in as far as E-P thinks that in the breast of Durkheim the former won against the latter, Durkheim would seem, rather grudgingly, to be counted among the Saved.

All the same, it was evidently rather a close thing. Irritation with Durkheim and his sins remains—his subordination of social phenomena to philosophic doctrine, his cloudy notion of collective consciousness, and his acute and ill-defined polarity of the sacred and profane. All this encourages E-P to make some characteristically acerbic observations about the "comparative method." Should anyone wonder what this secret and powerful method of sociologists consists of, it "means little more than that if one wishes to make a general statement about the nature of some institution one has first to examine it in a number of different societies." Here as elsewhere, E-P does little to protect our guild arcana.

More contentiously, he divides the comparative method into a two-stage operation. First, we must extract "the social fact from its cultural form"; and then, having done so, we look for generalizations. This is interesting a number of times over. The structure-culture contrast in anthropology is strikingly reminiscent of the old philosophical distinction between primary and secondary qualities. Primary qualities, structure, are *what is really there* and what plays a causal role; secondary qualities, culture, are appearances, causally epiphenomenal, engendered in the one case by the effect of reality on the sense organs of observers, in the other, by the (accidental?) choice of symbolic tokens by a given society. Funerals or weddings may be a structural necessity for a given society, but the sartorial and other conventions employed to define these occasions were thought to be contingent. (When *structuralisme* came to be fashionable, one of its basic ploys was not, as you might suppose, to concentrate on the old structure, but, on the contrary, to seek structure *in* culture, to say that culture too had its own structure, to claim to detect the rules by which cultural phenomena themselves were allegedly bound.)

E-P's implicit endorsement of the structure-culture distinction, as it had once been applied in British anthropology, is not altogether consistent with his often reiterated view that the comparative method has better prospects of completing its second and difficult stage (that of attaining generalizations), if it seeks them only within the limits of a fairly homogeneous cultural tradition. Maine, Fustel de Coulanges, and Robertson Smith are cited as having made at least some progress in this direction, thanks to having restricted themselves to single historical traditions. But if the limits of a single culture also set limits to the possibility of comparison and generalization, does this not suggest that culture is after all more important and crucial, less passive and superficial, than the initial sketch of the contrast would suggest?

Perhaps E-P did not bother his head with this question too much, because he was not overimpressed by the fruits of the comparative method even within the single-culture limitation, let alone outside it. Reflections on its failure goad him to offer, in this passage, a schematic history of anthropology which is even more blunt and brutal than his summing up of the essence of the comparative method. In the beginning, there were attempts to find general laws of social development; when this failed, it was replaced by the search for laws of social interdependence. This too was abandoned, etc.

The rest, you might conclude in this passage, is silence. The black mood, however, was not always with him, and even within his pessimism there were rival alternatives, nuances, and powerful ambivalences. He was a man pursued by doubts and ironies, but one thing is certain: it would be idle to seek in this anthropological testament those mealy-mouthed, anodyne and guardedly optimistic assertions which accompany applications for financial and official support for research or teaching.

The ambivalent fluctuations of mood go on. The strictures of Durkheim are surpassed by those on Malinowski. "Malinowski had no idea of abstract analysis, and consequently of structure." "All he tells us . . . could easily have gone into fifty pages rather than into over five hundred." Of a posthumous work of Malinowski he says: "It is a good example of the morass of verbiage and triviality into which the effort to give an appearance of being natural–scientific can lead one. Malinowski was in any case a futile thinker." But even the verdict on Malinowski is not as unambiguous as these sentences on their own might suggest, as we shall see.

Evans-Pritchard's account of the development of the ideas of his intellectual ancestors tells the story of the manner in which anthropologists have tried to grapple with the problem of human society as such, or primitive society, or the links between primitive and other societies. (This vacillation in the definition of the subject is of its essence.) The story, as he tells it, certainly has no happy end; the best you can say is that, happily, it is not ended. But it has a number of rather significant provisional endings, and Malinowski had his part to play in at least one of them.

For all his faults, about which E-P expresses himself with such characteristic vigor, Malinowski did achieve something decisive. He admits in the end that "we owe him [Malinowski] a great debt for acting as a critical dissolvent of accepted theory," where the theory in question is largely the collectivism of the French school, while nonetheless retaining its insistence on seeing practices and institutions in context. By means of sustained and context-sensitive fieldwork, the insights were retained, the errors overcome. But at the same time, the price of this was a theoretical impasse: a subject which could only offer either descriptions or theories which were camouflaged tautologies (as he hints in connection with the pursuit of laws of interdependence), and which lived intellectually on the theoretical capital inherited from a school it had repudiated: "the theoretical capital on which anthropologists today live is mainly the writings of people whose research was entirely literary. . . . When that capital is exhausted we are in danger of falling into mere empiricism. If a personal note be allowed, I would, though with serious reservations, identify myself with the *Année* school if a choice had to be made and an intellectual allegiance to be declared."

But there are alternative endings to the story. One is in the holocaust of the First World War. Had Hertz and others not perished in it, they might, Evans-Pritchard suggests, have overcome the weaknesses inherent in their armchair approach—perhaps without the defects which E-P attributes to the man who slayed them theoretically? And in connection with his admired friend Franz Steiner, one of the last thinkers to be mentioned in the book, E-P also alludes to the Holocaust of the Second World War, in which Steiner's family was murdered. So, some two centuries after the beginning of the story, E-P leaves us with a theoretical impasse in the study of savages, against the backcloth of savagery in which the killers and the victims were not the savages, but those who were to study them.

It was not given to Evans-Pritchard to complete and round off these conversations with his intellectual forebears. For this reason, it may perhaps be unfair to place them alongside his other work—in the sense that he might have given them further polish, qualification, and documentation, had he lived long enough to do so. But in another sense, this occasionally incomplete and rough work is all the more valuable, with all its bluntness and unresolved tensions. We learn the history *questions,* without the pretense of conclusive answers. Do we understand our humanity and our social nature through tracing the path by which we came to be what we are, or by seeing the interdependences between the various traits we possess? Was there any one single path? Do identical principles underlie the diversity of societies? Can we understand the links between the various traits by seeing them in diverse societies? If so, how can we make sure that the compared items are indeed comparable? Just how much elbow room is there, and how much need have we, for *inference* in anthropology? Is inference and speculation but a snare, leading us to support theories by data only constructed on the assumption of the truth of those various theories? Or is it essential, or inevitable? Can we credit ourselves with more reason than savages, and if so why? Is society the consequence of our individual traits or the other way round? (Evans-Pritchard does not seem to like either of these two options.) Can men live without the state, and how do they manage it? Is reason universal or tied to social order?

These questions have haunted anthropological thought. Evans-Pritchard had relatively few definite or dogmatic answers to them (he rejected some alternatives, but he embraced few without hesitation). In these dialogues with his predecessors—which he kept attractively simple, for they were meant to be overheard by students—we see him wondering, puzzled, quizzical, ironic, sometimes cross, but above all, *troubled*. This, in the end, is perhaps humanly the most attractive feature of the volume.

ERNEST GELLNER
Foxfield, April 1980

BIOGRAPHICAL NOTE

Professor Ernest Gellner has been Professor of Philosophy at the London School of Economics since 1962. He worked in North Africa, and knew Evans-Pritchard very well. His publications include *Saints of the Atlas* (Weidenfeld and Nicholson, 1969), *Legitimation of Belief* (Cambridge University Press, 1975), *Thought and Change* (Weidenfeld and Nicholson, 1965) and *Muslim Society* (Cambridge University Press, 1981).

A History of Anthropological Thought

Chapter 1
Montesquieu (1689–1755)

It is difficult to decide where, from a pedagogical standpoint, to begin an account of what today might be considered to be social anthropological thought. One can go back to Plato and Aristotle, or yet further back; and I used to give a course of lectures of Ibn Khaldun; but the break of centuries is too great. Then I have started with Machiavelli, nibbled at Vico and toyed with Montaigne, before finally deciding that if one has to begin somewhere or rather with someone, it must be with Montesquieu. I agree with Professors Aron and Durkheim that it is he who should be called, not a precursor of sociological thought, but its modern founder, on account of what was at the time of his writing it, a most remarkable, brilliant, and original, though rather chaotic, book, the *L' Esprit des lois* (1748). His other writings, the *Considérations* and others, are very inadequate history, showing clearly the influence of Machiavelli, but without his acute understanding of politics; they contribute little to sociological thought.

Little need be said about the life of Charles-Louis de Secondat, Baron de Montesquieu. He came, as his name shows, of an aristocratic family, he was a student of law first in Bordeaux and then in Paris, and he later became a lawyer of the courts. He was for his time a very learned man who enjoyed high repute among the savants of the salons of licentious Regency Paris, where he appears to have had a good time. Some have called him a libertine. He pictured himself as a *homme galant;* though he was also, some said, a bit parsimonious. He was much traveled in Europe, the two years he spent in England having made an especially deep impression on him, particularly in political matters. He was very tolerant, one might almost say liberal, and sometimes a bit muddled in his outlook. He was a Catholic, though no one seems to know for certain how much of the deference he paid to the Church was merely formal. Whatever he may privately have thought of its dogmas he was certainly not himself dogmatic. He was, I suspect, what in the eighteenth century would have been regarded as a Deist.

Montesquieu was one of the first writers to place emphasis on the idea that in any society all its institutions constitute a system of interdependent parts. The relations between them can be discovered by the comparison of observations made in a large number of different societies. "Laws in their most general signification, are the necessary relations derived from the nature of things. In this sense all beings have their laws ..." (1750, p. 1). By "necessary" he means no more than that given a certain type of social structure we will not normally find institutions in conflict with it. There is a certain consistency between one social fact and another and between a type of society and the environmental circumstances in which it is placed.

The size of population and hence of the political community depends on the mode of livelihood. Hunting peoples are widely dispersed and live in small communities. We find larger communities among pastoral peoples and larger ones still among agriculturalists. The line of distinction between savages and barbarians lies between hunters, who roam in independent hordes, and herdsmen and shepherds, among whom there is unity on a larger scale. This to Montesquieu is a "law." Another "law" is that the character and even the philosophy of a people are largely a product of climatic conditions, e.g., the Indians are naturally a cowardly people, and even the children of Europeans born in India lose the courage of the people of their homeland, being enervated by the climate.

Though his book is about "laws," he used this word in different senses in reference to the dual nature of man. That is to say, he distinguished between natural law, to which animals are subject, and positive law, which is characteristic of human societies. In matters of positive law man is a free agent, although a certain type of positive law is generally found in a certain type of society or, if it is not, it ought to be. "Man, as a physical being, is, like other bodies, governed by invariable laws. As an intelligent being, he incessantly transgresses the laws established by God, and changes those which he himself has established" (1750, p. 4). Note the two senses of "law" in that passage. I conclude that by the "laws" of a society, Montesquieu meant little more than what people of that society do (social facts), or at any rate what he thought they ought to do. On the whole he speaks of "law" in the modern scientific sense rather than in the moral sense of his time.

It being his point of view that where one finds one or other fundamental institution other institutions will conform to it, he proceeds to examine societies of which he had first-hand experience (those of Europe) and others about which he had read (Greece, Rome, China, India, Formosa, the Maldive Islands, the Arabs, the Hebrews, Turkey, Ethiopia, the Carthaginians, Franks, Germans, Mexicans, American Indians, and others), and to compare their different ways of social life. In the course of his lengthy treatise, in which he was much influenced by Aristotle, he discusses a very large number of topics: constitutions, education, the position of women, laws, customs, manners, luxury, war, currency, commerce, economics, taxes, climate, slavery, morals, religion, etc. A large part of it is taken up with a history of European feudalism. It is a general commentary of human affairs, of a sensible and reflective kind; and also a guide to rulers about what sort of institutions they should encourage: no wonder that, as he confesses, the labor of writing it nearly killed him. He obviously felt the need for discretion in discussing both political and religious subjects; and he sometimes sheltered behind irony, e.g., in his discussion of Negro slavery. Nevertheless, in spite of its many obscurities and diversions there is a clear and persistent attempt to make a scientific classification of types of human society and to reveal the significant features of each type.

In the earlier part of his book Montesquieu (following Aristotle) takes the form of government as his constant, to which all other institutions are variables. He classes governments into the three classical species: republican (democratic or aristocratic), monarchical, and despotic; but though using Aristotle's classification he employs it differently—Aristotle's knowledge having been more or less restricted to the Greek city states. These words indicate the nature of each, and Montesquieu then examines those laws, manners, customs, etc. which follow from the form of government, for what is proper to one form would be unsuitable in another. It becomes clear whether they are suitable or unsuitable once the principle (ethos) of each type of government has been isolated. "There is this difference between the nature and principle of government, that its nature is that by which it is constituted, and its principle that by which it is made to act. One is its particular structure, and the

5

other the human passions which set it in motion" (1750, p. 27). The principle of a democracy is virtue (probity); of an aristocracy, moderation (restraint) founded on virtue; of a monarchy, honor (grandeur); and of a despotism, fear. It does not, however, follow that in a particular republic the people actually are virtuous, though they ought to be, or that in a particular monarchy they are actuated by honor, but if they are not the government is imperfect. In other words, these were for Montesquieu what today would be called ideal types, to which actual societies approximate more or less. The corruption of a government generally begins with that of its principle; the spirit of equality becomes extinct; the power of the nobles becomes arbitrary; a prince deprives his subjects of their prerogatives and privileges.

Other institutions conform to the pattern of the government. Forms of education must evidently be consistent with its principle, e.g., in republics its aim will be to inculcate self-renunciation. Then "it is natural" for a republic to have only a small territory; a monarchy to have only a moderately big territory (if smaller it would become a republic, if larger the nobility would assert their independence, safe from swift retribution), and a large empire supposes a despotic authority (quick decisions can be taken, and fear keeps remote governors from rebellion). The spirits of states change as they contract or expand their limits. In monarchies which have also an hereditary nobility between the prince and the people, entails preserve the estates of families and are very useful; they are not so proper in other sorts of government. In despotisms punishments have to be very severe; in moderate governments (monarchical and republican), shame and a sense of duty act as restraints. Luxury is proper in monarchies and there should be no sumptuary laws, for were the rich not to spend their wealth the poor would starve. In democracies there can be no luxury. In monarchies women are subject to very little restraint; in republics they are free by the laws and constrained by manners; in despotisms they are chattels. Dowries ought to be considerable in monarchies to enable husbands to support their rank; in republics they ought to be moderate.

However, the ethos (*esprit*) of a people is not just determined by their form of government, though it is most clearly seen in this, but by their total way of life: "men are influenced by various causes, by the climate, the religion, the laws, the maxims of government; by precedents, morals, and customs, from whence is formed a general

6

spirit that takes its rise from these" (1750, p.418). Among different peoples one or other of these influences may be dominant and that of the others will then be weaker. "Nature and climate rule almost alone among the savages; customs govern the Chinese; the laws tyrannize in Japan; morals had formerly all their influences at Sparta; maxims of government, and the ancient simplicity of manners, once prevailed at Rome" (1750, p. 418). It follows that the introduction of new laws may alter the spirit of a nation. One should be careful!

Montesquieu's method of interpretation can readily be seen by taking a few typical examples from his book. They demonstrate his thesis: we should explain the laws by the laws, and history by history, as a social fact can only be explained in terms of other social facts, the totality of which it is a part. At Athens, for example, a man could marry a sister only on the father's side, and not a sister by the same venter. This rule originated in republics whose aim it was not to let two inheritances devolve on the same person. A man who married his father's daughter could inherit only his father's estate, but if he married his mother's daughter it might happen that this sister's father had no male issue and might leave her his estate; and so her husband would acquire two estates. Domestic servitude (as distinct from slavery) is explained by the fact that in hot climates girls are married between the ages of eight and ten and are old by the time they are twenty; so infancy and marriage go together, and hence the dependency of women in the home. He says this about polygamy: in Europe there are more boys than girls, and in Asia more girls than boys—hence monogamy in Europe and polygamy in Asia; but in the cold climates of Asia there are, as in Europe, more males than females, "and from hence, say the Lamas, is derived the reason of that law, which amongst them, permits a woman to have many husbands" (1750, p. 361), i.e., polyandry. We are told that "in the tribe of the Naires, on the coast of Malabar, the men can only have one wife, while women, on the contrary, may have many husbands. The origin of this custom is not I believe difficult to discover. The Naires are the tribe of nobles, who are the soldiers of all those nations. In Europe, soldiers are forbidden to marry: in Malabar, where the climate requires greater indulgence, they are satisfied with rendering marriage as little burdensome as possible; they give a wife amongst many men, which consequently diminishes the attachment to a family, and the cares of housekeeping, and leaves them in the free possession of a military spirit" (1750, p. 362). Among the Tartars the youngest of the males is always the heir because as soon as the older sons are capable of leading a pastoral life, they leave the home with cattle given them by their father and start a new home of their own. "The last of the males who continues in the house with the father, is then his natural heir. I have heard that a like custom (ultimogeniture) was also observed in some small districts of England. This was doubtless a pastoral law conveyed thither by some of the people of Brittany, or established by some German nation. We are informed by Caesar and Tacitus, that these last cultivated but little land" (1750, p. 401). Some of these explanations may seem to us today to be somewhat fanciful, but they are certainly an attempt at being sociological, even if they are entirely, or for the most part, unsupported by evidence.

There is a connection between forms of domestic and political government. The equal status of the citizens of a republic is consistent with the high standing of women in the home. When the climate demands that women be in subjection this fits in better with a monarchical form of government. This is one of the reasons why it has always been difficult to establish popular government in the east. But the abasement of women is most conformable to the genius of a despotic government, which treats all with severity. "Thus at all times have we seen in Asia domestic slavery and despotic government walk hand in hand with an equal pace" (1750, p. 365). "One thing is very closely united to another: the despotic power of the prince is naturally connected with the servitude of women, the liberty of women with the spirit of monarchy" (1750, p. 428).

Montesquieu had a clear idea of the integrative function of custom—and we may perhaps compare him to Confucius—"We shall now show the relation which things in appearance the most indifferent, may have to the fundamental constitution of China. This empire is formed on the plan of the government of a family. If you diminish the paternal authority, or even if you restrict the ceremonies, which express your respect for it, you weaken the reverence due to magistrates, who are considered as fathers; nor would the magistrates have the same care of the people whom they ought to consider as their children; and that tender relation which subsists between the prince and his subjects, would insensibly be lost. Retrench but one of these habits, and you overturn the state. It is a thing in itself very indifferent whether the daughter-in-law rises every morning to pay such and such duties to her step-mother: but if we consider that these exterior habits incessantly revive an idea necessary to be imprinted on all minds, an idea that forms the governing spirit of the empire, we shall see that it is necessary that such, or such a particular action be performed" (1750, p. 433).

On the prohibition of marriage between near kin Montesquieu says that the marriage of son with mother "confounds the state of things: the son ought to have an unlimited respect to his mother, the wife owes an unlimited respect to her husband; therefore the marriage of the mother to the son would subvert the natural state of both" (1750, p. 205). The prohibition of marriage between cousins-german is due to the fact that in the past it was customary for children on their marriage to remain in the home of their parents: "The children (sons) of two brothers, or cousins-germans, were considered both by others and themselves, as brothers" (1750, p. 207). Hence marriage was not permitted. These incest prohibitions are universal: "These principles are so strong and so natural, that they have had their influence almost all over the earth, independently of any communication. It was not the Romans who taught the inhabitants of Formosa that the marriage of relations of the fourth degree was incestuous: it was not the Romans that communicated this sentiment to the Arabs; it was not they who taught it to the inhabitants of the Maldivian islands" (1750, p. 207). However, religion sometimes permits, or even encourages, marriage to mothers and sisters, e.g., among the Assyrians, Persians, and Egyptians.

Montesquieu's point of view closely resembles that of later functionalists, and this is perhaps best seen in his discussion of religion. Even though a religion may be false it can have an extremely useful function. it will also be found to conform to the type of government associated with it. Christianity goes best with moderate government and Islam with despotic government. Northern Europe embraced Protestantism and Southern Europe stuck to the Catholic Church: "The reason is plain: the people of the north have, and will for ever have, a spirit of liberty and independence, which the people of the south have not; and therefore a religion, which has no visible head, is more agreeable to the independency of the climate than one which has one" (1750, p. 149). "In the countries themselves where the protestant religion became established, the revolutions were made pursuant to the several plans of political government. Luther having great princes on his side, would never have been able to make them relish an ecclesiastic authority that had no exterior pre-eminence; while Calvin, having to do with people who lived under republican governments, or with obscure citizens in monarchies, might very well avoid establishing dignities and pre-eminence" (1750, p. 150).

Even peoples whose religion is not revealed have one agreeable to morality (was not Lévy-Bruhl to urge us to this more than a century later?). All alike teach that men should not murder, steal and so on, and that they should help their neighbors. The philosophical sects of the ancients were a species of religion, e.g., the Stoics. Religion and civil laws ought everywhere to be in harmony. "The most true and holy doctrines may be attended with the very worst consequences, when they are not connected with the principles of society; doctrines the most false may be attended with excellent consequences, when contrived so as to be connected with these principles" (1750, p. 161). Neither Confucius nor Zeno believed in the immortality of the soul (so Montesquieu says) but both religions are admirable as to their influence on society. On the other hand, the sects of Tao and Foe believe in the immortality of the soul and have drawn from this doctrine the most frightful consequences, e.g., they encourage suicide. The sacred books of the Persians advised the faithful to have children because at the day of judgment children will be as a bridge over which those who have none cannot pass. "These doctrines were false, but extremely useful" (1750, p. 163). A people's religion is suited to their way of life. It is difficult to breed cattle in India (so he says), so a law of religion which preserves them is appropriate. India is good for cultivation of rice and pulse: a law of religion which permits of this kind of nourishment is therefore useful. The flesh of beasts is insipid (whatever he meant by that): therefore the law which prohibits the eating of it is not unreasonable. "It follows from hence, that there are frequently many inconveniences attending the transplanting a religion from one country to another" (1750, p. 167), e.g., the hog is scarce in Arabia but it is almost universal in China and to some extent a necessary nourishment. In India it is most meritorious to pray to God in running streams. How could this be performed in winter in climates such as our own?

Now, I say again, much of this was an attempt to present as an answer a bright idea, a logical presentation which often has little to support it in fact; much of it was naive guesswork. Perhaps it is for this reason we can see how close he was to much modern sociologi-

cal thinking. We have to remember that the study of social behavior in literature and in life was limited almost entirely to Montesquieu and what he knew about it was deficient. There is an unfortunate eighteenth-century tendency to moralize, but there is nevertheless an attempt at a cold dissection of the social body, to discover the functioning of its organs; and the belief that the principles of social life cannot be known by reasoning from philosophical maxims and axioms but only by observation, induction, and comparative study. If we can say that Machiavelli wrote a treatise on social psychology we can say that Montesquieu's treatise is sociological. In it we find most of the ingredients of sociological (socio-philosophical) thought, particularly as it developed in France from his day to Durkheim's and beyond: the insistence on the scientific, comparative study of society, the use of the data of as many societies as possible; the inclusion of primitive societies as examples of certain types of social systems; a need to start with a classification or taxonomy of societies based on significant criteria—the way zoology and botany, for example, have begun; the idea of inter-consistency between social facts (social systems), and that any social fact can only be understood by reference to other social facts and environmental conditions, as part of a complex whole; and the idea of this interconsistency being of a functional kind. Also we find clearly stated in the *L'Esprit des lois* the idea of social structure and of dominant values which operate through the structure. There is also the notion of an applied science of social life: what we learn from a comparative study of human societies helps us to shape the organization of our own. What is lacking in his writings—perhaps to his advantage—but which is prominent in those of social philosophers of a later date, is the idea of societies being natural in the same sense as the systems studied by the experimental sciences; the idea that sociological laws are as similar to the laws formulated in the natural sciences, general statements of invariable and inevitable regularities, with the related idea of an inevitable and unilinear development. (As Comte points out, he did not have the idea of progress at all.) Although we now know much more about human societies than Montesquieu and can see that some of his surmises were naive, it must nevertheless be allowed that so far as method and theoretical knowledge go we have not advanced much beyond Montesquieu. Even if this is n granted, at least it must be conceded that most writers concerr with social philosophy, social history, and sociology (including

cial anthropology) right up to the present day show his influence, whether direct or indirect; it is stamped plain on their writings. What a majestic thesis, and in what prose, was the *Esprit*. At the end of his life he said "I have but two things to do, to learn to be ill, and to learn to die."

Chapter 2
Henry Home, Lord Kames (1696–1782)

Lord Kames was the son of an impoverished Scottish laird, and he had a hard struggle both to obtain an education and to make a reputation at the Scottish bar; but with a brilliant mind and dogged persistence he reached a judgeship, taking his title as a Law Lord from his parental home.

If we may trust what his biographers have written, he was critically pertinacious to the point of wearing his correspondents out. We are told also that he was something of a Lothario and *bon viveur;* and if only half of what we read about him were true we might still have to conclude that he was not an amiable person.

In his early days he had been a Jacobite and Episcopalian. As far as religion is concerned, I suppose he may later be regarded, like Ferguson, as some sort of Deist, and in his writings there are frequent references to "the Author of our Being," "the finger of God," "Providential care," and so forth. He appears to have been very devout. However, his attempt to defend the Christian faith, or some aspects of it (*Essays on the Principles of Morality and Natural Religion,* 1751), against Hume was not very successful and proved to be a boomerang for, ironically, it brought against him a charge of infidelity. Besides being lawyer, author, and polemicist, Kames was a farmer who took great interest in his property, introducing new methods in farming, much to the disgust of the local farmers. Also, he corresponded on almost every subject—physics, physiology, natural history, literary criticism—with all the leading intellectuals in Edinburgh and beyond. A versatile man, he was a prolific writer, employing always an amanuensis; so prolific that his rival Law Lord, Montboddo, said to him in sarcastic wit that he (Montboddo) could not read as fast as he (Kames) could write. His writings are of considerable interest to the student of the social history of eighteenth century Scotland, but the only one which has much relevance for the history of sociological thought is his *Sketches of the History of Man* (1774) (I have used the three-volume edition of 1807). He intended to write a History of Man but he found the subject too vast, and himself too old, to complete it, so it was reduced to the more modest *Sketches*.

In some ways it may be said that all the Scottish moral philosophers wrote the same books. They started off with the idea that a study of man must be a study of social institutions of men in groups: Man, says Kames, is endued with an appetite for society, no less than the appetite he has for food, for in a solitary state he is helpless and forlorn. Also, Kames's book, like those written by his contemporaries, purports to be a history of man in his progress from savagery to the highest civilization and improvement. This was the aim of all the philosopher-sociologists of the period, and phrased in much the same words. And like them he employed for the purpose of historical reconstruction, Dugald Stewart's, "Theoretic or Conjectural History" (see *Collected Works of Dugald Stewart*, Thomas Constable, Edinburgh, 1854–58, volume x, "Theory of Moral Sentiments and the dissertation on the Origin of Languages," section ii), to which he gave unqualified approval.

Sketches starts off with a discussion, much in the air at the time, of whether there are different races of men or just one race with such differences as might be attributed to climate, soil, food, or other external causes. Although he was strongly influenced by the celebrated Montesquieu, as he acknowledges, and so was prepared to allow climate to have some effect on character, Kames comes down decisively in favor of the diversity of races, of what today we would call innate racial characteristics. He attempts to support his contention by a hotchpotch of information culled from travelers' reports from all over the world (American Indians, Melanesians, Polynesians, Lapps, Tartars, Chinese, etc.) and from classical Latin authors—much of which might fairly be said to be rubbish. He was certainly credulous and his reasoning highly conjectural; but we must not perhaps judge an author by what we know today, *ex post facto*. It is true, he says, that the Spanish of Southern America have lost their vigor, that the offspring of Europeans in Batavia soon degenerate, and that Portuguese long settled on the seacoast of the Congo retain scarcely the appearance of men; but neither climate nor any other extraneous influence can account for fundamental differences in dispositions or character, e.g., courageous and cowardly, pacific and warlike—differences in what today some people would call "ethos." Such being his view, it would seem to me that it was not very consistent of him to accept the biblical story of the Tower of Babel to account for the great number and variety of languages; the alternative, that "God created many pairs of the human race" (volume I, p. 59), he would not accept.

Like all other writers of the time on social institutions, his basic criteria for a classification of types of society are bionomic, based on modes of production such as hunting and collecting, pastoral, and agricultural; and like Ferguson, Condorcet, and others, he makes (volume I, chapter 2) the point that as population increases various social consequences follow. There is the same emphasis we find in these same writers, on the significance of property in the development of civilization. "Among the senses inherent in man, the sense of property is eminent" (volume I, p. 91), and this sense increases in the advance from savagery to higher types of culture; and desire for property is the mother of many arts: "without private property there would be no industry; and without industry, men would remain savages for ever" (volume I, p. 97). But property combined with opulence leads to decadence and depopulation: "cookery depopulates like a pestilence . . ." (volume I, p. 88). There is a good deal about the development of modes of exchange from barter to money.

These three volumes can be rather tedious reading, almost as tedious as *The Golden Bough*, an erudite catalogue of customs, many of which are cited on dubious authority. I give one quotation as an example. "The female Caribbeans and Brasilians are no less fond of ornament than the males. Hottentot ladies strive to outdo each other in adorning their crosses, and the bag that holds their pipe and tobacco: European ladies are not more vain of their silks and embroideries. Women in Lapland are much addicted to finery. They wear broad girdles, upon which hang chains and rings without end, commonly made of tin, sometimes of silver, weighing perhaps twenty pounds. The Greenlanders are nasty and slovenly, eat with their dogs, make food of the vermin that make food of them, seldom or never wash themselves; and yet the women, who make some figure among the men, are gaudy in their dress. Their chief ornaments are pendants at their ears, with glass beads of various colours. . . . The Negroes of the kingdom of Ardrah in Guinea have made a considerable progress in policy, and in the art of living. Their women carry dress and finery to an extravagance. They are clothed with loads of the finest satins and chintzes, and are adorned with a profusion of gold. In a sultry climate, they gratify vanity at the expense of ease. Among the inland Negroes, who are more polished than those on the coast, the women, besides domestic concerns, sow, plant, and reap. A man however suffers in the esteem of his neighbors, if he permit his wives to toil like slaves, while he is indulging in ease" (volume I, pp. 434–5).

Nevertheless, one may say, in reference to the above excerpt, that in spite of the inadequacy of his sources and of much sententious and dogmatic moralizing, Kames deserves credit for the attention he paid to the position of women and "the gradual progress of women, from their low state in savage tribes, to their elevated state in civilized nations" (volume I, p. 404). However, the progress of women is only one of his topics. Like Adam Ferguson, he wrote about every topic on which he wished to air his opinions. I mention just a few headings: Property, Commerce, Arts, Manners, Luxury, Forms of Government, War and Peace, Finances, the Army, Aristotle's Logic, Theology.

It would be time ill spent to discuss in detail all he wrote on so many topics, but I should like to quote what he has to say on government, a subject which dominated thinking about social institutions in England in the eighteenth century, and which shows the influence of Montesquieu. There is the familiar discussion in terms of democratic, monarchical, despotic, and so on. Kames tells us "of all governments, democracy is the most turbulent: despotism, which benumbs the mental faculties, and relaxes every spring of action, is in the opposite extreme. Mixed governments, whether monarchical or republican, stand in the middle; they promote activity, but seldom any dangerous excess" (volume II, p. 61). Again, "Democracy is contradictory to nature, because the whole people govern: despotism is not less so, because government rests in a single person. A republic, or a limited monarchy, is the best form; because in these every man has an opportunity to act the part that nature destined him for" (volume II, p. 75).

Like others before and after him, since Kames was aiming to write an account of social development, he had to make a classification of social types so as to relate these various topics to them. Like the others, he did this on criteria of production and productive relations; and it is difficult to see what other criteria he could have used. Moreover, they were strictly relevant in that it is evident that other social and cultural differences must, at any rate to a large extent, be determined by them.

So, "In the hunter-state, men are wholly employed upon the procuring of food, clothing, habitation, and other necessaries; and have no time nor zeal for the studying conveniences. The ease of the shepherd-state affords both time and inclination for useful arts; which are greatly promoted by numbers who are relieved by agriculture from bodily labour; the soil by gradual improvements in husbandry, affords plenty with less labour than at first, and the surplus hands are employed, first, in useful arts, and, next, in those of amusement. Arts accordingly, make the quickest progress in a fertile soil, which produces plenty with little labour. Arts flourished early in Egypt and Chaldea, countries extremely fertile" (volume I, p. 128).

We are not here to praise or blame Lord Kames, but merely to speak of him as a typical figure in that eighteenth-century Edinburgh circle which was profoundly interested in the development of social institutions and whose members certainly had great influence on the development of social anthropological thought. This may be clearly seen, I believe, in the writings of the two famous Scottish anthropologists McLennan and Frazer (see chapters 7 and 13).

In conclusion I would add that—although he often broke the rule himself—he laid down a very sound directive for anthropologists to follow: that one should never draw general conclusions from particular facts. Dominated by empirical fieldwork, many English-speaking anthropologists have forgotten this advice, which is very different from saying that we should not try to see the general in the particular.

Chapter 3
Ferguson (1723–1816)

Adam Ferguson was a remarkable person and, although much neglected, is one of the major figures in the history of sociological thought. The son of a minister and a child of the manse, he had the distinction, or we may say advantage, of having served for some years as Chaplain to the 42nd Regiment, or the Black Watch (he fought, so it is said, at the battle of Fontenoy); and he was unique among the Scottish moral philosophers in that he was a Gaelic-speaking highlander. He appears to have been a rugged character, sometimes rather difficult; an ultra-conservative and an anti-Stuart; and when one reads about his life one can well understand what he meant when he said that men are at the best when they have difficulties to surmount.

To estimate Ferguson one must see him and his writings in the intellectual setting of his time and place; and for this it is necessary to mention the Jacobite troubles, the suppression of Scottish independence, rapid economic changes, and the elements of provincial isolation and language difficulty. Without going into the historical and social setting in detail, however, it will be sufficient to note how much Ferguson was an intellectual child of his time if I mention the names of his contemporaries: Hume, Reid, Adam Smith, Lord Montboddo, Lord Kames, John Millar, and Ferguson's pupil and his successor in the Chair of Moral Philosophy at Edinburgh, Dugald Stewart.

Ferguson received recognition at the time he wrote, especially in Germany, where he had much influence on Schiller and others, and in France, where Saint-Simon and Comte owed much to him. In our own country, and later, J. S. Mill fully acknowledged his debt to him. Nevertheless he has since been forgotten, more or less, for over a century and a revival of interest, though not a general one, in his writings has only recently taken place—regretfully limited to America (Lehman, 1931, and Kettler, 1965) and Germany (Kaneko, 1904, and Jogland, 1959), and not in Britain.

Ferguson left the Ministry of the Church of Scotland in 1754 to become professor at Edinburgh first of natural philosophy and then of pneumatic and moral philosophy, and it was there he wrote his books on a variety of philosophical (as he and his contemporaries understood the word) subjects. His first and best-known work, the one I am for the most part going to restrict my comments to, was *An Essay on the History of Civil Society* (1766). I do not think his *Institutes of Moral Philosophy* (lecture notes, 1772) or his *Principles of Moral and Political Science* (two large volumes, 1792) add much of sociological importance to what he had said in his first book; in both there is much tedious moralizing and what eighteenth-century philosophers regarded as psychology; I suppose that was only to have been expected of a moral philosopher of the period, especially of a Scottish Calvinist one. All the same, one can at times sympathize with Hume's irritation and even Sir Leslie Stephen's stricture of superficiality. Ferguson's *The History of the Progress and Termination of the Roman Republic* (1783), a favorite topic among writers of the time, comprises five volumes of almost pure narrative spiced with some rhetoric. This work has little sociological value; but it is only fair to say that Ferguson was a very good classical scholar.

The *Essay* is a fascinating book if you like, as I do, the ornate, even florid or inflated English eighteenth-century style of writing. One has, it is true, to put up with a good deal of sententious verbosity (the book is 430 pages long), but in spite of all the moralizing there is much sound thought in the *Essay,* which, it should be said right away, shows throughout and very clearly the influence of Montesquieu, as Ferguson himself says. It should perhaps also be added that Hume—whose successor he was as Keeper of the Advocates' Library in Edinburgh—although they were great friends and much admired each other, regarded the book unfavorably with regard to both style and content (not that that should necessarily discourage us). If we are to make further comments on the author's personal life and values as reflected in his writings, it may be said that while he abandoned his clerical career, he did not go out of his way, like Condorcet for instance, to attack Christianity. After all, he had once been a minister and a chaplain. He became, I suppose, what one might describe as some sort of Deist: there is much of "The Author of Nature," and reasoning from "design."

Ferguson's book illustrates many of the basic assumptions we find in modern social anthropology. In the first place he says that the desire to give some account of the earliest form of human society has led to fruitless enquiry and wild suppositions because, while the natural historian thinks himself obliged to collect facts and not to offer mere conjecture, "it is only in what relates to himself, and in matters the most important, and the most easily known, that he substitutes hypothesis instead of reality . . ." (pp. 3-4). Here we have a clear statement of the scope of a study of human societies—they are part of nature and must be studied, as any other part of nature, by observation and induction.

It is especially important to avoid conjecture in the study of early man. It must not be assumed, as it so often is, that a mere negation of what we find among ourselves is a sufficient description of man in his original state. This is simply judging by our own standards and is, moreover, going beyond, or against, the testimonies of those who have had opportunities of seeing mankind in their rudest conditions. Nor can direct observation be replaced by the written traditions of a people about the earlier phases of their history. These are for the most part mere conjectures and fictions of subsequent ages and bear the stamp of the times through which a people has passed rather than that to which the descriptions are supposed to relate (he was thinking of the *Iliad* and *Odyssey* and also of writers like Virgil and Tasso, who give us historical information only about the conceptions and sentiments of the age in which they wrote). In spite of all this excellent advice Ferguson, like most of his contemporaries, relied largely on introspection, using historical examples, taken from such classical authors he knew, when they illustrated or corroborated conclusions reached by deductions from philosophical axioms or psychological speculations rather than from the facts themselves.

Now, when Ferguson speaks of human societies as being "natural," he has in mind the political theories of his day. He will have nothing to do with hypotheses such as those of Hobbes, Locke, and others, about a state of nature in which men lived without any form of order, and more particularly of government. That kind of state of nature will be found in the struggle between princes and subjects rather than among rude tribes. He is also scornful of those who imagine that they are studying "natural man" when they interview a wild man caught in the woods—an eighteenth-century pastime. Human nature is a product of social life and man is only "natural" in society, whether it be rude or polished. Therefore an eighteenth century gentleman is not less "natural" than a savage Redskin of North America; indeed, in one sense he is more so, because the potentialities of men in polished societies have greater scope for expression.

Therefore we must not oppose art (culture) to nature, for art itself is natural to man: "If we are asked therefore, where the state of nature is to be found? We may answer, 'It is here': and it matters not whether we are understood to speak in the island of great Britain, at the Cape of Good Hope, on the Straits of Magellan. . . . If the palace be unnatural, the cottage is so no less; and the Highest refinements of political and moral apprehension, are not more artificial in their kind, than the first operations of sentiment and reason" (p. 12). He also says "all the actions of men are equally the result of their nature" (pp. 14-5).

It may here be said, if only as an aside, that the idea that primitive peoples are in some sense more "natural" than civilized peoples is still an idea commonly met with in everyday thought. In Ferguson's day it was the center of much philosophical discussion. He held that it is futile to try to contrast hypothetical man living outside society ("natural man") with man living in society. Did not Aristotle long ago insist that man is by nature a political (social) creature? The question of what in a man in any society is to be attributed to biological inheritance and what to society and culture is altogether different and one which concerns equally both rude and polished man.

It is true that man, unlike the beasts, is endowed not just with instinct but also with intelligence and will and so shapes his own destiny up to a point, though, it must be added, only up to a point. For societies, being natural, do not develop by will or design but of their own nature, like trees: "He who first said 'I will appropriate this field; I will leave it to my heirs'; did not perceive that he was laying the foundation of civil laws and political establishments" (p. 186). Men, that is, arrive at ends they may not aim at; they are free to choose, but they cannot predict what will happen as a result of their choice, for societies arise from instincts and not from speculations, so that what happens is "indeed the result of human action, but not the execution of any human design" (p. 187). Institutions spring out of the general conditions of a society and are not the conscious creations of men, far less of any particular man, however gifted. Statesmen who think that they control events are like the fly in the fable who thought it was turning the wheel on which it sat. How often since have sociologists told us this, especially the Marxist ones!

Since man is essentially a social creature he cannot be understood except as a member of a group. So our first task is to get some idea of the nature of a social group. All accounts from all parts of the earth "represent mankind as assembled in troops and companies . . ." (p. 4). Therefore, "Mankind are to be taken in groups, as they have always subsisted. The history of the individual is but a detail of the sentiments and thoughts he has entertained in the view of his species: and every experiment relative to this subject should be made with entire societies, not with single men" (p. 6). Then again: "Mankind have always wandered or settled, agreed or quarrelled, in troops and companies. The cause of their assembling, whatever it be, is the principle of their alliance or union" (p. 23). In the *Principles* we read, "Families may be considered as the elementary forms of society or establishments the most indispensably necessary to the existence and preservation of the kind." The family in some form or other is universal. Comte was to say very much the same.

The study of man is therefore a study of institutions in relation to one another in the total conditions of life, including national character and climate (Ferguson picked up some odd ideas about the influence of climate from Montesquieu). He discusses at length, closely following the classification and method of analysis of Montesquieu, the nature of various forms of government, democratic, aristocratic, monarchical and despotic, observing the circumstances in which each is found and the various forms of other institutions found with each. He discusses the beginnings of property in agricultural and pastoral societies (this notion of property and the part it has played in social development was, perhaps rightly, an obsession among philosophers of the period) and the distribution of these two types of societies over the earth's surface with reference to climate and some of the main cultural features of each. Both, however, show the beginnings of property and the inequalities and subordination which go with it, and the jurisdiction and government which accompany them. Property comes about in passing from the savage to the barbarous state. He also discusses how superstition disputes with valor (he never quite ceases to be a soldier) the road to power: the "magic wand comes in competition with the sword itself" (p. 161). He discusses how population grows with increase in wealth and security and is always limited by the means of subsistence. He has an excellent discussion of the circumstances in which cultural borrowing takes place (pp. 25 *et seq*). Also how as a result of borrowing knowledge increases: "When nations succeed one another in the career of discoveries and inquiries, the last is always the most knowing. Systems of science are gradually formed. The globe itself is traversed by degrees, and the history of every age, when past, is an accession of knowledge to those who succeed. The Romans were more knowing than the Greeks; and every scholar of modern Europe, is in this sense, more learned than the most accomplished person that ever bore either of those celebrated names. But is he on that account their superior?" (p. 44). Anyhow, no people borrows from another unless it is ready for the loan. He discusses many other topics of anthropological interest which I cannot, obviously, enter into here. Throughout he adheres to his general viewpoint, that culture, like society, is a natural growth, collectively produced, and having its existence outside, and apart from individual minds, which it shapes. Was not Durkheim to say much the same as his main thesis a century later?

Since I cannot discuss all he wrote, I shall mention as examples of his sociological insights only two of the topics he treated—war and the division of labor—in both of which his idea of a society being some kind of system of balanced parts comes out quite clearly. A political structure is a system of opposed groups. The Hottentots, he says, quoting Kolben, raid each other for cattle and women, but they only do this to bring their neighbors to war: "Such depredations then are not the foundation of a war, but the effects of a hostile intention already conceived. The nations of North America, who have no herds to preserve, nor settlements to defend, are yet engaged in almost perpetual wars, for which they can assign no reason, but the point of honour, and a desire to continue the struggle their fathers maintained. They do not regard the spoils of an enemy; and the warrior who has seized any booty, easily parts with it to the first person who comes in his way" (p. 33). In other words, wars arise not so much from an opposition of interests as of sentiments, and the supposed causes of war are only its occasions—the real cause is to be looked for in the functioning of the political structure: "But it is in vain to expect that we can give to the multitude of a people a sense of union among themselves, without admitting hostility to those who oppose them. Could we at once, in the case of any nation extinguish the emulation which is excited from abroad, we should probably break or weaken the bands of society at home, and close the busiest scenes of national occupations and virtues" (p. 37). Again: "The society and concourse of other men, are not more necessary to form the individual than the rivalship and competition of nations are to invigorate the principles of political life in a state" (pp. 182–3). Athens was necessary to Sparta (for which state and way of life Ferguson had great admiration) as steel is to flint in making fire. When the kingdoms of Spain united and the great fiefs in France were annexed to the crown the nations of Great Britain were joined. Social groups, that is, maintain their cohesion through opposition to like groups. Hence the structural necessity of war—both hot and cold. In another part of his book he says "small and simple tribes, who in their domestic society have the firmest union, are in their state of opposition as separate nations, frequently animated with the most implacable hatred. . . . Even where no particular claim to superiority is formed, the repugnance to union, the frequent wars, or rather the perpetual hostilities, which take place among rude nations and separate clans, discover how much our species is disposed to opposition, as well as to concert" (pp. 30–1).

My second example is what Ferguson says about division of labor. A people can make no great progress in cultivating the arts of life until they have committed to different persons the several tasks which require a peculiar skill and attention. This cannot be done in the savage stage and only partly in the barbarian stage. All this changes with greater prosperity and the development of property, and then we get division of labor, not only in production but in all the activities of social life: politics, war, civil government, commerce, and so on. "These separate professions are made, like the parts of an engine, to concur to a purpose, without any concert of their own" (pp. 278–9). "The savage who knows no distinction but that of his merit, of his sex, or of his species, and to whom his community is the sovereign object of his affection, is astonished to find, that in a scene of this nature, his being a man does not qualify him for any station whatever; he flies to the woods with amazement, distaste, and aversion" (p. 278). Then again: "Even the savage still less than the citizen, can be made to quit that manner of life in which he is trained: he loves that freedom of mind which will not be bound to any task, and which owns no superior: however, tempted to mix with polished nations, and to better his fortune, the first moment of liberty brings him back to the woods again...." (p.145).

Division of labor is no less a ground for subordination than difference in natural talents and dispositions and the unequal division of property; and it results in different sets of values and modes of custom in each class or profession in society, just as types of society have their special character—the Roman is a soldier, the Carthaginian a merchant; and the subjects of a republic and a monarchy differ in their outlooks, aims, and behavior. Nevertheless, societies in which there has taken place division of labor, in spite of divergences, present a uniform structural similarity. The general point Ferguson is making is that just as a political society forms part of a system of such societies, maintained in a balance through opposition, so internally the same society is a system of classes, ranks, professions, etc., which have an interdependence, it being precisely this which determines the moral solidarity of a complex society. Furthermore he says, "But apart from these considerations, the separation of professions, while it seems to promise improvement of skill, and is actually the cause why the productions of every art become more perfect as commerce advances; yet in its termination, and ultimate effects, serves, in some measure, to break the bands of society, to substitute form in place of ingenuity, and to withdraw individuals from the common scene of occupation, on which the sentiments of the heart, and the mind, are most happily employed" (p. 334).

There are many correspondences one could draw attention to between what Ferguson is saying here and what others have said before and since, but I shall make only two comments. The first is a reference to the purely historical question, whether Ferguson got what he wrote about the division of labor, or at any rate an indication of its significance, from his coeval Adam Smith. Probably he did, through lectures and private converse. The second comment is that it has been said that Ferguson had the idea that what follows division of labor is what later came to be termed "alienation." For this he got a pat on the back from Karl Marx (*The Poverty of Philosophy*, 1910, pp. 109 and 187); and in a way it is true, for he saw, and clearly stated, that division and specialization can bring about what Durkheim called *anomie*, making a man feel that he does not belong fully to the society of which he is a member. What he wrote may also be linked to what has been written about *Gemeinschaft* and *Gesellschaft*.

As I have remarked earlier, Ferguson has much to say on many topics to which in a brief essay I can only allude. The anthropologist will note that he was very interested in primitive—what he called "rude" or "savage" or "barbarous"—peoples, a study of whose social life he considered most valuable in that it enables us to make significant comparisons between the simpler societies and the more complex. He gives a good account, based on Jesuit sources, of what was then known of the American Indians, and in his chapter "Of Rude Nations prior to the Establishment of Property" (pp. 125 *et seq*) he makes many sensible and penetrating observations about these savages, though on the whole he tends to romanticize them. His brilliant and acutely sensitive skit on travelers' reports is highly amusing.

However, leaving many topics aside, it will be evident from what has already been said that for Ferguson, conceiving as he did of societies being natural systems of some kind, and hence that they can be studied as such much as the natural sciences study the phenomena with which they deal, it was necessary to hold also that there are general sociological laws ("principles") to be discovered, by reference to which variations can be explained. "In collecting the materials of history, we are seldom willing to put up with our subject merely as we find it. We are loth to be embarrassed with a multiplicity of particulars, and apparent inconsistencies. In theory we profess the investigation of general principles; and in order to bring the matter of our inquiries within the reach of our comprehension, are disposed to adopt any system" (pp. 23-4). Again: "To collect a multiplicity of particulars under general heads, and to refer a variety of operations to their common principle, is the object of science" (p. 40). Quoting him again: "In order to have a general and comprehensive knowledge of the whole, we must be determined on this, as on every other subject, to overlook many particulars and singularities, distinguishing different governments; to fix our attention on certain points, in which many agree; and thereby establish a few general heads, under which the subject may be distinctly considered. When we have marked the characteristics which form the general points of coincidence; when we have pursued them to their consequences in the several modes of legislation, execution and judicature, in the establishments which relate to police, commerce, religion, or domestic life; we have made an acquisition of knowledge, which, though it does not supersede the necessity of experience, may serve to direct our inquiries, and, in the midst of affairs, to give an order and a method for the arrangement of particulars that occur to our observation" (pp. 97-8). Thus we have to fix our attention on the significant general features of social institutions and overlook many particulars and singularities—mere events and personalities, which are "accidents." A classification of types may then be made, and must be made if any general and comprehensive laws are to be reached; this is the manner in which all the natural sciences have proceeded: they have traced facts to their general laws. He lays the same emphasis on the difference between the mere recording of facts and their relation to laws in the *Institutes* and the *Principles:* history is concerned with the detail of particulars, science with general principles (laws).

If there are general principles they must be dynamic principles for, like most of his contemporaries, Ferguson was chiefly interested in the study of social development. Indeed, he tells us, the great difference between man and animals is that "in the human kind, the species has a progress as well as the individual; they build in every subsequent age on foundations formerly laid . . ." (p. 7). Every scholar in Europe is more learned than the most accomplished of the Greeks and Romans, though this does not mean that he is their superior. How often have we been told this, that dwarfs on the backs of giants see further than the giants themselves? If I may quote our author again: "This progress in the case of man is continued to a greater extent than in that of any other animal. Not only the individual advances from infancy to manhood, but the species itself from rudeness to civilization" (pp. 1-2). Adam Ferguson was a great believer in progress and laws of progress.

Now, the method to be used in making the historical reconstruction necessary for the earlier phases of a people's social development so that the principles of progress can be revealed is that of what Dugald Stewart called "conjectural"—that is, hypothetical—history. Every phase in the history of our own society can, it was supposed, be known by observation of how people now live who are still in those stages. "What should distinguish a German or a Briton, in the habits of his mind or his body, in his manners or apprehensions, from an American (Indian) who, like him, with his bow and his dart, is left to traverse the forest; and in a like severe or variable climate, is obliged to subsist by the chase. If, in advanced years, we would form a just notion of our progress from the cradle, we must have recourse to the nursery, and from the example of those who are still in the period of life we mean to describe, take our representation of past manners, that cannot, in any other way, be recalled" (p. 122). Ferguson's interest in savages was chiefly that they illustrated a phase, he supposed, in our own history; and the evidences of prehistory give support to his supposition.

As always, the conception of laws ("principles") combined with the notion of progress inevitably led Ferguson to formulate a paradigm of stages drawn up on criteria of production and productive relations. With these economic stages go certain types of institutions and certain cultural traits. The criteria of Ferguson were much the same, and understandably so, as those of other writers who reflected on the different forms of society still to be observed. The earliest stage is that of hunting, fishing, or collecting the natural produce of the soil; in which there is little property and scarcely even the beginnings of subordination or government. The next stage is that of herders, who have property and hence distinctions between rich and poor, patron and client, master and servant. This distinction "must create a material difference of character, and may furnish two separate heads, under which to consider the history of mankind in their rudest state; that of the savage, who is not yet acquainted with property; and that of the barbarian, to whom it is, although not ascertained by laws, a principal object of care and desire" (p. 124). Property is the mother of progress, for it implies laws and habits of industry. In all this Ferguson leans heavily on Montesquieu.

In fact, we see in this book the essential ideas which make Montesquieu's *Esprit* so brilliant and original a classic. There is the same insistence on an objective study of social facts and on the need to reach formulations of a general kind based on a systematic comparison of societies. There is also the same emphasis on the logical consistency between series of social facts that we are later to find so strongly emphasized by Comte, and the need to explain institutions by reference to their functions in the activities of the total society rather than by reference to doctrines or philosophical axioms about social life or human nature (not that he always lived up to his exhortations in this respect). Where he differs most from Montesquieu is in a more rigid, though far from mechanical, idea of what might constitute a sociological law, and in the notion of unilinear social development, stages through which all societies pass and which can be reconstructed by use of what later became known as the comparative method, a notion deriving from a combination of the ideas of law and progress, the first largely a product of discoveries in physics, the second, according to Comte, a consequence of the collapse of Catholic feudal institutions.

Chapter 4
Millar (1735-1801)

One of the most interesting and rewarding of sociological writers, though seldom mentioned, and even more seldom read, is John Millar, a pupil of Adam Smith and from 1761 Professor of Law in the University of Glasgow. His best-known book, and the one which is of importance to us as anthropologists, if we are concerned with the history of our thought, is *The Origin of the Distinction of Ranks or an Inquiry into the Circumstances which give rise to Influence and Authority in the different Members of Society* (1771; 4th edition with an introduction by John Craig, Edinburgh, 1806), a book which shows the strong influence of Montesquieu, Lord Kames and Adam Smith (the last two and Hume being Millar's friends). The idea of social progress, the child of the Enlightenment, was very much in Millar's mind, and not inappropriately. He aimed, as we all say we try to do, at separating what is general to mankind from what in particular societies is due to particular circumstances. By comparing different societies he sought "to deduce the causes of different laws, customs, and institutions which, previously, had been remarked merely as isolated and uninstructive facts" (p. xxv). In reconstructing the earlier stages of development from savagery to civilization he used what Dugald Stewart called theoretical or conjectural history. Using this comparative method he classified human societies into four types or states: hunters and fishers, pastoralists, agriculturalists, and those engaged in commerce. There was nothing very original in this classification. All writers about social progress of his time had much the same; and it goes back, without the idea of progress, it is true, to Aristotle. Millar did not, however, as some did, suppose that every society of necessity passes through all these stages. He adopted the division as the most convenient for his purposes, which were to bring out the most significant changes which have led to civilization; and to define these as general rules or principles in the light of which particular forms of institutions can be seen to be illustrations of the principles. Deviations from them are to be regarded as due to special and peculiar circumstances. In the course of his study he used such information as was available about what he regarded as simpler peoples: North American Indians, Hottentots, West African Negroes, Tartars, Arabs, the ancient Germans, Greeks, Italians, etc.

Differences of rank and power are everywhere due to sex and age, and also to the need for leadership. But particular systems of law and government have been affected by all sorts of conditions: the fertility of the soil, the nature of its productions, the size of the community, its cultural development, communications, etc. But in spite of these differences the similarity of man's wants and of his faculties has everywhere produced a remarkable uniformity in the several steps of his progression. "There is thus, in human society, a natural progress from ignorance to knowledge, and from rude to civilized manners, the several stages of which are usually accompanied with peculiar laws and customs. Various accidental causes, indeed, have contributed to accelerate or retard this advancement in different countries" (p. 4).

Among primitive peoples women are treated harshly, little better than slaves, and sexual congress is scarcely more than animal mating. However, in matrilocal and matrilineal societies they have a much higher position (so he thought), e.g., the Lycians, the ancient inhabitants of Attica, some of the North American Indians, and the Indians of the Malabar coast; also where polyandry is practiced, e.g., in parts of the Median empire, on the coast of Malabar, and in some of the Iroquois cantons. Woman's condition improves when more attention is paid to the pleasures of sex and where her economic role is more important and valued. This supposedly took place in the pastoral ages. In general it can be said that the domestication of cattle gave rise to a permanent distinction of ranks, some people becoming richer than others and passing on their possessions to their descendants. The influence and power these people obtained was thus passed to their heirs, so that the distinction of ranks was permanent. Woman's position was again advanced in the agricultural stage, which also gave rise to property in land and hence to an even greater disproportion between the fortune and rank of individuals. Finally, changes in woman's condition arose from the improvement of useful arts and manufactures. These improvements led to a wider society and one in which there was greater intercommunication. Women ceased to be restricted in their activities to the family and home, and they mixed in outside society. "In this situation, the women became, neither the slaves, nor the idols of the other sex, but the friends and companions" (p. 89). They were now valued for their useful talents and accomplishments; and, with the increase in wealth, women of condition were admired for their agreeable qualities and for the amusement their conversation affords. (He notes that no writer of the Augustan age left a work of imagination in which love is supposed to be productive of any tragical, or very serious effects.) The progress of women is thus part of the general history of society. The book is a great polemic, and a worthy one, in woman's cause.

Age is very important in primitive societies. Children are entirely dependent on their fathers; old men are always respected and have authority. "So inseparately connected are age and authority in early periods, that in the language of rude nations the same word which signifies an old man is generally employed to denote a ruler or magistrate" (p. 114). When families begin to unite in a larger society the father loses some of his authority to representatives of the whole society; and when there are commerce and manufactures the children are no longer to the same extent dependent on him. The family becomes dispersed, the children leaving it to receive instruction and settling afterwards where there is employment. Thus they are emancipated from parental authority. However, when there is polygamy the authority of the head of the family lasts. Children are so numerous that parental affection is lessened; and the dissension among the wives requires a firm hand.

Millar then discusses the authority of a chief over the members of a tribe or village. This arises because tribes are almost continually at war with one another and feel the need for a military leader. This leader is given the respect once given to the father. In the hunting and fishing stage the leader is chosen simply for superior strength, courage, and other personal accomplishments. But in the pastoral stage the influence of a leader depends also on his greater wealth, which makes others dependent on him. "The authority derived from wealth, is not only greater than that which arises from mere personal accomplishments, but also more stable and permanent. Extraordinary endowments, either of mind or body, can operate only during the life of the possessor, and are seldom continued for any length of time in the same family. But a man usually transmits his fortune to his posterity, and along with it all the means of creating dependence which he enjoyed. Thus the son, who inherits the estate of his father, is enabled to maintain an equal rank, at the same time that he preserves all the influence acquired by the former proprietor, which is daily augmented by the power of habit, and becomes more considerable as it passes from one generation to another" (p. 152). Hence the intense interest pastoral peoples have in their genealogies. Authority is further enhanced in a society with agriculture. The chief, with his superior wealth in cattle and his numerous retainers, acquires a much larger estate than anybody else; and his retainers are increased and, since they live on his land, are still more dependent on him. Also estates are less likely to be destroyed or impaired by accidents than are flocks and herds, "so that the authority which is founded upon it becomes more permanent, and is apt to receive a continued accumulation of strength by remaining for ages in the same family" (p. 160). The chief is first a military leader; then he begins to exert his authority in other ways, including jurisdiction in both civil and criminal cases. Then he gets a sacred character—for example, it is said that he is descended from the sun—and he assumes priestly functions, or controls them. Finally, he takes on legislative functions.

Millar has discussed the powers of husband, father, and civil magistrate. He concludes by a discussion of the relation between masters and servants or slaves. He notes that there are but few slaves among the greater part of the savages of America and says that the reason for this is that they have no opportunity of accumulating wealth and cannot therefore maintain servants. Therefore, also, they kill their prisoners. The Tartars, on the other hand, have great flocks and herds and support a number of domestics. Hence they treat their prisoners with moderation. Slavery in the end disappears because in a technically well-developed country little profit can be drawn from the labor of a slave who is not trained to manufacture. It is more profitable to pay wages than to maintain slaves.

Millar's book contains some ethnographical and historical errors, perhaps unavoidable at the time he wrote it, but it is in many respects nearer to a modern sociological treatise than any other eighteenth-century book; and I have always been grateful to G. D. H. Cole for bringing it to my notice. We find the same insistence as in Montesquieu and Ferguson that in any systematic scholarship one has to separate the general from the particular, and whilst accounting for the general by some theoretical formulae (principles or laws) which explain it, one must at the same time account for variations or irregularities by reference to variable circumstances (as we have to do, e.g., with the laws of projectiles or falling bodies). What chiefly interested Millar was a study of the development of institutions (progress), a study which for the earlier stages had to be carried out with the aid of what has often been called the comparative method, a method which gives us a schematic typology (stages), each stage having its special features by which it is defined. When he discusses the factors leading to changes in the status of women, children, and social leaders he never appeals only, or even much at all, to psychology or philosophy but to other social facts. His explanations are sociological, especially economic: chiefs arise through war; property enables aristocracies and dynasties to persist; prisoners are treated well or otherwise according to their economic value; slaves are maintained only in societies where they produce more than the cost of maintaining them.

This might well be a treatise in modern sociology with its elimination of incidents, perturbations, special and peculiar circumstances, elements and persons. His typology of societies, which runs right through our literature, is by mode of livelihood—"economic" for those who like the word. Then in relation to this classification he makes an analysis of rank, showing the causes and conditions of prestige and power and character in each type of socioeconomic community. On the whole it is a sober assessment, not didactic or dogmatic: a clear and consistent enquiry with the limited aim of discovering the origin and development of class structure. At the time it was written this was a remarkable achievement.

Chapter 5
Condorcet (1743-1794)

Marie-Jean-Antoine-Nicolas Caritat, Marquis de Condorcet, born in Picardy, may be regarded as the last of the "philosophers." He wrote much, mostly on mathematics, and on political and social topics, but only one of his writings has any particular interest for us, the *Esquisse*. Condorcet played a considerable part in the public life of France of his time. He was a strong supporter of the Revolution but fell foul of the Jacobins and had to go into hiding. When he emerged from it he was arrested; and he was found dead in his cell on the following morning; it is uncertain whether it was suicide. He was a pupil of Turgot, an *"homme éclairé"*; he supported all the liberal programs of his time and was a believer in the perfectibility of man. He was especially hostile to religion, and to priests; he would go into a frenzy about them—as ignorant, hypocritical, greedy, corrupt, and depraved.

There are different versions of the *Esquisse* and I have used that edited by O. H. Prior. It should be kept in mind that it was written with speed and in the difficult circumstances of Condorcet's concealment. It is typical of eighteenth-century writers about social institutions; and especially significant for us in that it was a lamp that guided Comte through the dark.

All peoples about whom we know, Condorcet tells us, fall somewhere between our present degree of civilization and what we are told about savage tribes. There is a chain which leads from the first peoples known to us to the present nations of Europe. For the earliest period we have to rely on what travelers tell us. There has in fact to be a good measure of conjecture about the cultural steps which mankind took toward a higher state, so we must make theoretical observations of a logical and deductive sort, bearing in mind that the great difference between man and other animals, who are in many respects like him, living in a regular and continuous society, is that man has culture (especially language and some morality and social order). After this we have historical, documentary, sources. But we have to combine the histories of different peoples to get a general view of the progress of mankind as a whole. So, in the *Esquisse* he presents to us, in the eighteenth-century manner, a sketch or plan for a universal history, less of events or about individuals, though a few names are scattered here and there, than of the development of ideas and institutions from the beginnings of human society to the French Revolution. It is a history of thought, and he engages in it by a classification of the social and cultural stages, or states, through which man has passed in his progress. But if the form is historical the content is sociological.

Condorcet, like many of his contemporary writers, was much impressed, as indeed he had a right to be, by the progress of physics, brought about by mathematics; and he advocated the use of quantitative methods in the study of social facts. There was to be a new science, *"la mathématique sociale."* He thought that knowledge of what he believed to be the laws of history would give us the keys to the future. His outlook was what some people might call more scientific than that of most of the social philosophers of his time; and he certainly had a good understanding of scientific methods and techniques.

But let us pursue the book. In the first stage, men are united into peoples—small societies of families subsisting by hunting and fishing and with only a simple, crude technology and what he called science, but with language and some moral ideas. Custom had the place of law and there was embryonic government. There was little time for reflection and there was little division of labor. Men at this stage were already corrupted by superstition, and those with a rudimentary knowledge of arts and religion became leaders. These were the first priests, or charlatans or sorcerers.

The second stage is from pastoralism to agriculture. Pastoralism gave a more abundant and assured food supply and hence greater leisure. So there followed an increase in knowledge and the arts, and also differences in wealth and the employment of labor and slavery (the labor of a man was now worth more than the keeping of him). Also, the greater variety of things used and their unequal distribution produced commerce, which necessitated currency. Increase in the means of life led to increase of population, which in turn led to greater complexity in social life. Some peoples have remained in this stage owing to climate, habit, love of independence, conservatism, laziness, or superstition.

We may here pause to make some comments: (1) he gives no examples of societies in these stages; (2) his classification of social types is on criteria of production and productive relations; (3) he demonstrates logically if not empirically (or thinks that he does) how certain changes in social institutions inevitably follow changes in modes of production; and (4) he gives, as did others of his time, chief place in social evolution to property, from which follow leisure, government, commerce, currency, etc.

The third stage is from the beginnings of agriculture to the invention of alphabetic script—to Condorcet a most important invention, for it more or less rendered impossible, especially when printing was later invented, what he called superstition. Agriculture attached men to the soil and hence there was greater stability and continuity in social life. Ownership became more distinct, as did capital also, in that the yield of cultivation gave a surplus. Division of labor now took place and specialized crafts and economic functions resulted. Commerce was also extended and there was a general cultural development. To the three classes which we can already distinguish in pastoral societies—owners, domestics attached to them, and slaves—we now add laborers of all kinds and merchants; and as new institutions arose or old ones developed, there was need for more extensive legislation. All sorts of other progressive changes began to creep in at this stage, e.g., in the manner of educating children, in the relation between the sexes and in political institutions. The power of leading families increased and their excesses and extortions brought about revolutions and the establishment of republics or tyrannies. An agricultural people who had been conquered could not abandon their land but had to work it for their masters, so we get various forms of domination. He makes another sound observation when he says that communication between peoples much accelerated their progress through cultural borrowing; and, though war and conquest may ultimately lead to cultural decline, they at first often bring about expansion of the arts and serve to improve them. Arts and sciences made slow progress, the progress being due to certain families and castes having made them the foundation of their power to exploit the common people. Like Saint-Simon and Comte, Condorcet recognized the value at a certain time of what

37

was later to be inappropriate and become decadent. The other stages are historical ones and Condorcet abandons speculation at this point. He describes the main phases of the history of thought in Europe. They are: stage IV, the progress of human thought in Greece to the division of the sciences about the time of Alexander; stage V, progress of the sciences from their division to their decadence (the period of Aristotle)—the decadence was due, as Gibbon also informs us, to Christianity, which was hostile to all spirit of inquiry, and to the Barbarians; stage VI, the decadence of enlightenment (*lumières*) to its restoration about the time of the crusades; stage VII, the first progress of the sciences after their restoration in the west to the invention of printing, which finally made the persistence of superstition impossible, scepticism being spread too far and wide; stage VIII, from the invention of printing to the time when science and philosophy broke the back of authority; stage IX, from Descartes to the formation of the French Republic; stage X, a vision of the future progress of the human mind (*esprit*).

There is no need to discuss his comments on these historical changes in detail. We may note, however, that he showed acumen in his selection of them and also in the sociological features he considered to be most significant of each; e.g., much progress was made in Greece because there the priests had no monopoly of learning—the crusades were favorable to liberty in that they weakened and impoverished the nobles and extended the contacts of European peoples with the Arabs which had already been formed in Spain and through the commerce of Pisa, Genoa, and Venice; the invention of printing led to a strong and free public opinion which could not be stifled; the fall of Constantinople to the Turks brought the original writings of Aristotle and Plato to the scholars of Europe; the discovery of America had, among other consequences, the advantage that it was then possible to study many new and different types of society (he did not mention particular primitive societies, but it is evident that he had read what had been written about them in his day); the use of vernacular languages in the place of Latin in all branches of philosophy and science rendered them accessible to the common people but made it more difficult for the savant to follow their general advance.

A few concluding observations may be appropriate. Condorcet was primarily a polemical writer and a social reformer who stood up to privilege and exploitation wherever he found them. He talked much about science, but as a student of cultural history he was not a very deep scholar—what he wrote about the Middle Ages displayed bias and left much to be desired in scholarship. Nevertheless, he is rightly regarded as a precursor of sociology and social anthropology in that he was speaking of social institutions and the history of thought rather than of political events in the narrow sense, and in a scientific, comparative way. He held that "The sole foundation of belief in the natural sciences is this idea, that the general laws, known or not known, which rule the phenomena of the universe, are necessary and constant; and for what reason would this sentiment be less true for the development of the intellectual and moral faculties of man, than for the other operations of nature?" (p. 203). Like his contemporaries he saw these laws as laws of cultural and concomitant social development or progress, and an essential feature of culture is that, in spite of backslidings, it is cumulative—a boy leaving school today knows more of mathematics than Newton knew. The laws have therefore to be formulated in terms of stages (*époques*) in each of which various social changes give rise to new needs (*besoins*) which in their turn bring about further changes. And though these changes may be associated in our minds with individuals, who may even give their names to an epoch, great social changes make them and not they the changes. Descartes was an important figure, but his importance is in his being a sign and product of, and a link in, a great movement in the history of thought—a way of looking at things akin to that of the Marxists. When Condorcet talks about the invention of printing he does not tell us its date or who the inventor was, for the only interest it has for him is that it was the culmination of social changes in one epoch and the cause of social changes in the next. And all this meant, to him at least, that a general theory could be formulated and, furthermore, that the history of any particular people could only be understood in the light of such theoretical knowledge based on universal history.

For Condorcet, the study of social facts must be by observation of actual relations. The religion of books is not the same as that of the people. Law and its execution are quite different things. So are the principles of government and its actualities and indeed any institution as imagined by its creators and how it works in practice. He here foreshadows social surveys and fieldwork.

His writing emphasizes that social facts must be studied in relation to each other as functioning parts of a total social system (*système social*)—e.g., the progress of science in any country depends on natural circumstances, political and social conditions, forms of religion and government, and economic circumstances. All parts of a social system are interdependent and this is necessarily so. Condorcet was a great believer in applied social science (*art social*), which will derive from a theoretical science of society. "In the same way as the mathematical and physical sciences serve to make perfect the arts employed for our most elementary needs, is it not equally in the necessary order of nature that the progress of the moral and political sciences should exercise the same action on the motives which control our sentiments and our actions?" (p. 227). In other words, greater knowledge invariably and inevitably leads to the cumulative amelioration of mankind. Perhaps he was over-optimistic; but his star *"brille encore. Elle brillera toujours."*

Chapter 6
Comte (1798–1857)

To understand the work of Auguste Comte fully, one would have to take into more detailed account things which colored his work to the point of dominating its themes: his royalist and Catholic family (he was always a paradox: a republican royalist, aristocratic proletarian, Catholic freethinker); also his acute paranoia, reaching heights of suicidal madness, and the megalomania that so often accompanies it, rendering him intolerable to anyone who might have thought of helping him attain academic status and a painful experience to those of his family and friends who sought to ease his condition only to be repaid by malice of an almost Corvoesque intensity. And then of course his women: the mistress passion of his youth, Pauline (the mother of his child); the ex-prostitute Caroline Massin, with whom in 1825 he made a disastrous marriage (in a ceremony well described as *lugubre*), a long-suffering lady who took much and could take more no longer and left him in 1842; and lastly in 1844 the beautiful (if we may judge by her picture) lady Clotilde de Vaux (her husband appears to have been in prison), whose role would scarcely be accepted as a character of make-believe, the Beatrice—his *"sainte patronne"*—who inspired the near lunacy of his last writings. The poor lady endured listening to his lectures, from which even her death in the following year did not release her, for Comte continued to deliver discourses at her graveside; yet who can read the *Dédicace* to the *Système* or its *Invocation finale* without being deeply moved?

Comte's opinions and even his character were very much shaped by the events of his time. France, bled almost to death in the Napoleonic wars, had to endure many vicissitudes and uncertainties in the years which followed, which drove Comte to near despair and convinced him more and more that the basic issues were not political but moral and could be decided only by a combination of the scientific study of the social problems involved with a radical

41

regeneration of the French people—a sincere acceptance of altruistic standards, values, and sentiments. France was defeated and defeatist and could, and must, rise again but this could be achieved only if knowledge and duty joined hands.

Then again, Comte's contribution to social studies must be seen in the perspective of the general history of ideas if the originality of his thought is to be appreciated, and his claim to be the founder of sociology upheld. Clearly, he was deeply influenced by Montesquieu, Turgot, Diderot, and the encyclopedists in general, and above all by Condorcet; also by de Maistre, and by Hume, Adam Ferguson, and Adam Smith, and by contemporary socialist propaganda. He was, of course, profoundly influenced also by Saint-Simon, whose secretary and collaborator he was for seven years, from 1817 to 1824 (and heaven forbid that we should enter into the tangled relationship between the two men). Equally clearly, much of what he regarded as his most inspired discovery—the positivist approach to the study of social institutions—was almost a commonplace among eighteenth-century philosophers, and his insistence on the need to reconcile such studies with an acceptance of order and authority was a familiar topic, especially in the Catholic France of the Restoration—indeed, a claim might be put forward on behalf of the triumvirate Bonald (1754-1840), de Maistre (1754-1821), Chateaubriand (1768-1848) for some of the credit that has gone to Comte.

But whatever claims might be advocated on behalf of others and however much he was both the intellectual child of his time and heir to the past—and no one in this broad sense can be regarded as an entirely original thinker—there can be no doubt about his enormous influence on nineteenth-century ways of looking at social affairs, an influence easy to discern in the writings of men like Herbert Spencer, J. S. Mill, Lecky and Morley in this country and Lévy-Bruhl and Durkheim in his own—none of whom were little fish. We can see his influence also on such historians as Mommsen and Grote and, so it is said, Taine and Renan.

But all this, however essential it would be to take into consideration in a biographical sketch, can be set aside in giving an answer to the question here asked: what in Comte's writings have significance for social anthropologists and sociologists, and not only for their historical interest but also for their relevance to our problems today? Many of the issues he raised are still unsettled, many of the questions he asked still unanswered or at any rate still disputed.

Born in 1798 and dead in 1857, Comte did not have a very long life, and considering also how it was beset by poverty, sickness, *dissentiments conjugaux*, and acrimonious quarrels of one sort or another it is surprising what he accomplished: six volumes of the *Cours de philosophie positive* (1830-42), four volumes of the *Système de politique positive* (1851-54), the *Catéchisme positiviste* (1852) and many *opuscules*. Much also has been written about him.

For our purposes we may give our attention mainly, though not exclusively, to the *Cours,* a stylistically repellent monstrosity of 2,582 pages and probably near a million words which makes its prolixity and didacticism an added aggravation to a test of endurance. The first three volumes of this vast encyclopedia of the sum of human knowledge (he and Spencer were the last two men who aspired to universal knowledge) deal with what today would be termed the natural sciences—inorganic and organic—and only the last three with social institutions and morals. The natural science volumes cannot, however, be ignored by the social scientist, because they form a prologue to the social science volumes and are a necessary introduction to them in two respects. Firstly, in Comte's view, some acquaintance with the natural sciences is required because the essential methodology of all the sciences is the same and the correct use of procedures of observation and analysis in the social sciences could therefore best be studied in those sciences which had preceded them and were more developed. Secondly, the sciences have a logical structure which must also be a chronological order and can therefore be best presented in a hierarchy of increasing complexity of content, with mathematics at one end and sociology at the other. The logical structure and chronological sequence of the series is inevitable because each depends on the truths of those which precede it.

J. S. Mill (*Auguste Comte*, 1961, pp. 37-8) states Comte's argument succinctly: "Thus, the truths of number are true of all things, and depend only on their own laws; the science, therefore, of Number, consisting of Arithmetic and Algebra, may be studied without reference to any other science. The truths of Geometry presuppose the laws of Number, and a more special class of laws peculiar to extended bodies, but require no others: Geometry, therefore, can be studied independently of all sciences except that of Number." And so on: "The phenomena of human society obey laws of their own, but do not depend solely upon these: they depend upon all the laws of organic and animal life, together with those of inorganic nature, these last influencing society not only through their influence on life, but by determining the physical conditions under which society has to be carried on."

The phenomena of each science are thus more complex than those of the preceding one, and if this is true, it is in consequence increasingly difficult as we ascend the scale to formulate any laws governing the phenomena being investigated. Even if, therefore, sociology finally succeeds in making general statements about its subject matter they are likely to have a smaller degree of generality than those in the inorganic and organic sciences and will anyhow, and inevitably, be reached only when the organic sciences have attained a high point of development. This does not mean, however, that the subject matter of any science in the ascending scale of the sciences can be organized and explained in terms found to be conceptually appropriate in the science preceding it. Each science is a new phenomenal level demanding its own explanations in its own specific terms, for each has its own specific, autonomous, character. The struggle to mark out an exclusive domain of inquiry in the social sciences—to determine what constitutes a social fact which is not any other kind of fact, what are sociological phenomena which are not any other kind of phenomena—was still a battle being fought by Durkheim more than half a century later in his manifesto: *Les Règles de la méthode sociologique.*

Here we may pause and ask some questions, but before asking them it has to be noticed, and of course often has been, that Comte does not include psychology in his series (to the annoyance, among others, of Mill and Spencer) and indeed expresses his utmost contempt for it—which made it easier to endow social phenomena with specificity. His contempt for the introspective observations which passed as psychology in his day may well have been deserved, but my impression is that he held that on logical grounds there could be no such science. Man is born into the world an animal. His moral and intellectual functions are what are implanted on the organism by society, the products of culture. Consequently, one must not define "humanity" by "man" but "man" by "humanity." Furthermore it is quite irrational to try to explain society, even in its simplest fetishistic stage, in terms of individual needs, it being the most vicious of metaphysical (Comte's dirtiest word) theories which derives faculties from needs of the individual. Men only respond to needs by creating new institutions, when social conditions determine the response.

So all in all what place could there be for an autonomous science of psychology in between physiology and sociology? What people might call psychology was to Comte a branch of physiology, what he called cerebral physiology, and he later, much to the embarrassment of some of his erstwhile admirers, advocated phrenology as the most appropriate means of studying mental phenomena. Leaving out the phrenology it seems to me that Durkheim took up much the same position, that there is no place for an intermediate science between the organic and the social sciences, though, so far as I know, he never actually said this in so many words.

What, now, about the hierarchy of the sciences based on the increasing complexity of their subject matter? Comte's classification of the sciences was for his time (though Karl Pearson did not think much of it) an original and illuminating piece of systematization, and as a logical paradigm it is convincing; though, as oversimplified by Comte, it is scarcely acceptable as a historical record of a unilinear order of development of the sciences, as Spencer was to point out.

The whole scheme makes certain basic assumptions which, though they seem to be still taken for granted by some anthropologists, are nevertheless questionable. The fundamental dogma is one shared by most eighteenth-century moral philosophers (Rousseau was an exception), that social institutions are just as much part of "nature" (one of their favorite metaphysical terms) as the phenomena studied by physicists and chemists. Comte states this without any equivocation, if not without evident contradictions. Earlier ideas about social institutions were either theological fictions, happily in decay, or, what was far worse, metaphysical entities, still alas only too much in evidence, and just theology (for which one could have some respect) gone bad. The Reformation and the Revolution had destroyed the Catholic–feudal structure of Europe, and the metaphysical notions which served to undermine its intellectual and moral basis were such rubbish that they could only be transitory, critical, negative, and illusory. What was wanted, and had to come, was a rational and scientific study of social life. Once theological dogmas and metaphysical jargon had given way to sober scientific research into the physical universe and the structure and functions of living organisms, man had acquired real knowledge, a knowledge of the laws of their existence, which he could apply to ameliorate, at any rate to some extent, his own circumstances. The old division of the Greeks between natural philosophy and moral philosophy must therefore go for ever. The pioneers of positive philosophy had long ago pointed to the path which must be pursued—Bacon, Galileo, Descartes; Bacon above all. We had now reached the point in the development of thought at which social phenomena could, and should, be studied by the same methods as had yielded such remarkable results in the natural sciences, and comparable results might be expected. The techniques employed, as distinct from the methods, would of course have to vary according to the nature of the phenomena under investigation. The methods are observation (including experiment), comparison, and generalization (which, when one comes to think of it, are processes common and essential to all thought, scientific or any other). The inductive method to be pursued in the social sciences is that of concomitant variation. The techniques employed will vary according to the situation in which observations are to be recorded. This is really mainly what Comte meant by "positive philosophy"—that we should in inquiring into the nature of social life be rigorously scientific, basing our procedures on the model of the well-established natural sciences. And I may add here that Comte has often been so misrepresented that he might have said that he was not a Comtist (positivist), as Marx had to say that he was not a Marxist; though, as Charlton remarks (1959, p. 24), to enquire how far Comte was a consistent positivist may seem not unlike asking whether the pope is a Catholic.

But what about the little word with the big—and, it seems to me, ambiguous—sense, "nature"? In one way of looking at the matter, everything which exists is "natural" and is also part of a system and has a structure, and can therefore be studied as such. But in this sense the concept is so amorphous, so all embracing, that it is of doubtful utility. When a word means everything it can also mean nothing. It is true that in this sense the planetary system and an Act of Parliament are equally parts of nature but they are phenomena of such different orders that one may indeed question whether much is gained by making the statement. To give any precision to the term "natural" it seems to me what is required is to define what is "nonnatural," and to furnish some examples to illustrate the use of that term. After all, Comte's scientific (positivist) philosophy is no less "natural," in the sense of being determined—as positivist philosophy must hold—by social conditions, than the theological and metaphysical philosophies he rejected —as indeed he might have admitted. So we are back to the old dilemma of the science of knowledge, a mirror facing a mirror with nothing in between. Who is the potter, pray, and who the pot?

But there is more to Comte than an insistence on scientific rigor in our study of social institutions if we are to discover the laws of their development. He claimed to have discovered the most fundamental of these laws, that of the famous three stages (or states)—actually first enunciated by Turgot. According to Comte, man first conceives of the world theologically, that is, anthropomorphically, first in the form of Comte's idea of what fetishism was; then polytheistically; then monotheistically. Monotheism in modern Europe faded after nationalism had ruined the Catholic Church and under the impact of the anarchy of Protestantism and rationalist criticism, deism, and finally a hotch-potch of absurd metaphysical notions advanced as explanations: ends, principles, causes, Nature, substance, essence, virtues, form and, on the political side, such sterile rubbish as liberty, equality, fraternity, the state of nature, and what have you! His particular dislike of lawyers was, among other things, on account of their constant talk about natural rights, a meaningless conception they got from Roman law.

Even the greatest philosophers of the seventeenth and eighteenth centuries belonged to this negative and sterile category; Hobbes, Locke, Voltaire, Helvetius, and Rousseau. They could not understand that the crisis of their time was a moral and spiritual one, so they thought their difficulties could be overcome by legislation. Their mistake was to suppose that intelligence and learning could by themselves do the trick: the worst of all illusions, the Greek utopian illusion. A pedantocratie (a word coined—in its English form—by J. S. Mill) just will not work. "Legitimate social supremacy does not belong, properly speaking, either to force or to reason, but to morality, dominating equally the acts of the one and the counsels of the other" (*Cours*, VI, p. 312).

Full justice has not been done to Comte in this matter of the three stages. He was saying little more than what was the thesis of his best biographer, Lucien Lévy-Bruhl, in his many books, that on the whole we may say that primitive and barbarous peoples tend to attribute events to what are commonly called supernatural forces of one kind or another (magic or religion) and that such interpretations slowly give way to rational-positive or scientific ones in the course of cultural progress; and he tried to show, which

Lévy-Bruhl did not, how this development might have come about. Who can, in the broad view, deny that he was right? Whether he was justified also in equating the ontogenetic and the phylogenetic, as Freud did in his theory of the libido, is another question: "Then, each of us, in contemplating his own history, does he not remember that he has been successively, with regard to his most important ideas, theologian in his infancy, metaphysician in his youth, and natural philosopher in his manhood" (*Cours*, I, p. 4).

It further follows from the logic of his argument that the theological or imaginative (*fictif*) type of explanation and the metaphysical or abstract type of explanation (in that order) of phenomena are ousted in favor of rational and experimental or positive ones in the sciences in their historical sequence: first in the inorganic sciences, then in the organic sciences, leaving only the social sciences cluttered up with a lot of idiotic verbiage which passed, and still passes, fraudulently as rational interpretation. Things are a bit more complicated than Comte made them out to be, but with certain reservations we may here again accept his thesis in broad outline. Nor did Comte hold, as some have given the impression that he did, that the three stages, or states, in cultural development—the theological, the metaphysical, and the positivist—were closed and exclusive systems of thought. This would have been nonsense to him, for his whole point was that while one of them is the dominant philosophy of each phase and tends to exclude explanations of phenomena which run directly counter to it the other ways of thinking are found together with it, and indeed must be, since the sciences advance from the theological phase to the positivist phase in chronological order. Moreover there could otherwise have been no progress, because progress comes about by the maturing in one phase of the seed which will come to flower in succeeding phases; so what appears as decadence may equally be viewed as commencement of new birth and what appears as the height of development in any stage may equally be viewed as an advanced symptom of its decline. Comte was under no illusions about current theological and metaphysical ideas coexisting with positivist ones; and indeed when we cast a brief look at the *Système* we shall abundantly appreciate that he, in his rather peculiar way of looking at things, understood that this must always be so.

Comte has, I think, also sometimes been misunderstood with regard to his attitude to the theological and the metaphysical. Naturally, he regarded the positivist philosophy as the best, both because it came last in the evolutionary series (evolution and progress were all the same for him) and because it had a more rational understanding of nature; but he also regarded the earlier stages in which different outlooks on the world were prevalent as inevitable and indispensable stages in the development of thought, and therefore, in an historical sense, as beneficial. Moreover, if there had not been a good deal of purely rational thought and empirical knowledge in the theological stage modern science could never have come into being. And was not religion the mother of culture and social order? So even Protestantism and metaphysical conceptions had to be, in that they played their part in the undermining of the Catholic-feudal society of Europe and, negative, anarchical, abhorrent, and puerile though they were to Comte, they performed this essential service, as a *lacune nécessaire,* as *provisoires,* and thereby brought about the emergence of the new positivist order, which was to be seen as a terminus, just as the dictatorship of the proletariat and the withering away of the state is envisaged as the final situation by Marxists. The inexorable, ineluctable laws of progress—against which it is useless to fight, our only freedom being to recognize them—seem to stop operating at this point. Man is master of the universe and master of man. But, as we shall see, Comte became increasingly convinced that it was an oversimplification—indeed, wishful thinking—to suppose that knowledge could by itself bring about the ordered social life demanded if science were to be applied to the amelioration of the appalling moral decadence and intellectual confusion he saw all around him in the France of his time. Only religion could do that—but not *la religion révélée;* only *la religion démontrée,* a sort of humanistic morality.

It will have been observed that Comte's whole thesis is a philosophy of history (as well as being a history of philosophy); not just a philosophy of science, but a philosophy of the development of thought in the history of mankind. We must be clear in our minds on this point what Comte and his contemporaries and immediate forerunners, and indeed also the anthropologists of the nineteenth century, in general, understood by the sort of history they thought worth pursuing, for their perspective has been largely lost, possibly to the detriment of our subject, which may have to some extent abandoned thereby what gave it its bearings and its consistency.

According to Comte, social studies consist ideally of two branches: social statics dealing with the laws of coexistence and social dynamics dealing with the laws of succession. He regarded this as a fundamental distinction found throughout the sciences, for example, in biology between anatomy and physiology; and it is necessary to distinguish radically, with regard to each political subject, "between the fundamental study of the conditions of existence of the society and that of the laws of its continuous movement" (*Cours*, IV, p. 167). But he thought that in practice in social studies it would be premature and inopportune at the time he wrote to try to keep them apart (and nobody has been able to do so successfully since). He tells us about social statics little more than that all social activities form a harmonious whole, a consensus: that economic, legal, religious, and aesthetic facts cannot be understood in isolation but only in their relation to one another. Beyond this somewhat bland assertion, this enunciation of what Mauss was to call a *fait total,* he gives by way of illustrative examples in support, little more than some very broad observations about such phenomena as militarism and industrialism. But he has plenty to say about the evolution of civilization, holding that it is on account of the nature of human society and culture that the method of analysis must be historical, for unlike biology (genetics?), for instance, sociology is concerned with the influence of different generations on those which follow them, a process of gradual but continuous accumulation; and this is true of both social dynamics and social statics, for the laws of coexistence manifest themselves above all in movement.

Earlier writers had the idea of law but they did not possess the essential concept of progress without which the idea of law is sterile, since the laws regulating social phenomena are essentially those of development or evolution or progress; or one can at least say that until the diachronic laws are discovered the synchronic ones cannot be discovered either. The "incomparable" Aristotle, for instance, or Montesquieu had not grasped the idea of progress, which alone could have given them a true understanding of the nature of social institutions, the meaning of which is to be seen in their movement in a certain direction. Without the notion of progress they were bogged down in vague and chimerical conceptions of oscillatory or circular movements. The idea of a definite and continuous movement in one direction was first brought about, according to Comte, by Christianity, but it did not go very far because social conditions were adverse and the natural sciences still nascent. The credit for the first consistent attempt to formulate laws of social progress must go to Condorcet. It was he who was, if not the first, the clearest exponent of what a sociological law should be: a formula derived from a study of cultural development. It was certainly one of Comte's contributions to social studies that he saw that to understand social phenomena it must be recognized that they are always in movement and can only be studied as such. The past is in the present and the present is in the future. As Lévy-Bruhl, in discussing Comte, puts it, "Man has knowledge of himself when he puts himself back in the evolution of humanity" (*La Philosophie d'Auguste Comte*, 1921, p. 243).

History, we must emphasize, did not convey the sense to Comte that it conveys to the modern reader of a book on the political history of a people. For the historical writings of his day he had nothing but scorn—they were literary, narrative, almost anecdotal exercises—but he would have shown little appreciation either of the historical writings of today, or most of them. They would have been for him mere chronicles of events, and of persons of no great significance. In the social histories of Comte and his eighteenth-century precursors there are no particular events or persons. You look in vain for dates and names and even for mention of peoples in Adam Ferguson (except in his history of the Roman Republic), Condorcet or Comte. What does it matter who invented printing or precisely when it was invented? These details are accidents not worth recording. There is no history worth recording other than universal history. There cannot be a history of mathematics for one side of the Alps and another for the other side.

And in all this Comte was very far from holding a materialist view of history. The vast social movements he was interested in are indeed brought about largely by economic—in the earliest stages, bionomic—changes, but these cannot be isolated from spiritual developments: "The grave error of historical philosophy . . . results evidently, in fact, from an exaggerated and almost exclusive preoccupation with the temporal point of view of human events . . ." (*Cours*, V, p. 47). Then again he tells us, "It is ideas which govern and disturb the world. . . . All the social mechanism rests finally on opinions. . . . The great political and moral crisis of present-day societies, derives, in the last analysis, from the intellectual anarchy" (*Cours*, I, p. 26). No one is agreed on the fundamental ideas and values, without which agreement stable social life is impossible. Once Comte starts chasing that hare there is no stopping him. We shall have a further look at the hare later.

In one respect Comte's view of history might shock many modern social scientists. In spite of all he says about the need for use of the comparative method (what he calls *la méthode historique*) in reaching general conclusions, he pretty well confines himself to the conjecture, common to social philosophers of the time, that all peoples, being all alike, fundamentally progress in the same manner; though some, for reasons of climate or race or other "inevitable secondary differences" (*Cours*, IV, p. 232), or because conditions may for a while be affected by "exceptional perturbations," progress slower or faster than others. Consequently he reaches the conclusion that to study the development of social institutions in general it is sufficient to trace their evolution to its highest point— the civilization of Western Europe (*la civilisation occidentale*), and in particular France—*"centre normal de l'Occident"* (*Système,* I, p. 62). This may be a fiction but it is methodologically required. To bother about the history of India and China would merely create confusion and be a vain concession to concreteness and a display of sterile erudition. It is indispensable to have the hypothesis of a single people to whom can be ideally related all the consecutive social modifications actually observed among distinct populations. Without this abstraction, this rational fiction, this theoretical framework, sociology would be no more than a barren, pointless, merely empirical collection of endless facts—a vain accumulation of incoherent monographs—which is what he would have said it very largely is, and what social anthropology could become.

Science is essentially composed of laws and not of facts. Mere accumulation of facts leads nowhere. Individual histories have no meaning except when viewed in the light of universal history and the laws of its determination. Bossuet understood this, although he was a theologian; so did Turgot and Condorcet. The particularities of history do not give us its laws; it is the laws which will ultimately account for the particularities, make them significant, even give them meaning for him who contemplates them: *"la notion philosophique de 'loi' naturelle consiste toujours à saisir la constance dans la variété"* (*Système,* II, p. 41). Particular histories are only useful to provide sociology with data for the testing of hypotheses and with illustrations for its theoretical conclusions; and they do not even do that if their authors are unaware of the hypotheses in the first place. All this is indeed sound reasoning, if, as Comte supposed, social phenomena are of the same order as those of the physical world: an apple falling or the trajectile of a bullet are to be understood in the light of well-established laws of physics of one sort or another. Certainly Comte is right when he says that no observation is really possible at all except in so far as it is directed and interpreted by some theory; people who think that theory arises from bare observations themselves are quite wrong. Even in the simplest researches, scientific observations have to be preceded by some conception of the corresponding phenomena.

Even so, if all this be accepted—and in general much of it has to be—we must not expect results from the application of scientific methods of research to social facts commensurate with what has been achieved in the natural sciences. Social facts are much more complex, and in any case we are, says Comte, speaking of his time (and he might have said the same today), only at the threshold of positivist sociology, the situation being exactly like it was before astronomy replaced astrology, chemistry alchemy, and a system of medical studies the search for a universal panacea. We must not, therefore, expect to reach, perhaps ever, laws of a high level of generality; and even to reach generalizations on any level some modifications in general methodological conceptions are required in dealing with social phenomena.

The first and fundamental adjustment is necessitated by the very nature of these phenomena. In the inorganic sciences, even in the biological sciences, one seeks to study the simplest phenomena first and then the more complex, to break complex reality into simpler and simpler elements, so isolated for study. An analysis of this kind is inappropriate in the case of social phenomena, which are completely meaningless when broken into elements and can only be studied as wholes. What we know is the whole, so one should follow the sound rule of science, that one should proceed from the known to the unknown, and hence in the social sciences one should reverse the procedure of the inorganic sciences and proceed from the complex to the simple. Consequently every social fact "is explained, in the true scientific sense of the term, when it has been suitably connected with either the totality of the corresponding situation or the totality of the preceding situation" (*Cours*, IV, p. 214). It follows from this idea of a total situation that social relations, ideas, and customs form a system in which every part is functionally dependent on every other part for both its operation and, for the observer, its meaning: "This preliminary aspect of the science of politics supposes then evidently, of complete necessity, that contrary to present-day philosophical habits, each of the numerous social elements, ceasing to be envisaged in an ab-

solute and independent manner, must always be exclusively conceived of as relative to all the others, with which it is intimately
and always bound up in a fundamental solidarity" (*Cours*, IV, p.
171). "Then, the scientific principle of the general relation consists
essentially in the evident spontaneous harmony which must always
tend to rule between the whole and the parts of the social system,
of which the elements cannot avoid being finally combined among
themselves in a manner fully conforming to their own nature"
(*Cours* IV, p. 176).

In other words, and as said earlier, at any stage political, moral,
economic, domestic, religious, intellectual, and aesthetic phenomena all hang together and form a complex unity, the solidarity of
which is derived from some dominant principle. There is an *"intime
solidarité nécessaire entre les divers aspects quelconques du mouvement humain"* (*Cours*, VI, p. 61). This was Montesquieu's thesis and it is
still, or was until recently, a dogma, or at any rate a methodological axiom, among many social anthropologists. Comte saw that
this is a very difficult proposition and that (I must say it again) to
combine static with dynamic studies—in a very general sense, sociological with historical studies—is easier said than done, for the
data are not only those at any one time existing but also those from
which they have evolved, and they have furthermore to be viewed
in relation to their evolutionary potentialities, what they are becoming or are to become.

I do not pursue Comte's discussion into the social phase of positivism, for he was speculating on the future—even more hazardous
than speculating on the past—and he more or less regarded himself, with his usual superb self-confidence, as the only person who
had knowledge of it: of the new world of science and technology, of
rationalism, humanism, agnosticism, industrialism, pacifism, altruism, etc. We will rather ask what was supposed to be the outcome and purpose of this lengthy inquiry.

The outcome was to be the establishment of the laws of social
life, it being understood that such laws are never absolute but relative to our knowledge at any given stage—absolute knowledge of
reality is unachievable. There are two kinds of natural sciences: the
one abstract, general (nomothetic), which has for object the discovery of the laws which govern the different classes of phenomena
(Comte's use of the concept of "law" seems to me to come perilously near to what he denigrated as "metaphysical"); the other,
concrete, particular (ideographic) and descriptive, consists in the

application of these laws to the effective history of the different existing beings. I regard this distinction as being in practice hard to maintain and serving little useful purpose; but for Comte the first, the speculative sciences, are fundamental and the second, the applied, are secondary. Now Comte, the philosopher, was concerned only with the speculative and general. It can be said that he gave us excellent directions for how to find these laws, but it cannot be said that he discovered any—the so-called law of the three stages, even if true, is scarcely a law in the sense the word can be used in the natural sciences, and as defined by him. In the absence of a developed body of theory, he held, as is understandable, that while the natural and advanced sciences may be taught dogmatically, the social sciences, being in a nascent stage, should be taught historically.

But in spite of his personal interest in the speculative, he considered it a complete waste of time to acquire knowledge of the laws of social life unless there could be based upon them an applied science of sociology. Not that he believed that research for useful ends at the expense of speculative research was anything but a mistake, even from the point of view of utility itself. But knowledge, to be worth pursuing, must be applicable. His oft-quoted formula was *"Science, d'où prévoyance; prévoyance d'où action!"* He would have agreed with what is written on Karl Marx's headstone in Highgate Cemetery, "The philosophers have only interpreted the world in various ways: the point, however, is to change it."

But, says Comte, one can only modify social conditions to a very slight extent by a scientific study of them, and what can be done can only affect the pace of development and not its direction or outcome, which are determined by inexorable natural laws. There is plasticity only in so far as, since social progress does not follow a straight line but advances by a series of oscillations, an exact knowledge of these movements enables us to diminish the oscillations and the gropings (*tatonnements*), procedures by trial and error, which correspond to them; and also to exercise some control over lesser crises by rational prevision. Not, he hastens to add, that any hope can be expected from statesmen and other men of affairs, who are under the illusion that social phenomena can be indefinitely and arbitrarily modified. All that results from their fumbling is disorderly experimentation. Comte's attitude in this matter resembles in general that of the Marxists, or what used to be their attitude: we must on the whole admit and accept our impotence when confronted with great social and cultural movements. We may say about all this that while it is evident that one cannot have developed applied science until one has a developed theoretical science to apply—no developed medicine, for example, without a developed physiology—empirical knowledge is capable of application up to a point, and always has been; and it can be further held that learning may be useful in other than a strictly (and perhaps narrowly) positivist sense. Comte scarcely enters into these questions, but it is evident from the *Système* that the moral regeneration he proposes to impose can in no conceivable way be said to arise from sociological enquiries into social phenomena or from the hoped-for laws that are supposed to govern them.

So far we have considered a few points made by Comte in his vast *Cours,* such points as it would seem still as worth emphasizing today as when he made them. We cannot accept all of them without reservations; and we must pass judgment on him for his almost total disregard of facts (it comes almost as a surprise when he begins in the third volume of the *Système* to record some events in European history or perhaps we should say his estimation of them). But we must not judge him too severely on this score, for he was delivering lectures on the philosophy of science and on the history of science (he may be said to have been the first historian of science) and not on science. He has also been often rebuked for his mania for systematization, his *"esprit de système"* as Renan called it. The most damaging criticism is, I think, his *post factum* interpretation of history—and of a limited history in a particular region and restricted in time—as a sequence of events which was "inevitable," "inexorable," "necessary" (metaphysical terms if ever there were any!), allowing nothing to choice and intention, making man the spectator and not the shaper of his destiny. It has fairly been asked whether Comte could, with all his talk of methodology and laws, have predicted any event in history, even events of fundamental significance in the history of mankind, those great movements of which he spoke so much. Certainly his predictions were very wide of the mark. "The owl of Minerva spreads its wings only with the falling of the dusk."

But in spite of all its defects it is true what John Morley said of the *Cours,* that "This analysis of social evolution will continue to be regarded as one of the great achievements of the human intellect." As social anthropologists we may reflect on the vast influence he has had on our subject, both directly and indirectly. It is customary, and right, for us to pay tribute to Durkheim but there is little of general methodological or theoretical significance in his writings that we do not find in Comte if we are earnest and persevering enough to look for it; and I would go so far as to say, though he was not a person of Durkheim's stature, that there is nothing in Radcliffe-Brown's theoretical formulations of a century later that is not as clearly and cogently enunciated by Comte. We may leave him now at the end of the first part of his journey with: "Now that the human mind has founded celestial physics, terrestrial physics, both mechanical and chemical, organic physics, both vegetable and animal, it remains for it to complete the system of the sciences of observation in founding *social physics*" (*Cours*, I, p. 12).

What about the second part of his journey, the *Système?* He himself contrasts what he calls his two *carrières*, the Aristotle-Comte of the *Cours* and the St. Paul-Comte of the *Système*, the scientist and the prophet. But there was no blinding light on the road to Damascus. All the essential ideas of the *Système* (another 2,613 pages!) are to be found in embryo in his earliest writings, as they are in those of Saint-Simon also; so that the surprised indignation of some of his friends, such as Littre and Mill, at what appeared to them to be a sudden conversion and recantation is scarcely warranted. Much of it is indeed a polemical and rather turgid repetition of what was said in the *Cours*, with the addition of a rather tedious prescription for the future of society. All the same, one can understand the dismay with which some of his admirers greeted it; and it must be admitted that Comte was a bit mad—madder even than Saint-Simon and Fourier had been—or at any rate that most people would have regarded his later actions and writings as symptoms of instability, what Littre called a *"crise de folie."* Look at his portrait: "His eyes have all the seeming of a demon's that is dreaming." One need not go into details; one or two examples of his obsessional state will suffice. There was nothing unreasonable in his conviction that science and Catholicism were natural allies, but it was going a bit far in his efforts to combine positivism with moral regeneration to dispatch an emissary to arrange an understanding with the general of the Jesuits (whom he regarded as the real head of the Church, the pope being little more than the bishop of Rome). Comte, like Renan, never ceased to be a Catholic of a kind. His whole proposed organization for his Religion of Humanity, with its liturgical calendar and its sacraments (for Comte, cult came before dogma), was modeled on the structure of the Church of Rome. One need not be surprised that towards the end of his life the *Imitation* was his daily reading. Then, his new society ruled by industrialists in the place of warriors, and scientists in the place of priests, representing the temporal and the spiritual powers (another of Comte's notions taken from medieval times), was to be regulated on a scale communists might envy. Every person was required before the age of twenty-one to have a knowledge of all the abstract sciences, also Greek and Latin and the five principal modern languages. Mill also complained in sorrow that Comte had selected 150 volumes of science, philosophy, poetry, history, and general knowledge (not at all a bad selection) and proposed a systematic holocaust of all books except these. He had also made a rule for himself to abstain from all reading whatsoever, except a few favorite poets, for the sake of mental health (*hygiène cérébrale*)—which Mill regarded as evidence of decline, but might on the contrary be regarded as a very salutary regimen to adopt. But though some of these aberrations could be regarded as no more than eccentricities, more serious symptoms of derangement could be thought to be his increasing passion for systematization to the point of mania, systematization both intellectual—I have earlier alluded to that—and moral.

It might be thought that a treatise containing so many apparently odd ideas, and those mostly lacking in scientific interest, is not worth further consideration; though what he has to say on some topics, e.g., the family and language, is of value. However, I speak of the *Système,* if only briefly, for two main reasons. Firstly, Comte understood that science is by itself neutral. It can discover for us the facts and the laws which determine them but it cannot decide for us how we are to act on our knowledge (there is here an obvious contradiction, for if there are inexorable laws we have no choice). It can, so Comte thought, even inform us of the inevitable course of social evolution but it cannot ensure that there will be any society to evolve (again a contradiction). For science to be of benefit to man there must be social harmony, which derives not from positivist philosophy alone, or even at all, but from a morality which arises from a sense of duty (the emphasis is on duties, not on rights, which are an obnoxious metaphysical concept), and charity and love. We must live for others (*vivre pour autres*). It is true, as Aron says (*Les étapes de la pensée sociologique*), that for Comte history must be the development of human intelligence, but it is also the development of sentiment and morality, for what determines action is sentiment; intelligence serves only to attain the ends: *"Agir par affection, et penser pour agir"* (*Système*, I, p. 688). There must be a synthesis of heart and mind, but the heart must lead, the intellect follow. There is a *logique de l'esprit* and a *logique du coeur;* and *"Le sentiment . . . doit toujours dominer l'intelligence"* (*Système*, I, p. 435).

But morality ultimately rests not just on love, necessary, ultimate, and final though love is, but also on direction, discipline, regimentation, and force. I suppose that in modern terminology Comte might be labeled by some a "fascist" for, for him, institutions stem from beliefs and have vigor and stability only if everybody accepts—is made to accept in the absence of any others—the same imposed and obligatory beliefs. The fanatical harshness and arbitrariness of such rule was in some way to be softened by the influence of women in their roles of mother, sister, spouse, and daughter; a wife being the *"Centre moral de la famille"* (*Système*, II, p. 204). In the positivist society sentiment, reason and action will correspond exactly to the three *"Éléments nécessaires, féminin, philosophique, et populaire, de l'alliance régénératice"* (*Système*, I, p. 215). Comte was not being sentimental about women, and it should be understood that for him marriage must be both monogamous and indissoluble; and the wife must be subordinate to the husband, for there can be harmony only if one commands and the other obeys (needless to say, he and Mill did not see eye to eye in this matter). It must also be said that in Comte's wild and magnificent imaginings his proposed reforms and Madame de Vaux were mixed up together. At the end of the *Système* he wrote: *"Dès 1845 j'avais pleinement apprécié, sous sa sainte influence, l'ensemble de ma carrière, dont la seconde moitié devait transformer la philosophie en religion, comme la première avait changé la science en philosophie"* (*Système*, IV, pp. 529-30). So if there was no blinding light there was an angelic vision.

The second reason why I speak briefly of the *Système* is that Comte had the idea of history as the evolution of humanity, the Great Being (*Grand-Être*), of which the dead and the living both form part: in his memorable words *"L'Humanité se compose de plus de morts que de vivants"* and *"Les morts gouvernent de plus en plus les vivants."* As individuals we do not exist, but where the mystic might say that we exist in God in whom we are all members one of another, for Comte we exist only in the Great Being humanity, in whom our little separate beings are merged and in which, if we have given what we have to give to humanity and not just taken what we could take, we are immortal, that is, our name is immortal, not our person (an unsatisfactory solution to the problem of survival for those who give and are forgotten). This was Comte's positivist conception of the Church Militant, the Church Suffering and the Church Triumphant. As I have said earlier, the individual for Comte is an abstraction. Society, in the widest sense of humanity, is the reality. Art, philosophy, science may get labeled with the names of individuals, but properly conceived of they are the creation of humanity, even though their collective nature has to be expressed through individuals. Famous men in history are heirs, not authors; they do not make history, history makes them. Surely it is from Comte that Durkheim derived his theory of religion, that it is society which men venerate when it is gods they think they worship, an illusion Comte wanted to make reality; and he took from the same source his whole conception of culture and society as collectively created and for the individual obligatory. Some may regard the *Grand-Être* as sentimentality. I would prefer to say sentiment, and to regard it as a great conception of history—ethical, if you like, rather than scientific—which far from conflicting with the positivist programme of the *Cours* seems to me to be a restatement of it in terms of morality, charity, and poetry, but if we so regard it, it is only in a very vague and peculiar sense that, for all his talk of inevitability, Comte can be said to be a determinist.

You may ask yourselves as I conclude this essay what is the point of digging up the past. Comte has himself answered that question as far as social studies are concerned: one can only understand ideas about social life when one knows something of the history of their development. For anthropologists it teaches also, I hope, a lesson in humility. "After me cometh a builder. Tell him, I too have known!"

Chapter 7
McLennan (1827-1881)

McLennan was a member of the Scottish Bar and a founder member with Robertson Smith of "The Edinburgh Evening Club." He later settled in London. His main writings are *Primitive Marriage* (1865), republished in 1876 together with various other essays under the title *Studies in Ancient History;* and a second volume with this title was published after his death. *Patriarchal Theory*, a refutation of Maine's theories, was also published posthumously (1885). McLennan was a hard-hitting critic; he was especially critical of Morgan, whose thesis in *The Systems of Consanguinity and Affinity* (1871) he describes as a "wild dream—not to say nightmare." He also accuses Morgan of stealing from Lafitau without any acknowledgment. He treats Sir John Lubbock's *The Origin of Civilization* (1870) with derision. But perhaps his sharpest criticisms were those directed against Maine's *Ancient Law* (1861): he concludes that neither the potestas nor agnation, in the sense of Maine and of the Roman Lawyers, were anywhere or at any time found outside historic Rome, and consequently that there was no evidence at all that the patriarchal family was primeval and universal. Nor would he accept that agnation derives from the potestas—it can easily be explained by patriliny and exogamy without bringing the potestas into consideration. Moreover, if Maine were right, it is odd that in Rome the potestas should have survived agnation. On this issue his most damaging argument is that the structure of what we call today a lineage with matrilineal descent is the same as that of a lineage with patrilineal descent without the former being associated with the potestas of a matriarch. The difference of opinion between these two men went deeper than this particular issue; it concerned the origin of society—for Maine it was an enlargement of the family; for McLennan relationship does not begin in the

family but in totemic stock-groups, from which the family eventually emerges as a distinct social group.

McLennan was a great believer in sociological laws. A comparison of primitive and ancient societies had led him to conclude that
"the history of human society is that of a development following
closely one general law, and that the variety of forms of life—of
domestic and civil institutions—is ascribable mainly to the unusual development of the different sections of mankind" (1896, pp.
9 *et seq*). This development is by virtue of the operation of the internal forces of society. Since it is unilinear, a classification of primitive societies will give us a chronological sequence, i.e., stages. The
chronology is, however, of a logical, and not of a purely or simply
historical kind. Granted that all societies pass through the same
stages, historical reconstruction is possible. McLennan was no fool.
He recognized that his reconstructions were doomed to failure if
the evidence on which he relied was unreliable, especially when a
cumulative argument is based on circumstantial evidence, i.e., is a
series of logical inferences; and he had to confess that the accounts
of primitive peoples were thin and vitiated by personal bias and ignorance. He knew also that his conclusions would be to some degree conjectural and that they would carry little conviction unless
positive evidence could be produced in support of his series of developmental stages and showing how each stage prepared the way
for the next. So he used a method which enabled him to prove that
the series constructed by logical criteria were also historical
stages—the study of what he called "symbols," social survivals
comparable to the rudimentary organs found in some animals and
to the mute letters in words. He thought that when a custom or institution passes away it often leaves evidences of its former existence in archaic observances. When we find these observances,
practices which do not make sense in their present setting, we assume that they are relics of a preceding stage of social development. Now, he believed, if we find among primitive peoples just
such institutions as would naturally assume such symbolic forms as
we find surviving among more advanced peoples, we may safely
conclude that the more advanced societies were once like the more
primitive.

A theory of unilinear development, of a law of social growth, a
diachronic law implies also laws of a functional and synchronic
kind, it being assumed that a change in one or other institutions
has brought about everywhere the same corresponding changes in

other institutions, since all form together a rigidly interdependent complex at each stage. Therefore, "a full explanation of the origin of exogamy requires it to be made out that wherever exogamy prevailed, totemism prevailed; that where totemism prevailed, blood-feuds prevailed; that where blood-feuds prevailed, the religious obligation of vengeance prevailed; that where the religious obligation of vengeance prevailed, female infanticide prevailed; that where female infanticide prevailed, female kinship prevailed" (1896, p. 27).

In *Primitive Marriage*, McLennan set out to discover the origin and meaning—words which had for him much the same sense—of what he thought to be in one form or another an almost universal custom, that of marriage by capture. This can be real or symbolic, the symbolic form being a survival of the real form. Now, what could have been the kind of society in which it was the regular practice to capture women, necessarily from other tribes, for wives? Obviously it could only have flourished where the groups concerned were politically autonomous. According to him, these groups were groups of kindred with common interests and possessions living together in a defined territory and under the leadership of a paterfamilias. We may further suppose that these groups were exogamous, for otherwise there would have been no need to capture wives and marriage by capture would not have arisen. (Exogamy is defined as "the law prohibiting marriage between persons of the same blood or stock as incest"—its opposite, endogamy, as "the law prohibiting marriage, except to persons of the same blood or stock" [volume II, p. 46].) So small independent tribes, exogamy and abduction of wives go together, and since they must go together, where we find either capture or exogamy we may assume that the other was once present. However, owing to exogamy the mothers in each tribe were foreigners, and since the tribes were matrilineal their homogeneity broke down and marriage by betrothal or sale became possible.

These postulates and inferences are a purely logical construct, but it can be said to McLennan's credit that he tried to demonstrate how one stage of development might have passed into the next; and also that he made some effort to support his thesis by appeal to the body of ethnographic facts then known (these are published in volume III from the notebooks). He thought that it required little demonstration to show that the usual relations of primitive groups to one another were those of war and unrelieved hostility, and he had no difficulty in proving that exogamy is a most widely prevailing principle of marriage among primitive races. He thought also that he could show that in a number of instances among primitive peoples today tribal exogamy, hostility as the prevailing relation between tribes, and a system of capturing wives are all found together in actual combination; and that from this we can assume that the combination has at one time existed wherever we find any one of the three elements of it.

But why should exogamy have prevailed? It arose from the practice of female infanticide, which, he believed, was a common practice among savages everywhere, on account of hard conditions of subsistence. This of necessity led to the capture of women from without, and also to the practice of polyandry within the tribe. Female infanticide is thus added to the cluster of adhesions. It follows logically also that kinship was traced through females only. The idea of exogamy cannot be detached from that of kinship, and man of necessity first sees that he is of the blood of his mother. We are therefore justified in assuming that when societies developed from stages, admittedly hypothetical but logically required, of promiscuity between the sexes they entered into a stage of kinship through females only. Indeed matriliny must have come before exogamy, for kinship depends on the idea of the unity of blood and without recognition of kinship there could have been no social group to be exogamous. McLennan was satisfied that the facts lent support to this part of his thesis (he believed that kinship through females only prevailed universally among the Australian blacks, among the majority of the nations of the American red men, and also among the South Sea Islanders). All this is legitimate reasoning. It is sound science to deduce from postulates, on condition that negative cases are accounted for and that the data are sufficient to confirm the hypotheses.

To this cluster of logically interdependent and, as he presents them, also mechanically interdependent institutions—small tribes of kindred, exogamy, marriage by capture, female infanticide, and kinship through females—McLennan, who was nothing if not rigidly consistent, now adds polyandry. He thought that polyandry was a widespread practice and that traces of it are found wherever there are traces of kinship through females only, that is, almost everywhere. It must be regarded as an advance from promiscuity. He distinguished two forms of it, the ruder, found always with matriliny and matrilocality and typified by the Nair system, and a less rude, which developed out of it, patrilineal and patrilocal and typified by the Tibetan system. In the Nair form the husbands are not brothers, and in the Tibetan form they are. When fraternal polyandry is combined with patrilocality patriliny results. The levirate is a relic of the Tibetan form. The levirate next died out and the family slowly assumed the form to which we are accustomed, and in the course of this development exogamy broke down. "The order of social development, in our view, is then, that the tribe stands first; the *gens* or house next, and last of all, the family" (pp. 154-55).

Most of McLennan's work after *Primitive Marriage* was amplification, but he made an original contribution by his discussion of totemism, which, together with the blood-feud, he added to his cluster of adhesions. His earlier attempt to explain by female infanticide alone why men of a tribe had to capture their wives from other tribes now appeared to him to be inadequate. He supplemented it by the following propositions. Primitive stock-groups were held together by common religious regard for their totems and by the obligation of the blood-feud. When, on account of female infanticide, marriage by capture began to be customary, the totemic stock-groups were broken up and distributed as *gentes* among different local (tribal) groups, such as we find in Australia today. There would therefore be a limitation on capture with regard to women of any tribe of the same totemic stock as oneself, since capture could hardly be accomplished without the shedding of blood and hence to a violation of the obligation of the blood-feud obtaining among kindred. There was no other way of getting a wife except by capture, and since a man could not capture women who were kin he could not marry them. He could therefore only marry unrelated women. This was the origin of exogamy.

The final thesis is as follows. The earliest societies were homogeneous stock-groups with totemic associations and practising the blood-feud. Marriage was at first unknown. Then the attachment of children to mothers led to subdivision of the groups into rude family groups of the Nair type and to the most ancient social system in which the idea of blood relationship is embodied, that of kinship through females only. While things were in this state, the practice of capturing women arose, owing to female infanticide, and was followed by the rise of the law of exogamy. By the joint operation of the system of capture, exogamy, and female kinship the original homogeneity of the group was destroyed. The stock-groups lost their character as such and became local tribes, each having within it a number of *gentes* of different stocks. Eventually the Nair system of polyandry gave way to the Tibetan form and the system of kinship through females only was succeeded by one which acknowledged kinship through males also, and which, in most cases passed into a system which acknowledged kinship through males only. (In his early writings McLennan thought that agnation commonly supervenes on the acknowledgment of kinship through males; later he came to the conclusion that it was peculiar to Roman society.) Real marriage does not come about till the stage of Tibetan polyandry and descent through males. On the practice of capture arising the Nair system would be changed. The captives would be the slaves of their captors and wife would become synonymous with subject, and then marriage proper begins. McLennan finally brings caste and endogamy into his general scheme by suggesting that a local tribe, having reached a patrilineal stage and grown proud through success in war, might decline intermarriage with other tribes, becoming an endogamous caste, feigning themselves, after the universal tendency of rude races to eponymy, to be all derived from a common ancestor.

Now all this reads like a just-so story. But we owe a great debt to McLennan. He was the first to make a comprehensive analysis of everything known about primitive peoples. He was not just a dipper into travel books. He was indeed the first to use the comparative method on a world-wide scale. Moreover, his interpretations were strictly sociological, e.g., marriage by capture and exogamy are explained by reference to other institutions found with them or out of which they might have developed. Also he eschewed *a priori* reasoning: he undoubtedly started with preconceptions but he did not, like the Scottish moral philosophers, explicitly start from certain postulates about human nature and reason deductively from these premises. However wrong the facts and interpretations may be, he started from the facts, or what he believed to be the facts and shaped his theories, if not always to accord with them, at least not to conflict with them. Also, out of the comparative method, as he used it, there came by sifting of the general from the particular, certain classificatory concepts of importance: *exogamy, matriliny, totemism*, and *marriage by capture*.

He can be criticized on the basis of fact, inference, and method. I indicate only a few points under each heading. As Lowie points out (*Primitive Religions*, p. 43 *et seq*) the facts do not support his conclusions that an unrelieved state of hostility is normal between primitive peoples; that female infanticide is a widely prevalent practice; that polyandry is a common institution; that exogamy regularly accompanies bride-abduction; that there are any societies in which kinship is recognized through one parent only; and that totemism implies worship or is the exclusive content of primitive religion. To these I may add that kinship is not necessarily conceived of in terms of blood (Australian patrilineal peoples profess ignorance of paternity); that it is untrue that the system of kinship through females only "is found to prevail amongst the great majority of existing rude races" (p. 198) and that he was especially in error in supposing that all the Australian Blackfellows were matrilineal. Again, nothing in the nature of marriage by capture as the normal way of obtaining wives probably exists anywhere. Many statements on other matters are quite unsupported by the facts as we now know them, e.g., that "women among rude tribes are usually depraved, and inured to scenes of depravity from their early infancy" (p. ii). No logical construction has any value if it is contradicted on so many vital points by the facts.

Lowie (p. 44) gives it as his opinion that as a purely logical construct McLennan's scheme inspires respect. It is true that, being a lawyer, he argues his case well; but when we examine the argument closely we see flaws fatal to it. How can one reconcile female infanticide with marriage by capture? If there were reciprocal raiding between adjacent tribes to obtain wives, how can this be reconciled with matriliny and the blood-feud? Surely a homogeneous stock-group, matriliny, and exogamy are incompatible! If the reason for infanticide was the low level of subsistence why are not people presented as doing so in the earliest stage postulated? There are many other inconsistencies.

One of the main causes of confusion, not only in McLennan's writings but also in those of his contemporaries, is a blindness to the social priority of the family. Among all the most primitive peoples the institutions of marriage and the family are found irrespective of the wide diversity of the other institutions with which they may be associated; but McLennan's thesis depends absolutely on the dogma that neither exist in early society. This was an axiom of the time (Maine was a notable exception; the idea was not dispelled until Westermarck and Malinowski). Another cause of confusion was the still not uncommon error of regarding lineage affiliations and kinship ties as relations of the same order. He

consequently thought that because it is customary in primitive societies to trace descent through one parent alone for certain purposes this meant that kinship with relatives on the other side was
not recognized in other contexts; e.g., he attacks Maine on the
grounds that the recognition of jural relations between a man and
his mother's kin, as in the incest prohibition in respect of them, was
evidence against agnation. He thought that patriliny and matriliny were absolute opposites. A further, and disastrous, error was
his confusion of descent groups with political or local and community groups, and of the clan with what he calls the tribe. On this
point he was severely handled by Morgan, who had suffered from
his vindictiveness. Exogamous tribes are an essential part of his
theory. Morgan held that tribal exogamy does not exist. Morgan
was undoubtedly right—cases apparently to the contrary are probably due to kinship relations between the members of small local
communities. Within the ordinary local community, even among
the most primitive peoples, there are women whom it is permissi-
ble to marry. There is the maximum of confusion here, largely due
to McLennan's highly ambiguous use of terms.

McLennan can be criticized on more general lines, which apply
also to most, if not all, of his contemporaries. They fought each
other on interpretations but their methods of analysis and the kind
of conclusions they formulated were the same. I mention them very
briefly. Fundamentally the hypotheses were posited on the facts
and did not derive from them. There is no real evidence advanced
for his series of stages of social development. Then McLennan was
a realist who thought of totemism, exogamy, matriliny, etc., as
things, and everywhere the same things, which can therefore be regarded as units and counted. His stages are a sort of conglomerate
of these things. Unsatisfactory as his stages must now seem to us
and devoid of the support of historical evidence, they were forced
on him, as they are on all those who try to reduce social development to scientific laws. All this can perhaps best be understood by
viewing McLennan and his contemporary anthropologists in relation to the general climate of thought of their time. Primitive peoples were seen through the lenses of mid-Victorian smugness: ma-
terialism, rationalism, puritanism, laissez-faire capitalism and
deep feelings about class. It was taken for granted that the antithesis of Victorian culture was the lowest possible stage of culture,
and their general ignorance of history and of societies other than
their own was abysmal.

Chapter 8
Robertson Smith (1846-1894)

William Robertson Smith was a very distinguished Semitic and biblical scholar who turned his attention to anthropological questions in these fields, largely under the influence of his friend and fellow countryman McLennan. This influence is particularly evident in his discussion of totemism and matrilineal descent in ancient Arabia. Smith was a man of wide learning. He was at one time a teacher of physics and could have taken Chairs of mathematics and logic had he been prepared to abandon his vocation for the ministry. His father was one of the Free Church secessionist ministers from the Established Church of Scotland, and he was brought up in the strict and narrow piety of manse and kirk. After a brilliant career at the University of Aberdeen, Smith was appointed to the Chair of Hebrew and Old Testament Exegesis in the Free Church College of Aberdeen in 1870. Then in 1875, some articles he had contributed to the ninth edition of the *Encyclopaedia Britannica*, especially the article "Bible," scandalized a section of the Free Church, particularly his remarks about the dating and composition of the Book of Deuteronomy. His arraignment before the courts of the Free Church on charges of heresy lasted on and off from 1875 to 1881. In the end, although he was not convicted of heresy and remained a minister to the end of his life, he was dismissed from his Chair for causing apprehension and disturbance and on account of the tendency of his teachings, which it was held, not without reason, might cause loss of faith in his students for the ministry. He then joined the staff of the *Encyclopaedia Britannica* as a joint editor. In 1883, he was appointed Lord Almoner's Reader in Arabic at Cambridge in the place of Palmer, who had been killed by the Arabs of the Sinai Peninsula. In 1885, he was elected to a Fellowship at Christ's College; in 1886, he was appointed University Librarian; and in 1889, he was elected Sir Thomas Adams

Professor of Arabic. (See *The Life of William Robertson Smith* by J. S. Black and G. Chrystal, 1912.)

Smith was a prodigious worker and he published several books of outstanding scholarship: *The Old Testament in the Jewish Church* (1881), *The Prophets of Israel* (1882), *Kinship and Marriage in Early Arabia* (1885), and *The Religion of the Semites* (1889); and a collection of his papers was published after his death under the title of *Lectures and Essays of William Robertson Smith* (1912). I propose to examine *Kinship and Marriage in Early Arabia* and *The Religion of the Semites,* which well illustrate his methods of sociological analysis. Both books were based primarily on literary sources, but these were supplemented by travels in Egypt, Palestine, Syria, Arabia and Tunisia.

In both books, Smith mainly restricted himself to the Semitic field, and his object was to reconstruct the earliest forms of Semitic institutions, especially those of the Bedouin Arabs before Muhammad and of the ancient Hebrews. Thus, unlike McLennan, he was comparing cultures which were not only similar in many respects but genetically related as well, like de Coulanges's attempt to reconstruct the earliest Indo-European institutions, especially those of ancient Italy. There is nothing inherently wrong in making such attempts—they had proved brilliantly successful in philological studies and had yielded results in the study of law and mythology. There is no reason why one should not try to reconstruct the social institutions of a people, at a time for which adequate historical evidences are lacking, from a study of the historical form of them and a comparison with those of other peoples who, we have good reason to suppose, formed a common society with a common culture. The reconstruction can only have a higher or lower degree of probability, but Smith knew this perfectly well. Unfortunately, however, he took over McLennan's paradigm of unilinear stages of social development and tried to make the evidences of ancient Arabia conform to it, to show that they were a particular instance of it. Hence he sought the origin of the patriarchal and patrilineal Bedouin clans, such as we find from the days of Muhammad till today, in an earlier stage of tracing descent through women. And he sought the origin of sacrifice, such as it is portrayed in the Old Testament, in totemism. Like all his contemporaries, he believed that the only satisfactory explanation of any institution is in terms of its historical development. It is therefore completely understood if we can determine its earliest forms. But like McLennan and others he was trying to combine this approach with the formulation, or rather, in his case, the assumption of general propositions about the development of human societies, and, like them, in this endeavour was compelled to rely on the notion of unilinear stages. A consequence of this assumption was that at times he not only used the evidence uncritically but also prevented himself from arriving at much simpler and more satisfactory interpretations than those he put forward. I will give some examples.

Kinship and Marriage in Early Arabia is typical of the theoretical orientation of the second half of the nineteenth century. Its thesis was, very briefly, this: there must have been in all human development, and therefore in the history of the pre-Islamic Arabs of Arabia, a stage when sexual relations were unregulated, a stage of primitive promiscuity. From this condition the Arabs emerged into a social state in which local hordes were composed of persons related to one another through female descent. They were matrilineal stock-groups with polyandrous sex relations. Through war, women from other stock-groups were introduced into the horde and were kept by the men of the horde as a whole for common cohabitation. This new form of polyandry resulting from marriage by capture brought about a change in the manner of counting descent. Matrilineal stock-groups became patrilineal stock-groups, and as marriage by capture slowly gave way to marriage by purchase (*mahr*), in course of time polyandry gave way to monogamous marriage, the custom of the levirate remaining as a survival of the earlier system.

As with McLennan, Smith put forward the stage of primitive promiscuity as a logical deduction required to round off his paradigm of social development. He offered no evidence in support of it. There were likewise no genuine historical evidences of a former condition of matriliny, so Smith had to fall back on the notion of survivals to prove his case, a case which rested in fact on little more than *a priori* ethnocentric assumptions. Historical evidences show us that at the time of the Prophet, and therefore long before his time also, the Bedouin of Arabia were divided into a number of local, or tribal, groups, the members of which were bound together by traditional sentiment, expressed in what they believed or feigned to be a unity of blood, and by the recognition and exercise of mutual obligations and social duties and rights. As Smith points out, these groups, each commonly called a *hayy*, were corporate descent groups, what we would call today lineage groups and not merely groups between the members of which there was kinship. These lineages were parts of lineage systems. They were represented as branches of a genealogical tree of descent, two or more minimal branches forming a minor branch and two or more minor branches forming a major branch in relation to another major branch, and so on. All tribal groups were groups of the same order and differed from one another only in size, genealogically represented in distance from a common ancestor (pp. 3–4). Furthermore, any groups living a common political life together as a tribe in one way or another forged a genealogical link with the dominant lineage of the tribe and took its *nisba,* gentile surname, and its war cry. The Arab genealogists brought all the lineages of Arabia into one big genealogy, the backbone of which was the line of the prophet Muhammad. In the process they had to euhemerize tribal names and, in order to make the representation of inter-tribal relations in the structure of the genealogy appear reasonable, were forced to invent dummy names so that the lines supposed to have descended from the same ancestor were of more or less equal length. These names were placed at nonarticulative points in the tables.

The largest constant political group was the tribe (*hayy*), which made war and prosecuted the blood-feud; and the tribe was thought of as a lineage, within a system of lineages, a system which corresponded to the political system of tribes. When tribes became too large for the tribal territory and for prosecution of the blood-feud—too large, in short, for corporate action—they split up and there took place a corresponding bifurcation in the tree of descent. When a tribal unit became too small for self-defense it joined a stronger tribe, and this accretion was registered by some fiction in the genealogy of the larger tribe. This process of splitting and aggregation was a constant feature of the tribal life of Old Arabia. This analysis and description of the Bedouin tribe was brilliant.

But what evidence does Smith produce to sustain his thesis that this pre-eminently patrilineal society was ever matrilineal. I mention a few as examples of his line of reasoning, which today appears fantastic. We have to remember, however, that in his day it was an axiom that matriliny everywhere preceded patriliny; otherwise progress and development could not be established.

His demonstration of the axiom had for one of its chief arguments the survival of certain usages. Now, the doctrine of the unity of tribal blood is found everywhere in Arabia, as appears from the prevalence of the blood-feud. The tribe is of one blood (I consider this to be a questionable proposition). Therefore, says Smith, where there is patrilineal descent, as in historic Arabia, we would expect to find that the eponymous ancestor of the tribe was a man. On the contrary, in a society with matrilineal descent we would expect to find that the eponymous ancestor was a woman. Therefore, when we find that a good number of the tribes of Arabia refer their origin to a female eponym there is a strong case for assuming that at one time the tribes, though now patrilineal, were matrilineal (p. 29). Smith put forward this explanation of female eponyms against two simpler explanations which carry more weight. One of these was Nöldeke's explanation, that as Arabic grammar treats all tribal unities as collective terms and as collective terms in Arabic are constantly feminine and take feminine pronouns and verbal forms it is not surprising that some tribal names had a feminine form. The other explanation was put forward by Dr. Redhouse in his defense of the Arab genealogists against Professor Wilken. He observed that in a polygamous society the children of one father may be distinguished into groups by the use of their mothers' names and this adequately explains the manner in which lineages with female eponyms are derived. This second explanation accords with more recent studies of lineage systems (Peters, 1960). Smith, moreover, cannot be excused for rejecting it on the grounds that the facts in support of it were unknown in his day, for lineages among Bedouin Arabs are still sometimes, even frequently, named after the wives of their founders today when the Bedouin have traced their descent exclusively through males for at least 1,500 years. This is the most convenient way of differentiating between lines descended from one man if the founders of the separate lines were born of different women. The further linguistic evidence he cites fails to support his contention for the same reason and for the further reason that kinship is always through the mother, even kinship with the father's side, for a child is a man's son because his mother is the man's wife: that the word *umma*, community, is derived from *umm*, mother; that the bonds of kinship are expressed in Arabic and Hebrew by the words *rehem* and *rahim*, the womb; that in all parts of Arabia one of the terms for a lineage is *batn*, belly, particularly the mother's belly, of its synonym *lahm*, flesh; and that the words *bait*, tent, and *ahl*, equivalent to the Hebrew *ohel,* tent (which in ancient Arabia belonged to the wife and not to the husband) are used to describe family and kinship groups.

Another of Smith's arguments is that when there is kinship through women, bars to marriage can arise only on this side; and not seldom it is found that, after fatherhood has begun to be recognized, a relic of the old law of kinship subsists in the law of prohibited degrees, which still continues to depend on mother kinship. Now, evidence that in historic times a man could marry his paternal half-sister is forthcoming (e.g., Abraham and Sarah), and when marriage with a half-sister is allowed it cannot be supposed that there is any bar to marriage in the male line, unless that a man cannot marry his own daughter. It is in fact known that in pre-Islamic Arabia men married their paternal nieces and cousins. On the mother's side, marriage with the mother herself was forbidden, and, though the evidence is indirect and inconclusive, Smith considered it fairly certain that a man could not marry his uterine sister. Though the evidence again is very weak, there is some reason to suppose that the mother's sister and the sister's daughter were also forbidden degrees. From what seems to me to be this very slender evidence of isolated instances in the literature Smith concludes that on the mother's side all relationship nearer than cousinship barred marriage. In his view, the law introduced by Muhammad therefore simply extended the marriage prohibition to cover the relatives on the father's side corresponding to those already forbidden by the old custom of Arabia on the mother's side.

Here Smith has landed himself in confusion. It does not at all follow from the fact that descent is traced through either males or females to the exclusion of the other sex that relationship through the other parent is not recognized and cannot be a bar to marriage. The confusion is due to not keeping distinct the tracing of descent in one line for certain purposes and the recognition of kinship, of various categories, through both parents for other purposes. It is the distinction between lineage affiliation and categories of kinship. The fact, therefore, that the Bedouin Arabs of today are patrilineal but still prohibit marriage with certain very close uterine kinswomen is in no way evidence of an earlier matrilineal mode of tracing descent.

A further example of Smith's handling of evidence is that, following McLennan, he thought it probable that it could be shown that not only were the Bedouin of ancient Arabia matrilineal but also totemic (this is also the assumption on which his theory of sacrifice is based, as we shall see). Just as he reasoned that logically matriliny is more primitive than patriliny because although there could be no doubt about who was a child's mother there might be doubt about who was his father, so totemism must be older than exogamy because the idea of exogamy "could not be conceived by savages in an abstract form; it must necessarily have had a concrete expression, or rather must have been thought under a concrete and tangible form, and that form seems to have been always supplied by totemism." Smith considered that he had demonstrated the existence of exogamy among the prehistoric Bedouin, so that there was, on this reasoning, an *a priori* probability of totemism. (He had, in fact, done nothing of the kind—he had merely shown that a man could not marry very close maternal kinswomen. This is not exogamy and therefore the correlation of exogamy and totemism, even if it were as general as he thought, would in no way support his argument that the Bedouin must at one time have been totemic.) Now, it is quite clear that the Bedouin of historic times are in no sense whatsoever totemic. Smith had therefore once again to rely for evidence on survivals, the relics of a totemic system. The characteristics of totemism in his day were considered to be the existence of stocks named after some animal or plant, the conception that the members of the stock are of the same blood as, or are sprung from, the animal or plant, and the sacredness of the totem. If all these features occur among the same people the proof of totemism is, Smith thought, complete, but even when this is not so—and it is not so for the Bedouin of ancient Arabia—the proof is, he said, "morally complete," if all three marks of totemism are found in the same race.

In ancient Arabia many Bedouin tribes had an eponymous ancestor with an animal name, and the Arab genealogists believed, or affected to believe, that this was the proper name of the ancestor, even when it was in the plural. Apart from the fact that on Smith's theory the tribes were then matrilineal—they had ancestresses and not ancestors—it appeared to him that this could not be the correct explanation. (He was possibly right in holding that, at any rate in some cases, these animal names were in the first place stock, or lineage, names; but, on the other hand, it is not at all uncommon to give a man an animal sobriquet.) There is not, however, the slightest evidence, as Smith had to admit, that the tribes with animal names had any attitude which could be called totemic towards the animals after which they were named. All he could attempt to show therefore was the possibility of such an attitude, that the Bedouin had a totemistic mentality: among them there is believed to be affinity between some men and hyenas; the Prophet disliked eating hares and hyenas because he believed that these animals menstruated; in Arabian folklore human stocks are transformed into animals and behave like persons, and a certain clan, though not a gazelle clan, mourned over dead gazelles. A further step in the argument was that side by side with tribes that called themselves by animal names, and hence sons of the animal, were numerous tribes which called themselves after one or other of the gods of pre-Islamic times. Smith thought that it was because these tribes believed themselves to be children of the gods, and hence of one blood with them, that they took their names, and that, by analogy, one might suppose that it was because the other tribes thought themselves to be children of the animals that they called themselves after them. (The evidence that tribes did regard themselves as children of the gods in a physical sense is highly uncertain. This was another basic assumption in Smith's theory of sacrifice.) In the absence of any direct evidence that these tribes at any time venerated the animals whose names they took, Smith was forced to buttress his argument with some very remote parallels: animals, or representations of them, were venerated in pre-Islamic times; e.g., Yaghuth, the lion-god, and the gods Ya'uc and Nasr, represented by the figures of a horse and a vulture; there were sacred doves at Mecca; the *jinn* often appeared in animal form (Smith held them to be survivals of pre-Islamic household gods); and among the northern Semites many of the animals after whom tribes are called among the southern Semites had a sacred character.

Clearly, Smith made out no case for the ancient Bedouin being totemic, unless almost any interest in nature is to be labeled totemism. Indeed, we may go so far as to say that the evidences he cites were inconclusive, furthermore that they are far from proving his case with regard to both matriliny and totemism, and that they are sometimes farfetched interpretations of the facts.

There is no better example than this book of the influence of what I believe to be faulty theoretical assumptions, which not only lead to highly doubtful conclusions but also block a correct understanding of the phenomena under investigation. This, in the case of this book, may have been due partly to the insufficiency of the historical data, but it was mainly due to a blind acceptance of

McLennan's formulations, which, as we have seen, are weak in logical construction and insupportable by the facts. I do not criticize Smith for trying to discover the earlier forms, if any, of Bedouin institutions but for his implicit acceptance of unilinear stages of social development or, in other words, of laws of social development. These laws were not generalizations from the facts but were deductions from a combination of the notions of law and progress.

Lectures on the Religion of the Semites (1889; the 3rd edition of 1927 has additional notes by Stanley A. Cook and runs to 782 pages) is an attempt to apply anthropological methods and concepts to interpret certain religious practices of the Hebrews. All Semitic sources are used, and occasionally classical data and information about primitive societies. Smith believed that while we moderns are accustomed to look on religion from the side of belief rather than of practice, "the antique religions had for the most part no creed, they consisted entirely of institutions and practices" (p. 16). The rite was connected not with dogma but with a story, a myth; and the myth is no explanation of the rite but itself requires to be explained by the ritual and religious custom to which it is attached. Here, as elsewhere, practice preceded theory: "political institutions are older than political theories, and in like manner religious institutions are older than religious theories" (p. 20).

He claimed that the basic rite in ancient religion is that of sacrifice, so to understand the religion we have to know the meaning of the *sacrificium,* and since sacrifice is so general an institution we have to seek its origin in general causes (the comparative method separates the general from the particular and the essential from the accidental).

One fact of importance, he continues, is that the gods of antiquity were thought to be literally the progenitors of their worshippers, god and men being of one stock and of one blood. It was a relationship of kinship, the only social relationship recognized in early society. The bond of religion was originally coextensive with that of blood, so at this stage we are dealing with closed kin-groups, each with its ancestor-god.

Briefly, then, he showed that in levitical law there were two main types of sacrifice: (1) the whole burnt offering, which was made over to the god in its entirety, and (2) a sacrifice followed by a meal shared by the god and his worshippers, the god getting the blood (poured on the altar) and some special pieces of the flesh (burnt) and the worshippers getting the carcass. To this second class belonged the *zebahim* or ordinary animal sacrifices, and it is therefore here that we must look for the origin and significance of sacrificial worship. What we find is that it is "an act of social fellowship between the deity and his worshippers" (p. 224). "The leading idea in the animal sacrifices of the Semites . . . was not that of a gift made over to the god, but of an act of communion, in which the god and his worshippers unite by partaking together of the flesh and blood of the sacred victim" (p. 238). Here we have the concept of origin in three forms: first form, simplest form, and most significant form.

Smith now introduces some other considerations. Sacrifice was a public event with the god presiding—a clan festival and a sacrifice being the same thing. Sacrifice is essentially a social act. Also, people who eat together are kin; in virtue of their kinship all have commensal rights, and those who do not eat together are aliens. Hence the sacrificial communion emphasizes that god and worshippers are kin, with all the reciprocal duties that implies. Furthermore the sacrificial victim was sacred—not made sacred by being devoted to the deity, but in itself. He was convinced that the old Semites were totemic, i.e., they believed that the totemic animal of their clan and they were of one stock. Hence the slaughter of animals was legitimate only in collective sacrifices. Among primitive peoples the only values are those of kinship. Consequently the rule that domestic animals could only be killed in sacrifice must have rested on the principle of kinship, and therefore the victims were holy. He supported his argument by a claim that pastoral peoples in various parts of the globe, especially in Africa, revere their flocks or herds, for they have a nature akin to gods. If this is not strictly totemic, it is a totemistic attitude. God, men, and victim are thus all kin, and when the clan partake of the victim's flesh they "cement and seal their mystic unity with one another and with their god" (p. 312)—each member of the clan incorporating a particle of the divine life of the victim into his own individual life. (Smith was later frightened of the implications of his theory—Frazer, *The Gorgon's Head,* 1927, pp. 278-90.)

So we have the following components in sacrifice: (1) animals are sacred and kin to men and gods; (2) it is an act of a kin-group; (3) it is a communion of men and gods; (4) it is a sacrament by which men and gods partake of the divine life. Communion, the idea of the kin-group and blood-group, totemism, the tribal god as a symbol of the unity of the group seem to Smith to band together.

There is really little evidence in the literary sources in support of the theory. It is little more than a plausible guess about what might have been the origin of sacrifice. The inconsistencies are in Smith's own mind.

Sacrifice is thus a communion. It is not a covenant—an idea which arose much later. Nor is the idea of atonement prominent, and any element of the piacular there may be in it, is subordinate to that of communion. Nor is it a sacred tribute. It is probable that sacrifice is older than the idea of private property. Moreover, this conflicts with the relations between chiefs and their tribesmen. Only a client tribe paid tribute, so it cannot be held that the typical form of Semitic religion is clientship (a sociological interpretation). The gift idea may be present in sacrifice but it is not the governing feature. The idea of communion is the central one and it governs the evolution of faith and worship to a later date.

As for later times all the evidence is against this theory: Smith has to suggest the stages by which the idea of sacrifice changed its significance and piacular, gift, and eucharistic meanings took the place of that of communion. We need not follow this part of his thesis in detail, as an assessment of its value requires a considerable knowledge of exegetical writings and Old Testament history. In brief: first, god and men were thought to partake together of the raw and living flesh (St. Nilus's camel). Then the blood comes to be regarded as the vehicle of the life and is no longer drunk by the worshippers but is sprinkled on their persons and later is poured on the altar, the carcass being cooked and eaten by priests or worshippers as the case might be. At this stage other notions, especially piacular ones, enter, but the later sin-offerings and the holocaust are descended from the ancient ritual of communion, as is also the ordinary sacrificial meal of later Hebrew times, and in these later sacrifices there are features of the earlier form (survivals). Finally, after the exile, animals could only be sacrificed in Jerusalem in the temple there, and when killed elsewhere their slaughter ceased to have any religious significance. Already in pre-Islamic Arabia all that was required when slaughtering a beast was that it was slain in the name of a god.

Much of Smith's argument is tortuous and based on tenuous evidence. The worst excesses of the comparative method are avoided by keeping to the Semitic field, but even here the evidence is not in his favor. Buchanan Gray and others have shown that if the idea of communion is present at all in the earliest Hebrew sacrifices known to us, there are also present piacular and other ideas. The Arabian material is also very inconclusive, and it may be doubted whether there is, properly speaking, sacrifice at all in orthodox Islam. The theory is also vitiated by the evolutionary bias of his time, all early religions being played down as superstitious and materialistic (concrete) to enhance the spirituality of later times (he had very much a Victorian Protestant's view of the antithesis between social and personal religion).

Nonetheless, this is an important book, and not only historically. It is in the best sociological tradition. It is a social history or the history of institutions and ideas. It is not a study—could not be—of persons and events, but of social development and of the interconsistency between institutions and ideas. Some general practice (sacrifice) due to general causes is studied from a functional point of view. Stanley A. Cook, in his notes to *The Religion of the Semites,* puts this well: "Whatever consciousness there may have been among rudimentary peoples in prehistoric ages of the Supreme Being, the social–religious system of the day must always have been in an intelligible relationship with the current physical, economic, moral, mental and all other non-religious conditions" (p. 531). As Cook also says: "The idea of a social system embracing all aspects of life and thought—social, economic, political, and religious—and connecting gods and men, stamps the whole book" (pp. 503-4). Moreover, throughout the book is the idea of everything being related to the fundamental social structure. It is the stock-group of McLennan; the god is little more than a reflection, or a symbol, of the mystical unity of the group. All the way through the book there is this structural way of regarding religion.

A good example of a structural explanation is Smith's discussion of kingship in Europe and Asia. In Greece and Rome it fell before the aristocracy; in Asia it held its own. "This diversity of political fortune is reflected in the diversity of religious development. For as the national god did not at first supersede tribal and family deities any more than the king superseded tribal and family institutions, the tendency of the west, where the kingship succumbed, was towards a divine aristocracy of many gods, only modified by a weak reminiscence of the old kingship in the not very effective sovereignty of Zeus, while in the east the national god tended to acquire a really monarchic sway. What is often described as the natural tendency of Semitic religion toward ethical monotheism, is in the main nothing more than a consequence of the alliance of religion with monarchy." (pp. 73–4). This is very naive history, very simple sociology, and very poor ethnography.

The most damning case against Smith's theory of a communion-sacrifice rests, however, on the reasoning that if all primitive sacrifices have the same features and the most fundamental of these is the idea of communion, then he should have shown that primitive peoples do, in fact, have that idea and that it predominates. He does not do this. He cannot do this. All he does is to guess about a period of Semitic history for which there are no contemporaneous evidences. His attempt at reconstruction from survivals was as unsuccessful as other such attempts and as unsatisfactory, and it contained the usual and fatal ambiguity of the concept of origin, with its double sense of earliest form and simplest form, involving at the same time both historical and logical analysis. The best one can say for it is what Cook says (and that is questionable), that Smith's "theory of the 'totem origin' or sacrifice is true, therefore, in the sense that in totemism we find the most primitive types of belief and practice that we can well conceive, and that, as Durkheim clearly showed, it contains in rudimentary form some of the significant features which mark the higher religions" (p. 685).

The criticism of all anthropological writers of this period by later writers (e.g., Malinowski and Radcliffe-Brown) is that whilst their use of the comparative method was justifiable, indeed, laudable, it was used for the wrong purpose, for the reconstruction of the earliest form of an institution, leading to laws of social development (causal laws), rather than for the formulation of laws of interdependence (functional laws). It is debatable whether this criticism is valid, or entirely so—the purpose of the method was justified in comparative philology, jurisprudence, and mythology. What is perhaps more to the point is the fact that the information at their disposal was much less, and much less accurate than that at the disposal of critics of a later generation—the result of field research. Of both the nineteenth-century writers and their critics, it may be said that little regard was paid to the first rule in science: negative instances must be sought for and accounted for in terms of the theory put forward.

Chapter 9
Maine (1822-1888)

Henry Maine was variously Regius Professor of Civil Law at Cambridge, Reader in Roman Law and Jurisprudence at the Inns of Court, legal member of the Council of India, Corpus Professsor of Jurisprudence at Oxford, Master of Trinity Hall, Cambridge, and Whewell Professor of International Law, Cambridge. His best-known work, *Ancient Law* (1861), is not only a classic of jurisprudence but may also be regarded as a classic of anthropology, and the author was a man of great learning and much insight. It is true that the book is addressed primarily to persons interested in legal theory and mainly treats of highly technical problems in Roman law and its European developments—legal fictions, the Law of Nature and *Ius Gentium,* testamentary succession, primogeniture, the law of property, theories of prescription, the nature of legal contracts, and the like—but it deals with them in a highly systematic and comparative manner, seeking to reach general statements of a sociological kind. It deals with these problems for the most part in the earliest known forms of European societies (mainly Roman, though also Greek, Hindu, Germanic, and Slavonic) and is therefore of interest to anthropologists both with regard to method and to the type of social structure with which they are mostly concerned.

Maine was a great believer in the historical and comparative method. By this he meant that aprioristic speculation from philosophical and psychological axioms did not help one at all to understand the development of legal institutions; they only led to false deductions; e.g., all sorts of fancy theories have been put forward to explain the disappearance of the death penalty from the penal system of Republican Rome, whereas a study of the facts shows that it was purely fortuitous (p. 395). "The inquiries of the jurist are in truth prosecuted much as inquiry in physics and physiology was prosecuted before observation had taken the place of assumption. Theories, plausible and comprehensive, but absolutely unverified, such as the Law of Nature or the Social Compact, enjoy a universal preference over sober research into the primitive history of society and law" (p. 3). Existing theories of jurisprudence, with the exception of those of Montesquieu (for whom Maine had great respect), omit one thing: "They take no account of what law has actually been at epochs remote from the particular period at which they made their appearance. Their originators carefully observed the institutions of their own age and civilization, and those of other ages and civilizations with which they had some degree of intellectual sympathy, but, when they turned their attention to archaic states of society which exhibited much superficial difference from their own, they uniformly ceased to observe and began guessing" (pp. 128–9). "What mankind did in the primitive state may not be a hopeless subject of inquiry, but of their motives for doing it it is impossible to know anything. These sketches of the plight of human beings in the first ages of the world are effected by first supposing mankind to be divested of a great part of the circumstances by which they are now surrounded, and by then assuming that, in the condition thus imagined, they would preserve the same sentiments and prejudices by which they are now actuated—although, in fact, these sentiments may have been created and engendered by those very circumstances of which, by the hypothesis, they are to be stripped" (pp. 266–7).

What was required was research into the way in which social institutions have in fact developed. Maine was primarily interested in understanding how modern law came to be what it is, or was, in the light of what we can discover about its earliest forms and what is known of the great historical movements which have shaped its development. We may say that his chief interest was in the origins of legal institutions. If he had made it quite clear that the conclusions he reached applied only to the Indo-European peoples under investigation he would have avoided much criticism on the part of McLennan and others who pointed out that they are not valid generalizations about primitive societies as a whole. Indeed, in the preface to the tenth edition (1884), Maine had to admit that "the observation of savage or extremely barbarous races has brought to light forms of social organization extremely unlike that to which he [Maine himself] has referred the beginnings of law, and possibly in some cases of greater antiquity" (p. v–vi). He admits, moreover, in the body of the book (p. 129), that one of our sources for a knowledge of early society are accounts by contemporary observers of civilizations less advanced than their own, but by this he meant people like Tacitus; and he ignores completely all writings about primitive peoples of the modern world. In spite of this fact and a number of faulty interpretations, it is true, as Pollock says, that Maine created the natural history of law.

Although Maine was acidly critical of the sweeping generalizations made by philosophers and others about legal institutions and in spite of his insistence of a mastery of detail he was far from being just an empiricist or from regarding history as a meaningless succession of accidents. On the contrary, he put forward a large number of general statements, some limited in scope, others wider. For example, customary law was codified (e.g., the Twelve Tables of Rome) in Greece, in Italy, and on the Hellenized seaboard of western Asia, "at periods much the same everywhere, not, I mean, at periods identical in point of time, but similar in point of the relative progress of each community" (pp. 12–3). As Pollock (*Principles of Contract,* p. 22) points out, when stages are spoken of, we need not think of an inevitable succession but of an irreversible order; some peoples may have had lawgivers as early as they had judges, but no people, having acquired a body of legislation, has reverted from it to pure customary law. Now it is of the highest significance at what stage of their social progress peoples had their laws put into writing. In the Western world the plebian, or popular, element in each state overcame the oligarchical monopoly of law and obtained an early codification, but in India the aristocracies tended to become religious rather than military or political, and they held on to their power. Codification was therefore much later than in the west and was not merely a collection of customary rules but also of Brahminical precepts, what they thought ought to be the law, thereby increasing and consolidating priestly authority—hence the caste system. "The fate of the Hindoo law is, in fact, the measure of the value of the Roman code." The Roman code was compiled "while usage was still wholesome, and a hundred years afterwards it might have been too late. The Hindoo law has been to a great extent embodied in writing, but ancient as in one sense are the compendia which still exist in Sanskrit, they contain ample evidence that they were drawn up after the mischief had been done" (pp. 14–18). "The rigidity of primitive law, arising chiefly from its early association and identification with religion, has chained down the mass of the human race to those views of life and conduct which they entertained at the time when their usages were first consolidated into a systematic form. There were one or two races exempted by a marvelous fate from this calamity, and grafts from these stocks have fertilized a few modern societies" (p. 83).

A generalization is implied in the following: Maine was surprised that so little attention had been given to the question of why Western theology differed so much from Eastern. The answer is that Western theology combined with Roman jurisprudence. Consequently while the Greeks were primarily interested in metaphysical questions (e.g., the doctrine of the Trinity), the Latins were not and just accepted Greek definitions. Indeed, when they discussed metaphysical questions at all they did so in Greek or, later, in a dialect of Latin constructed to give expression to Greek conceptions (pp. 362-3). It is a remarkable fact that no Greek-speaking people has ever been seriously perplexed by the question of free will and necessity. We are to account for this by the fact that no Greek society "ever showed the slightest capacity for producing a philosophy of law. Legal science is a Roman creation, and the problem of Free Will arises when we contemplate a metaphysical conception under a legal aspect" (p. 363). The Latins rather threw themselves with great enthusiasm into a discussion of such matters as could be treated legalistically: the nature of sin and its transmission by inheritance, the debt owed by man and its vicarious satisfaction, the necessity and sufficiency of atonement, etc. "Theological speculation had passed from a climate of Greek metaphysics to a climate of Roman Law" (p. 366). Theology in the West was permeated with forensic ideas and couched in a forensic phraseology. The adoption of Aristotle by Latin Christianity modified the forensic side to Western theology but this modification was lost by the Reformation. Calvinism and Arminianism have a remarkably legal character.

Another general statement declares that criminal law derives from and is preceded by civil law. In all ancient law the proportion of criminal to civil law is exceedingly different. Indeed, the civil part appears to have trifling dimensions because what we are wont to regard as civil law is for the most part lacking; e.g., it is impossible to have a law of persons (or status) in a society where all forms of status are merged in common subjection to paternal power, or laws of property and succession so long as land and goods devolve within the family, or a law of contract where contract is almost totally absent (no society is totally destitute of contract, but the conception in early society is rudimentary). But the predominance of "criminal" law is only apparent. It is not true criminal law because the offenses are not against the community (crimes, *crimina*) but against the individual (wrongs, *delicta*). The penal law of ancient societies is the law of wrongs or torts or delicts. In Roman law offenses we would regard as crimes are treated as torts (e.g., theft, assault, slander, etc.), or sometimes as sins. When the community intervenes to compel the wrongdoer to compound for his wrong it does so as arbitrator, and what have sometimes been taken for fines are in reality fees (*sacramenta,* the Anglo-Saxon *bannum* or *fredum*). The primitive history of criminal law divides itself into four stages (pp. 392-3). (1) The commonwealth interposed directly, and by isolated acts, to avenge itself on the author of the evil it suffered. (2) The multiplicity of crimes compels the legislature to delegate its powers to particular *quaestiones* or commissions, each of which is deputed to investigate a particular accusation and to punish the wrongdoer. (3) The legislature, instead of waiting for the alleged commission of a crime as the occasion of appointing a *quaestio,* periodically nominates commissioners on the chance of certain classes of crime being committed. (4) The *quaestiones* become permanent benches or chambers.

The part of *Ancient Law* which has had most influence on anthropological theory, arousing violent disputes, was that dealing with agnation and patria potestas. The old Roman law establishes "a fundamental difference between "agnatic" and "cognatic" relationship, that is, between the Family considered as based upon common subjection to patriarchal authority and the Family considered (in conformity with modern ideas) as united through the mere fact of a common descent" (p. 61). The evidence derived from comparative jurisprudence establishes the Patriarchal Theory. The eldest male parent—the eldest ascendant—is absolutely supreme in his household. The earliest forms of societies known to us are aggregates not of individuals but of families, each under the unqualified dominion of its patriarch: "The unit of an ancient society was the Family, of a modern society the individual" (p. 134). By "family" Maine meant not what we think of as the family—the elementary family—but what is known as the joint family or *Grossfamilie;* but his usage is not always free from ambiguity. In primitive societies the elementary group is the family, in this sense, the aggregation of families forms the gens or house, and the aggregation of houses makes the tribe; and the aggregation of tribes constitutes the commonwealth. All these groups considered themselves as a common stock, descended from a common ancestor. "The history of political ideas begins, in fact, with the assumption that kinship in blood is the sole possible ground of community in political functions" (p. 137)—it being understood that kinship in blood includes aliens attached by the fiction of adoption. Herein lies one of Maine's most important generalizations: kinship and *not* contiguity is the basis of common political action in primitive societies. Only later does the principle of kinship become supplanted by that of local contiguity as the binding force of the political group (pp. 131 *et seq*).

The parent had the *jus vitae necisque,* the power of life and death in his family—he can do what he likes with his children under the patria potestas of the Romans, the prototype of the primeval paternal authority. The duties the sons later owed to the state, especially service in war, eventually tempered, and finally broke down, paternal authority. The father also had full powers over his sons' property. On the other side, the head of the family had the duty of providing for his dependents and was responsible for their delicts.

That the patria potestas was a universal institution is shown by the widespread agnatic usage derived from it (chapter V). Agnates "are all the cognates who trace their connection exclusively through males" (p. 153). *"Mulier est finis familiae,"* "A woman is the terminus of the family"—"A female name closes the branch or twig of the genealogy in which it occurs"(p. 154). Why this arbitrary way of tracing descent? The answer is: "The foundation of Agnation is not the marriage of Father and Mother, but the authority of the Father. All persons are Agnatically connected together who are under the same Paternal Power, or who have been under it, or who might have been under it if their lineal ancestor had lived long enough to exercise his empire. In truth, in the primitive view, Relationship is exactly limited by Patria Potestas. Where the Potestas begins, kinship begins; and therefore adoptive relatives are among the kindred. Where the Potestas ends, Kinship ends; so that a son emancipated by his father loses all rights of Agnation" (p. 154). Hence the descendants of females are not kin, for their children fall under the patria potestas of their husbands, and a person could not be subject to two different patriae potestates. Hence also, uterine brothers, sons by the same mother but by different fathers, are not kin, whereas consanguineous brothers, sons of the same father by different wives, are kin. It is true that the paternal powers are extinguished on the death of the parent, "but Agnation is as it were a mould which retains their imprint after they have ceased to exist" (p. 155). Here Maine is setting forth the principle of lineage identity. In Roman jurisprudence it is the principle "that a man lives on in his heir—the elimination, if we may so speak, of the fact of death" (p. 202). "The life of each citizen is not regarded as limited by birth and death; it is but a continuation of the existence of his forefathers, and it will be prolonged in the existence of his descendants" (p. 270). Hence where we find agnation there must once have been patria potestas.

There were three forms of marriage in ancient Rome, *confarreatio, coemptio,* and *usus.* Through these a husband acquired wide rights over the person and property of his wife, but he acquired them by his wife becoming his daughter. She passed *in manum viri. Manus* was the power exercised by the patriarch, whether over the family or the material property—over children, slaves, wife, flocks, and herds, but in later Roman times power became discriminated, both in word and in conception, according to the object over which it is exerted; exercised over material commodities or slaves, it has become *dominium*—over children, it is *potestas*—over persons whose services have been made away to another by their own patriarch, it is *mancipium*—over a wife it is still *manus* (p. 330).

It follows from the agnatic principle that children of women cannot inherit. By the canons of Roman jurisprudence first the *sui,* or direct descendants, inherited. On the failure of the *sui,* the nearest agnates succeeded; then the *gentiles* (p. 211).

As we have seen, relations between persons in early society were almost entirely determined by their relative status. From this follows what is perhaps Maine's most famous generalization: "The movement of the progressive societies has been uniform in one respect. Through all its course it has been distinguished by the gradual dissolution of family dependency, and the growth of individual obligation in its place. The individual is steadily substituted for the Family, as the unit of which civil laws take account" (p. 172). This was brought about by contract, a substitution of free agreement of individuals for a condition of society in which all relations of persons are summed up in the relations of family. The status of slave has become the contractual relation of servant to master. The status of female under tutelage has given way to contractual relations.

etc. "The word Status may be usefully employed to construct a formula expressing the law of progress thus indicated, which, whatever be its value, seems to me to be sufficiently ascertained. All the forms of Status taken notice of in the Law of Persons were derived from, and to some extent are still coloured by, the powers and privileges anciently residing in the Family. If then we employ Status, agreeably with the usage of the best writers, to signify these personal conditions only, and avoid applying the term to such conditions as are the immediate or remote result of agreement, we may say that the movement of the progressive societies has hitherto been a movement *from Status to Contract*" (pp. 173–4).

Maine undoubtedly made a number of errors of interpretation, even, we can say now in the light of greater knowledge of the facts, in his own province of Roman law. Some of these involve technicalities of Roman law. Others concern wider issues of a sociological kind. As Pollock points out (p. 184) Maine exaggerated the victory of Contract over Status. In the law of corporations, they have a collective character, e.g., trade unions, which is of great importance today. Professor Dicey (*Law and Public Opinion in England*, p. 283) says that "the rights of workmen in regard to compensation for accidents have become a matter not of contract, but of status."

In seeking to defend Maine for ignoring the many societies which have matrilineal modes of descent, inheritance, and succession and in which the potestas is not at all in the hands of the *pater* but of the *avunculus,* Pollock says, "Whatever else it is or has been, primitive it (the matriarchal or maternal family system) is not" (p. 179). This is true, but Maine's contention about the universality of agnation is contradicted by ethnographical facts, for certainly a considerable number of matrilineal peoples are hunters and collectors.

However, we can forgive Maine this deficiency. He was a fine scholar and both in the handling of his data and the restriction of his field of inquiry to a limited range in which any fact could be ascertained and given its due weight, he broke away from the attempt to formulate general laws of universal validity. In doing so he gave us many of our more important technical terms: contract, status, delict, crime, agnation, etc., with a new sociological significance attached to them. He also gave us several sociological hypotheses of great value and displayed in doing so a clear understanding of sociological method, giving explanations in terms of relations between social phenomena by showing how one set of ideas or institutions affect others. This is a wide departure from eighteenth-century writings and their themes, dominated as they were by conjectural history and the notion of societies as natural phenomena with discoverable laws and stages of development.

Chapter 10
Tylor (1832–1917)

Sir Edward Tylor was keeper of the Pitt-Rivers Museum; reader in anthropology; and later, professor of anthropology at Oxford. Among his best known works were *Anahuac* (1861), *Researches into the Early History of Mankind* (1865), and *Primitive Culture* (1871) but, from the point of view of method, Tylor's most interesting contribution to anthropology was not his better-known book *Primitive Culture*, but a paper he gave to the Anthropological Institute in 1888 and which was published in the following year under the title, "On a Method of Investigating the Development of Institutions; applied to Laws of Marriage and Descent" (*J.R.A.I.*, XVIII, 1889). Anthropology could, he thought, never be finally accepted among reputable men of science until it could present its findings in numbers, statistically. "For years past it has become evident that the great need for anthropology is that its methods should be strengthened and systematized" (p. 245). His aim, therefore, was "to show how the development of institutions may be investigated on a basis of tabulation and classification." He examined the literature on about 350 different peoples for their rules of marriage and descent, and he scheduled these out into tables to ascertain what he called "adhesions" or correlations, found in a sufficient number of cases to make it unlikely that the association was a chance one. This procedure would give us causal explanations of universal validity.

He began with the custom of "avoidance." He found that there were forty-five cases of avoidance between the husband and his wife's relatives, eight cases of mutual avoidance, and thirteen cases of avoidance between the wife and her husband's relatives. He wanted to show that there was a relation between the distribution of this custom in its different forms and according to different modes of residence; and he therefore tabulated modes of residence under the headings of matrilocality (65), temporary matrilocality giving way to final patrilocality (76), and patrilocality (141). Then, by comparing the two sets of tables he reached the conclusion that the concordances he found were above the ratio of chance and that therefore they could not be regarded as independent associations but must be regarded as adhesions: "There is a well-marked preponderance indicating that ceremonial avoidance by the husband of the wife's family is in some way connected with his living with them; and vice versa as to the wife and the husband's family" (p. 247).

He then took the custom of naming the parent after the child, for which he coined the word "teknonymy" (by paying no attention to the naming of women after their first-born he displays a lack of scientific rigour which much weakens his observations on this custom). He found that teknonymy with regard to the father is often found in societies with matrilocal residence, and that it is even more closely attached to the practice of ceremonial avoidance by the husband of the wife's relatives. It occurs fourteen times where accident might have given four.

Returning to a further consideration of the association of forms of avoidance with modes of residence, he presented his tables in diagrammatic form to demonstrate better what he considered to be an evolutionary trend (p. 251).

But what about the negative instances—when, for example, there are found together both patrilocality and avoidance by the husband of his wife's parents? Tylor gets round this difficulty in the same manner as McLennan, by contradicting, it seems to me, his whole concept of adhesions; he says that this is a survival (for him a "geological" notion) from a stage of matrilocality. On his own showing, however, mode of residence is the constant and avoidance the variable, so one would wish to have it explained why when the constant changed the variable did not also change and why what survived in some societies did not survive in others. Not only does Tylor avoid the issue by appeal to the notion of survival, but he also makes further use of the notion to give support to his main thesis, an evolutionary one. His diagram is designed to show that the three modes of residence—matrilocality, "removal," and patrilocality—are something more than types of residence, being also historical transitions or stages, for had historical development been in reverse order the wife's avoidance would have survived into the matrilocal stage. This argument subsumes a theory of survivals for which no evidence is adduced.

He next discusses patriliny (paternal), matriliny (maternal), and dual descent (maternal–paternal), including under these headings a variety of forms of succession—of the family name, of property, of office, of authority. Here again, he wants to show that mankind has consistently moved from the maternal kind of society to the paternal kind. His test is the levirate (he does not distinguish between the levirate and widow-inheritance). He says that the levirate is a custom of substitution, "belonging to the period when marriage is a compact not so much between two individuals as between two families." The social distribution of the levirate extends through all three stages. In the paternal–maternal stage it comes into competition with inheritance of widows by sons. "Looking at the distribution of these groups of customs, it is seen to be only compatible with the view that the paternal rule followed the maternal, bringing with it even while its prevalence was but partial, the principle of widow-inheritance" (p. 253-4). (Inheritance, that is, by sons—not by brothers.)

He then turns to the custom of the couvade, this "farcical proceeding," as he calls it. It does not appear in the maternal stage. It arises in the maternal–paternal stage (twenty cases) and then dwindles as a survival into the paternal stage. He agrees with Bachofen that the couvade belongs to "the turning-point of society when the tie of parentage, till then recognized in maternity was extended to take in paternity, this being done by the fiction of representing the father as a second mother." Thus the couvade "proves to be not merely incidentally an indication of the tendency of society from maternal to paternal, but the very sign and record of that vast change."

The proof to him that the typological classification is also a record of historical stages lies in the absence of survivals extending into the maternal stage, which they frequently do into the paternal stage. "The argument is a geological one." The determining cause of the clusters of customs we call the maternal and paternal systems is mode of residence. The maternal system and matrilocality go hand in hand, as do the opposites. "In the one simple fact of residence we may seek the main determining cause of the several usages which combine to form a maternal or paternal system."

He next examines the custom of marriage by capture, once

again to throw light on "the great social transformation." Over 100 of the peoples scheduled have this custom in one or other of its three forms: hostile capture, connubial capture, and merely formal capture. "The effect of capture in breaking up the maternal system, and substituting the paternal for it, has thus to be taken into account as a serious factor in social development."

Lastly, he examines together, as part of a single complex, exogamy and the classificatory system. The latter derives from the rule of exogamy in a society consisting of only two intermarrying groups, and is thus connected with cross-cousin marriage. He considers this to have been the original form of exogamy. The schedules show a much higher than chance correlation between the classificatory system and exogamy. There is the same correspondence with cross-cousin marriage, but here "the relation is not one of derivation, but of identity, the cross-cousin rule being actually a partial form or imperfect statement of the law of exogamy itself." Exogamy has for him a political function, the strengthening and enlarging of the political community by ties of marriage and admixture of clans: "Again and again in the world's history, savage tribes must have had plainly before their minds the simple practical alternative between marrying-out and being killed out."

He concludes his paper: "The key of the position is, as that veteran anthropologist, Professor Bastian, of the Berlin Museum, is never weary of repeating, that in statistical investigation, the future of anthropology lies."

Some weaknesses of Tylor's thesis emerged in the discussion which followed the presentation of this paper. Mr. Galton pointed out that it is essential that the degree in which the customs compared together are independent should be known, for they might be derived from a common source and be duplicate copies of the same original as would be the case, shall we say, with the spread of the English language or parliamentary system. Also, as Professor Flower observed, it was obvious that the method depended entirely on the units of comparison being of equivalent value. Are, for example, "monogamy" among the Veddalis of Ceylon and "monogamy" in Western Europe units of the same kind or is "monotheism" in Islam equivalent to "monotheism" among the Pygmies?

Chapter 11
Pareto (1848-1923)

This chapter aims to show how Vilfredo Pareto's work is directly relevant to the methods and observations of social anthropology. Further, it is the chronicle of an attempt by Pareto to apply to documents about civilized peoples the same comparative analysis as was applied to documents about savages in the great classics of social anthropology, *Primitive Culture, The Golden Bough, Les Fonctions mentales,* etc. When we realize that Pareto reached the same conclusions about "civilized" behavior as Lévy-Bruhl reached about "savage" behavior, it will readily be granted that his writings are of concern to anthropologists and that if the rigid division of social studies into those that deal with civilized peoples and those that deal with primitive peoples is to be maintained it can only be as a temporary convenience.

In Pareto's vast *Trattato di Sociologia Generale* (English translation, *The Mind and Society*), over a million words are devoted to an analysis of feelings and ideas. The treatise is always amusing and is born of wide reading and bitter irony. But Pareto must be classed as political philosopher rather than sociologist. His were the brilliance and shallowness of the polemicist and the popularizer of scientific method. Like so many Italian students Pareto was a quarter of a century behind the rest of the scientific world, and his constant jibes and jeers at phantom enemies become tedious. It is surely unnecessary to spend two thousand pages in controverting the opinions of philosophers, priests, and politicians. Moreover, Pareto was a plagiarist, and a very foolish one. He appeared to be unaware of contemporaneous sociological literature. He does not mention the works of Durkheim, Freud, and Lévy-Bruhl, to cite only three savants, though they had dealt with the same problems of sentiments, rationalizations, and nonlogical thought that he was enquiring into. Even if ignorant of these works he certainly took many of his ideas, without due recognition, from earlier writers whom he often repaid with abuse. Of these I will mention only Bentham, Marx, Nietzsche, Le Bon, James, Sorel, Comte, and Frazer. Many authors are held up to derision because they use metaphysical terms, for Pareto, throughout his prolix and ill-arranged arguments, makes much ado about remaining in the scientific (logico-experimental) field. Nevertheless, he is often as open to criticism on this score as those whom he ridicules.

Why trouble to digest a book which is so bad? Pareto tried to solve a number of genuine problems, and we can learn as much from his failure as from his success about the nature of the problems themselves and the terminological and methodological difficulties involved in an enquiry into them. The data he cites and his treatment of it also provide an illuminating commentary of the theories of a number of writers, especially on Lévy-Bruhl's theory of primitive mentality, because both men were trying to classify types of thought and to discover their interrelations.

The treatise contains five major propositions:

1. There are sentiments ("residues") making for social stability ("group persistences") and sentiments making for social change ("instinct for combinations"). The study of these sentiments, of their persistence, distribution, and interrelations, in individuals and groups, is the whole subject-matter of sociology.

2. Sentiments are expressed not only in behavior but also in ideologies ("derivations"). These are of very little social importance compared with sentiments and the only point in studying them is to discover the sentiments they both express and conceal.

3. Individuals are biologically heterogeneous. In any society a few are superior ("elites") to the rest and are the natural leaders of a community.

4. The form and durability of a society depends on (1) the distribution and mobility of these superior persons in the social hierarchy and (2) the proportion of individuals in each class who are mainly motivated by sentiments that make for stability ("rentier" type) or by sentiments that make for change ("speculator" type).

5. There are alternating periods of change and stability due to variation in the number of biologically superior persons in the classes ("circulation of elites") and to the proportion of rentier and speculator types in the governing class ("distribution of residues").

The first two propositions are more directly relevant to a study of primitive mentality than the others.

There are six classes of residues: (1) instinct for combinations, (2) group-persistences (persistence of aggregates), (3) need of expressing sentiments by external acts (activity, self-expression), (4) residues connected with sociality, (5) integrity of the individual and his appurtenances, and (6) the sex residue.

Most actions that are expressions of these residues are nonlogical in character and are rigidly distinguished by Pareto from logical actions which derive from and are controlled by experience. Pareto includes thought (speech-reactions) as well as behavior in his concept of "actions." Logico-experimental thought depends on facts and not the facts on it and its principles are rejected as soon as it is found that they do not square with the facts. They assert experimental uniformities. Nonlogico-experimental theories are accepted *a priori* and dictate to experience. They do not depend on the facts but the facts depend on them. If they clash with experience, in which term Pareto includes both observation and experiment, arguments are evoked to reestablish the accord. Logical actions derive mainly from processes of reasoning while nonlogical actions derive mainly from sentiments. Logical actions are found connected with arts, sciences, and economics and in military, legal, and political operations. In other social processes nonlogical actions predominate.

Genera and Species		Have the Actions Logical Ends and Purposes?	
		Objectively	Subjectively
Class I	Logical actions (The objective and subjective purposes are identical)	Yes	Yes
Class II	Non-logical actions (The objective end differs from the subjective purpose)		
Genus 1		No	No
Genus 2		No	Yes
Genus 3		Yes	No
Genus 4		Yes	Yes
	Species of the genera 3 and 4		
	3a, 4a The objective end would be accepted by the subject if he knew it		
	3b, 4b The objective end would be rejected by the subject if he knew it.		

97

The test between logical and nonlogical actions is whether their subjective purpose accords with their objective results, i.e., whether means are adapted to ends. A logical proposition is demonstrable by observation and experiment. The sole judge of the logico-experimental value of a notion of action is modern science.

Pareto quotes Hesiod, "Do not make water at the mouth of a river emptying into the sea, nor into a spring. You must avoid that. Do not lighten your bowels there, for it is not good to do so" (1935, p. 79). Both of these injunctions are nonlogical. The precept not to befoul drinking water has an objective result, probably unknown to Hesiod, but no subjective purpose. The precept not to befoul rivers at their mouths has neither objective result nor subjective purpose. The precepts belong to Class II Genus 3 and Class II Genus 1 in Pareto's synoptic scheme of classification.

"The ends and purposes in question are immediate ends and purposes. We choose to disregard the indirect. The objective end is a real one, located within the field of observation and experience, and not an imaginary end, located outside that field. An imaginary end may, on the other hand, constitute a subjective purpose" (1935, p. 78).

If there is no real end, an action or proposition cannot very well by judged by reference to scientific value because it lies outside the logico-experimental field where alone science can operate, e.g., "When St. Thomas [Aquinas] asserts that angel speaks to angel, he sets up a relation between things about which the person keeping strictly to experience can say nothing. The case is the same when the argument is elaborated logically and one or more inferences are drawn. St. Thomas is not content with his mere assertion; he is eager to prove it, and says: 'Since one angel can express to another angel the concept in his mind, and since the person who has a concept in his mind can express it to another at will, it follows that one angel may speak to another.' Experimental science can find no fault with the argument. It lies altogether outside its province" (1935, p. 289).

Pareto is aware that from the standpoint of formal logic the validity of premises is irrelevant, all that is required being sound reasoning from the premises. However, he chooses to speak of thought and action as logical when they are in accord with reality and are adapted to the end at which they aim and as nonlogical when they are not, from the point of view of science, in such accord nor so adapted.

Every social phenomenon may be considered under two aspects: as it is in reality, and as it presents itself to the mind of this or that human being. The first aspect we shall call *objective,* the second *subjective.* Such a division is necessary for we cannot put in one same class the operations performed by a chemist in his laboratory and the operations performed by a person practising magic; the conduct of Greek sailors in plying their oars to drive their ship over the water and the sacrifices they offered to Poseidon to make sure of a safe and rapid voyage. In Rome the Laws of the XII Tables punished anyone casting a spell on a harvest. We choose to distinguish such an act from the act of burning a field of grain.

We must not be misled by the names we give to the two classes. In reality both are subjective, for all human knowledge is subjective. They are to be distinguished not so much by any difference in nature as in view of one greater or lesser fund of factual knowledge that we ourselves have. We know, or think we know, that sacrifices to Poseidon have no effect whatsoever upon a voyage. We therefore distinguish them from other acts which (to our best knowledge, at least) are capable of having such an effect. If at some future time we were to discover that we have been mistaken, that sacrifices to Poseidon are very influential in securing a favourable voyage, we should have to reclassify them with actions capable of such influence. All that of course is pleonastic. It amounts to saying that when a person makes a classification, he does so according to the knowledge he has. One cannot imagine how things could be otherwise.

There are actions that are means appropriate to ends and which logically link means with ends. There are other actions in which those traits are missing. The two sorts of conduct are very different according as they are considered under their objective or their subjective aspect. From the subjective point of view nearly all human actions belong to the logical class. In the eyes of the Greek mariners sacrifices to Poseidon and rowing with oars were equally logical means of navigation. To avoid verbosities which could only prove annoying, we had better give names to these types of conduct. Suppose we apply the term *logical actions* to actions that logically conjoin means to ends not only from the standpoint of the subject performing them, but from the standpoint of other persons who have a more extensive knowledge—in other words, to actions that are logical both subjectively and objectively in the sense just explained. Other actions we shall call non-logical (by no means the same as "illogical") (1935, pp. 76–7).

Besides asking (1) whether a belief is scientifically valid ("objective aspect"), we may also ask (2) why do certain individuals assert the belief and others accept it ("subjective aspect") and (3) what advantage or disadvantage has the belief for the person who states it, for the person who accepts it, and for society as a whole ("aspect of utility"). Like many other writers (Mill, James, Vaihinger, Sorel, etc.), Pareto emphasizes that an objectively valid belief may not be socially useful or have utility for the individual who holds it. A doctrine which is absurd from the logico-experimental standpoint may be socially beneficial and a scientifically established doctrine may be detrimental to society. Indeed Pareto states it as his aim to demonstrate "experimentally the individual and social utility of non-logical conduct" (1935, p. 35).

How does nonlogical behavior gain acceptance among people capable of logical behavior? Why do people believe in foolish doctrines? Tylor and Frazer say it is because they reason erroneously from correct observations. Lévy-Bruhl says it is because they passively accept collective patterns of thought in the society into

---

Class I   Instinct for Combinations

Ia. Generic combinations
Ib. Combinations of similars or opposites
    1. Generic likeness or oppositeness
    2. Unusual things and exceptional occurrences
    3. Objects and occurrences inspiring awe or terror
    4. Felicitous state associated with good things; infelicitous state associated with bad things
    5. Assimilation: physical consumption of substances to get effects of associable, and more rarely of opposite, character
Ic. Mysterious workings of certain things; mysterious effects of certain acts
    1. Mysterious operations in general
    2. Mysterious linkings of names and things
Id. Need for combining residues
Ie. Need for logical developments
If. Faith in the efficacy of combinations

Class II   Group-persistences (Persistence of Aggregates)

IIa. Persistence of relations between a person and other persons and places
    1. Relationships of family and kindred groups
    2. Relationships with places
    3. Relationships of social class
IIb. Persistence of relations between the living and the dead
IIc. Persistence of relations between a dead person and the things that belonged to him in life
IId. Persistence of abstractions
IIe. Persistence of uniformities
IIf. Sentiments transformed into objective realities
IIg. Personifications
IIh. Need of new abstractions

which they are born. According to Pareto the answer is found in their psychic states expressed in residues, the six classes of which have been enumerated. As Pareto does not pay much attention to the last four classes of residues we will transcribe the subdivisions of the first two classes only. This classification will strike the reader as being a number of arbitrary, haphazard, categories, but it is only fair to an author to try to discover the meaning behind his words so we will give one illustration of each sub-division of Class I and seek in these for an interpretation of "residues."

Ia   GENERIC COMBINATIONS

Example: Pliny gives as remedies for epilepsy bears' testicles, wild boars' testicles, wild boars' urine (which is more effective when allowed to evaporate in the animal's bladder); hog's testicles dried, triturated, and beaten in sow's milk; hares' lungs taken with frankincense and white wine (1935, p. 522). (This residue comprises those magical associations of which Tylor says that they either never had rational sense or if they once had rational sense it has been forgotten, i.e., we can perceive no ideal link between the diseases and the drugs intended to cure them.)

Ib (1)   COMBINATIONS OF SIMILARS OR OPPOSITES

Generic likeness or oppositeness. (These are the principles of *similia similibus curantur* and *contraria contrariis*.)
Example: The witch in Theocritus says, "Delphis (her lover) has tormented me. A laurel-branch I burn upon Delphis. Even as this crackles aloud when it is kindled, and burns in a flash so that not even its ashes do we see, so may the flesh of Delphis be consumed by the fire. . . . Even as I melt the wax with the help of a God, so may Delphis the Myndian be likewise melted with love; and as I turn this rhomb of bronze, so may he (Delphis) be turned by Aphrodite towards my threshold" (1935, p. 533). (This residue comprises associations of ideas in magic of which Tylor wrote and which are analyzed at length by Frazer and classed by him as "Homeopathic magic.")

Ib (2)   UNUSUAL THINGS AND EXCEPTIONAL OCCURRENCES

Example: Suetonius records that "Once upon a time a thunderbolt fell on the walls of Velitrae [Vellitri], and that incident was taken as a presage that a citizen of that city was to hold supreme power. Strong in that faith the Velitrians made war on the Romans, but with little success. 'Not till years later did it become manifest that the presage had foretold the advent of Augustus,' who came of a family of Velitrae" (1935, p. 541). (This residue includes omens and portents.)

Ib (3)   OBJECTS AND OCCURRENCES INSPIRING AWE AND TERROR

Example: "This residue appears almost always by itself in certain situations of which the following is typical. Speaking of the Catiline affair, Sallust relates, *Bellum Catilinae*, XXII: 'There were those at the time who said that after Catiline had finished his address he pressed his comrades in crime to take an oath, and passed around bowls of human blood mixed with wine, whereof after they all had tasted, with imprecations upon traitors, as is the custom in solemn sacrifices, he made known his design to them, saying that he had done as he had to the end that each having such a great crime to the charge of the other, they would be the less likely to betray one another. Some hold that these and many other stories were invented by certain individuals who thought to mitigate the unpopularity that later arose against Cicero by stressing the enormity of the crime of the men who had been punished.' Whether this story be true or a fabrication, the fact of the association of two terrible things remains: a drinking of human blood and a conspiracy to destroy the Roman Republic" (1935, pp. 552–3).

Ib (4)   FELICITOUS STATE ASSOCIATED WITH GOOD THINGS;
INFELICITOUS STATE, WITH BAD

Example: "The ancient Romans credited the gods with the successes of their republic. Modern peoples attribute their economic betterment to corrupt, ignorant, altogether contemptible parliaments. Under the old monarchy in France the king partook of the divine. When something bad occurred, people said: 'If the King only knew.' Now the republic and universal suffrage are the divinities, 'Universal suffrage, the master of us all.' Such the slogan of our Deputies and Senators who are elected by the votes of people who believe in the dogma, *'Ni Dieu, Ni Maître!'* " (1935, p. 558).

Ib (5)   ASSIMILATION (Physical consumption of substances
to get effects of associable, and more rarely of opposite, character)

Example: "In view of and considering the strength, courage, and fleetness of foot of Achilles, some were pleased to assume that in his childhood he had been fed on marrow from the bones of lions and others specified bear's marrow and the viscera of lions and of wild boars" (1935, p. 561). (This residue corresponds to Frazer's category of "Contagious magic.")

Ic   MYSTERIOUS WORKINGS OF CERTAIN THINGS: MYSTERIOUS
EFFECTS OF CERTAIN ACTS

This residue figures in amulets, oaths, ordeals, and taboos.

Ic (1)   MYSTERIOUS OPERATIONS IN GENERAL

Example: "According to Tertullian 'Among the heathen there is a dreadful thing called the *fascinum,*' 'the spell,' which comes as the unfortunate result of excessive praise and glory. This we sometimes believe to be the work of the Devil, because he hates whatever is good, sometimes the work of God, for of Him comes judgement on pride in an exalting of the lowly and a humbling of the haughty" (1935, pp. 572-3).

Ic (2)   MYSTERIOUS LINKINGS OF NAMES AND THINGS

Example: St. Augustine says, "In a perfect number of days, to wit, in six, did God finish his handiwork" (1935, p. 586).

Id NEED FOR COMBINING RESIDUES

Example: "The human being is loth to dissever faith from experience; he wants a completed whole free from discordant notes. For long centuries Christians believed that their scriptures contained nothing at variance with historical or scientific experiences. Some of them have now abandoned that opinion as regards the natural sciences but cling to it as regards history. Others are willing to drop the Bible as science and history, but insist on keeping at least its morality. Still others will have a much-desired accord, if not literally, at least allegorically, by dint of ingenious interpretations. The Moslems are convinced that all mankind can know is contained in the Koran. The authority of Homer was sovereign for the ancient Greeks. For certain Socialists the authority of Marx is, or at least was, just as supreme. No end of felicitous sentiments are harmonised in a melodious whole in the Holy Progress and the Holy Democracy of modern peoples" (1935, p. 588–9).

Ie NEED FOR LOGICAL DEVELOPMENTS

"The demand for logic is satisfied by pseudo-logic as well as by rigorous logic. At bottom what people want is to think it matters little whether the thinking be sound or fallacious. ... We should not forget that if this insistence on having causes at all costs, be they real or imaginary, has been responsible for many imaginary causes, it has also led to the discovery of real ones. As regards residues, experimental science, theology, metaphysics, fatuous speculations as to the origins and the purposes of things, have a common point of departure: a resolve, namely *not* to stop with the last known cause of the known fact, but to go beyond it, argue from it, find or imagine something beyond that limit. Savage peoples have no use for the metaphysical speculations of civilized countries but they are also strangers to civilized scientific activity; and if one were to assert that but for theology and metaphysics experimental science would not even exist, one could not easily be confuted. Those three kinds of activity are probably manifestations of one same psychic state, on the extinction of which they would vanish simultaneously" (1935, p. 590–1). Example: None is specially cited but the entire collection of derivations afterwards enumerated by Pareto exemplify this residue.

If FAITH IN THE EFFICACY OF COMBINATIONS

Example: "Speaking in general, the ignorant man is guided by faith in the efficacy of combinations, a faith which is kept alive by the fact that many combinations are really effective, but which none the less arises spontaneously within him, as may be seen in the child that amuses itself by trying the strangest combinations. The ignorant person distinguishes little if at all between effective and ineffective combinations. He bets on lottery numbers according to his dreams just as confidently as he goes to the railroad station at the time designated in the time-table. He thinks it quite as natural to consult the faithcurer or the quack as to consult the most expert physician. Cato the elder hands out magical remedies and directions for farming with the same assurance" (1935, pp. 593-4).

Pareto does not consider that logical actions are to be distinguished from nonlogical actions on psychological grounds. "If a person is convinced that to be sure of a good voyage he must sacrifice to Poseidon and sail in a ship that does not leak, he will perform the sacrifice and caulk his seams in exactly the same spirit" (1935, p. 210).

It is not entirely clear what Pareto means by residues. Evidently he knew very little psychology and preferred to be as vague as possible about the concept. His critics and disciples do not enlighten us about residues. Borkenau says that the concept has the qualities of being unchangeable, meaningless, and unintelligible (Borkenau, 1936, p. 48). Sorokin says that they are relatively constant "drives" which are neither instincts nor sentiments. He compares them, among other things, to "dispositions" and "complexes" (Sorokin, 1928, p. 48). Bousquet says that they are certain tendencies, certain sentiments (Bousquet, 1925, p. 135).

I interpret his writings like Homans and Curtis who describe residues as the common element in "certain utterances and writings," as an abstraction from "the observed sayings of men" (Homans and Curtis, 1934, pp. 87-9). Nevertheless, in their exposition they prefer to apply the term also to certain hypothetical sentiments. They say, "Strictly, they (residues) are not parts of a conceptual scheme, but uniformities abstracted from the observed sayings of men. Common sense, however, has set up a conceptual scheme which in our habits of thought is so closely joined with observations that it is inconvenient to separate them. We all observe that we say and do certain things, but we all feel as well that we have sentiments connected with these sayings and doings. Therefore the word 'residues' will be used to mean 'sentiments.' For it is not worthwhile to sacrifice the directness of the language of common sense for the sake of a consistent rigour."

Pareto himself often speaks of "sentiment" instead of "residue." In an address at Lausanne (Homans and Curtis, 1934, appendix) he said, "*L'activité humaine a deux branches principales: celle du sentiment et celle des recherches expérimentales. On ne saurait exagérer l'importance de la première. C'est le sentiment qui pousse à l'action, qui donne la vie aux règles de la morale, au dévouement, aux religions, sous toutes leurs formes si complexes et si variées. C'est par l'aspiration à l'idéal que subsistent et progressent les sociétés humaines. Mais la seconde branche est aussi essentielle pour ces sociétés; elle fournit la matière que met en oeuvre la première; nous lui devons les connaissances qui rendent efficaces l'action et d'utiles modifications du sentiment, grâce auxquelles il s'adapte peu à peu très lentement, il est vrai, aux conditions de l'ambiant.*

"*Toutes les sciences, les naturelles comme les sociales, ont eu, à leur origine, un mélange de sentiments et d'expériences. Il a fallu des siècles pour opérer une séparation de ces éléments, laquelle, à notre époque, est presque entièrement accompli pour les sciences naturelles et qui a commencé et se poursuit pour les sciences sociales.*"

But Pareto uses the word "sentiment" only as a useful concept and not as something which can be observed. Though he often speaks of sentiments and residues as though they were interchangeable terms in his scheme they strictly refer to quite distinct things. We observe that men act in certain ways in certain situations and we find that there is a common factor in their behavior. This constant element in the behavior patterns is the residue and is the important variable in a complex of real behavior. What is inconstant are the derivations which are the unimportant variables in the complex. The residues and the derivations are therefore observed facts and the sentiment is a conceptualization of the facts, i.e., the facts translated into a system of ideas.

We can best understand Pareto's scheme by quoting examples. We see that certain insects (*Eumenes* and *Ceroes*) prepare a food supply for their worms and that all members of these species prepare it in very much the same way. What is variable in their behavior is a derivation. What is common to all insects of the species is a residue; i.e., what remains after all variations have been abstracted (it is the purest type nonlogical action and belongs to

Genus 3 in Pareto's synoptic scheme). We conceptualize this common behavior and call it instinct. We do this for our own convenience. Similarly it is convenient to speak of an instinct for nest-building in birds since it obstructs thought if we have always to describe the whole range of like behavior for which the word "instinct" stands in a conceptual scheme. Those who do not like the word may substitute for it the behavior. When we speak of instinct we make no statement about the psychophysiological action that may accompany, or even cause, behavior, but we speak of observed behavior alone.

The word "sentiment" is used in the same manner. A residue is what is constant in a range of behavior, i.e., it is a constant uniformity. An observer notes that in England people react in certain situations to certain symbols such as "King" and "Union Jack." He abstracts from their behavior what is constant in individuals and ceremonies. This is the residue. It is a pure abstraction because it will not be observed except in combination with the variable elements in real behavior but it is observable behavior none the less. For the sake of convenience we refer to the residue as the "sentiment of patriotism," and we say that the behavior both expresses and strengthens the sentiment. This hypothetical entity denotes a psychological state and therefore may not refer to anything observable and describable, but it is useful because it enables us to relate a great number of facts to each other in the same way as the notion of gravitation enabled people to relate falling apples, the motion of the planets, and many other observations.

Pareto finds in his survey of literature that in many countries and times when a storm arises at sea people do something to quell it. They may make magic, or pray to the gods, or do something else. Exactly what they do is, from his point of view, irrelevant. That they feel something can be done to quiet the storm and that they do this something, are the important facts. Men have always feasted but many different reasons are given for their banquets. "Banquets in honour of the dead become banquets in honour of the Gods, and then again banquets in honour of saints; and then finally they go back and become merely commemorative banquets again. Forms can be changed, but it is much more difficult to suppress the banquets. Briefly (and therefore not very exactly) one might say that a religious custom or a custom of that general character offers a less resistance to change, the farther removed it stands from its residues in simple associations of ideas and acts, and the larger proportion it contains of theological, metaphysical, or logical concepts" (1935, p. 607). The banquet is the residue; the reason for holding it is the derivation. But it is no special kind of banquet but simply the act of banqueting at all times and in all places that is Pareto's residue.

I will give two final examples to illustrate Pareto's use of "residue" and "sentiments."

CONCEPTUAL PLANE	OBSERVATIONAL PLANE	
Sentiment	Residue	Real Behavior
A	a	abc
		ade
		afg
		ahi

Let us take a hypothetical African people who in drought perform a ceremony to make rain. Their rites are *abc*. Christian missionaries convert them, and now when they want to make rain they go into a church and the minister prays for rain. These Christian rites = *ade*. The people, however, become converted to Islam and adopt new rites to obtain rain, namely *afg*. Later they relapse into paganism again but having forgotten their ancient rites of rain-making, borrow those of a neighboring people, namely *ahi*. When we compare all these rites we find they have a common element, *a*, in that in the situation of drought a ceremony is held to obtain rain, and there may be common elements in the rites themselves, e.g., prayers to a divinity and so forth. However, in real situations these common elements are always found with the other and variable elements. The residue is an abstraction from these real situations. Those who find that it helps them to understand the facts better by saying that this African people have a social sentiment, *A,* in regard to rain and account for the constant behavior they observe by attributing it to the sentiment are in no danger so long as they realize what they are doing, i.e., that they are merely conceptualizing the residue.

We need not have taken a hypothetical African tribe. Let us take *abc* = Christianity, *ade* = Islam, *afg* = Hinduism, *ahi* = Christian Science. The theologies and rites of these religions are very different. Let us consider only one element in the complex, namely moral conduct. All these religions condemn adultery, theft, murder, incest, etc., and the peoples in those societies where the religions hold sway express horror at the breach of the moral code; the great majority observing it and punishing those who break it. Conduct is constant and uniform. Only the reasons given for the conduct and the sanctions which are associated with it differ in many particulars. This is an observable fact. Those who like to conceptualize it by referring to religious sentiments are at liberty to do so.

From what has been said about "residues," the meaning Pareto attaches to "derivations" will be apparent. Strictly, derivations are relatively inconstant elements in a range of behavior. In the above diagram they are *b, c, d, e, f, g, h, i*. But Pareto generally uses the term to denote what are often called ideologies or speech-reactions, i.e., the reasons men give for doing things. He thus contrasts the sentiment and the action which expresses it with the explanation men advance to justify their action. He recognizes, however, that sentiments are expressed in both action and ideologies because men not only have a need for action but also a need for intellectualizing their actions, though whether by sound or absurd arguments matters little. What is done and said may have no direct relation to a sentiment but serves to satisfy these needs.

Pareto saw the sentiment, the behavior, and the ideology as existing in a functional relationship. The behavior and the ideology are derivatives of the sentiment and of these two the relatively constant behavior is the more important variable.

Above all, Pareto objected, like Durkheim, Lévy-Bruhl, and many other writers, to theories which interpret behavior by reference to the reasons that men give to explain it. He severely criticizes Spencer and Tylor for suggesting that primitive peoples argued logically from observation of phenomena that souls and ghosts must exist, and that they instituted a cult of the dead in consequence of their logical conclusions. Likewise he criticized Fustel de Coulanges for saying that from the religion of the hearth human beings learned to appropriate the soil and on their religion based their title to the soil. Pareto remarks that religion and ownership of land are likely to have developed side by side. Coulanges further said that the family, which by religion and duty remained grouped around its altar, became fixed to the soil like the altar itself. Pareto comments that what obviously happened was that certain people came to live in separate families fixed to the soil and one of the manifestations of this mode of life was a certain kind of religion which in its turn reacted on the mode of life and contributed towards keeping the families separate and fixed to the soil. The relationship is not a simple cause–effect relationship but one of reciprocal interdependence. Family life, cult, and system of beliefs interact and strengthen one another.

Nevertheless although ideologies may react on sentiments, it is the sentiments that are basic and durable. A particular ideology may change but the sentiment that gave rise to it will remain, and an entirely different ideology may take the place of the previous one. In fact the same residue may give rise to opposed derivations, e.g., the sex residue may be expressed in a violent hatred of all sex manifestations. Therefore the derivations are always dependent on the residue and not the reverse. It is a one-sided functional relationship.

Hospitality is universal, so that when the Greeks said that a man must be hospitable to strangers because "Strangers and beggars come from Zeus" we can leave Zeus out of consideration. The Greeks "were merely voicing their inclination to be hospitable to visitors, and Zeus was dragged in to give a logical colouring to the custom, by implying that the hospitality was offered either in reverence for Zeus, or to avoid the punishment that Zeus held in store for violators of the precept" (1935, p. 215). Other peoples give different reasons for hospitality, but all insist on the hospitality. The giving of hospitality is the residue; the reason for giving it is the derivation. The feelings and the behavior to which they give rise are the important things. The reasons for the behavior do not matter. Almost any reason will serve the purpose equally well, and therefore, even if a man can be convinced that his reasons for doing something he is very desirous of doing are erroneous, he is unlikely to cease his action but will rather look for a new set of reasons to justify his conduct. Hence Pareto, unexpectedly, quotes Herbert Spencer with approval when he says that not ideas but feelings, to which ideas serve only as a guide, govern the world.

"Logically," Pareto wrote, "one ought first to believe in a given religion and then in the efficacy of its rites, the efficacy logically being the consequence of the belief. Logically, it is absurd to offer a prayer unless there is someone to hearken to it. But non-logical conduct is derived by a precisely reverse process. There is first an instinctive belief in the efficacy of a rite, then an 'explanation' of the belief is desired, then it is found in religion" (1935, p. 569).

In fact there are certain elementary types of behavior, found in all societies, in similar situations, and directed towards similar objects. These, the residues, are relatively constant since they spring from strong sentiments. The exact manner in which the sentiments are expressed and the ideologies that accompany their expression are variable. Men in each society express them in the particular idiom of their culture. Logical interpretations especially "assume the forms that are the most generally prevalent in the ages in which they are evolved. These are comparable to the styles of costume worn by people in the periods corresponding" (1935, p. 143). If we want to understand human beings, therefore, we must always get behind their ideas and study their behavior; and once we have understood that sentiments control behavior it is not difficult for us to understand the actions of men in remote times, because residues change little through centuries, even millenia. How could we still enjoy the poems of Homer and the elegies, tragedies, and comedies of the Greeks and Latins if we did not find them expressing sentiments that, in great part at least, we share? Pareto's conclusion may be summarized in the dictum "Human nature does not change," or, in his own words, "Derivations vary, the residue endures" (1935, p. 660).

I will now note some comments on, and criticisms of, Pareto's theories about residues and derivations. In harmony with the diffuse and disjointed structure of the book I will not attempt general criticism but will isolate a number of points for remark. I select particularly those problems that are relevant to a study of primitive mentality.

Pareto like Tylor, Frazer, and Lévy-Bruhl, employed a faulty comparative method. He took beliefs from here, there, and everywhere, and fitted them into his theoretical mosaic. What I have said elsewhere (Evans-Pritchard, *B.F.A.*, 1933 and 1934) in criticism of this way of writing applies also to Pareto's treatise.

He had an advantage over contemporary anthropologists in that he did not have to rely on what travelers and missionaries said about savage superstitions. By restricting his field to classical and postclassical times in European countries he was able to use what the natives themselves said about their beliefs. His main texts were Greek, Roman, and medieval books. He had a further advantage in that he was in a sense a fieldworker. It is true that he took all his data from books and newspapers and also that he made a study of ideologies rather than behavior. But his life was not spent in the study, and the walls of a college were not the limits of his experience. In his early life he had been a practical man of affairs and had learnt by observation that there are wide differences between what men say are their aims and what they really want to do. Nevertheless, he could, as a rule, only indirectly apply his observations of human behavior to interpret his data. Hesiod, Plato, Aristotle and Suetonius cannot be cross-examined and we cannot do fieldwork among the ancient Greeks and Romans.

I criticize Frazer (see chapter 13) for comparing the scientist in modern Europe with the magician and priest in savage and barbarous societies, and Lévy-Bruhl (see chapter 12) for comparing the modes of thought of an educated European in the twentieth century with the beliefs of primitive peoples. Pareto does not make this mistake. He intends to study the part played by logical, and the part played by nonlogical, thought and behavior side by side, and in interaction, in the same culture. His intention was excellent. In fact, however, he does not adhere to this plan. He writes at great length about fallacious beliefs and irrational behavior but he tells us very little about commonsense beliefs and empirical behavior. Therefore just as Lévy-Bruhl leaves us with the impression of savages who are continuously engaged in ritual and under the dominance of mystical beliefs, so Pareto gives us a picture of Europeans at all periods of their history at the mercy of sentiments expressed in a vast variety of absurd notions and actions. If Pareto for civilized peoples, and Lévy-Bruhl for savages, had given us a detailed account of their real life during an ordinary day we would be able to judge whether their nonlogical behavior is as qualitatively and quantitatively important as the writers' selective methods would lead us to suppose. Actually, I would contend, nonlogical conduct plays a relatively minor part in the behavior of either primitive or civilized men and is relatively of minor importance.

Pareto's work is an amusing commentary on Lévy-Bruhl's books. Lévy-Bruhl has written several volumes to prove that savages are pre-logical in contrast to Europeans who are logical. Pareto has written several volumes to prove that Europeans are nonlogical. It would therefore seem that no one is mainly controlled by reason anywhere or at any epoch. The situation is yet more amusing when we remember that Lévy-Bruhl excused himself from describing the characteristics of civilized mentality on the grounds that ancient and modern savants have adequately defined them, and Pareto bases his contention that civilized thought is primarily nonlogical on the writings of these same savants (Myres, *Folklore*, 1925, vol. 36).

Indeed one of the reasons why I have chosen to analyze Pareto's treatise is to bring out the fact that a study of unscientific thought and ritual behavior cannot be restricted to primitive societies but must be extended to civilized societies also. He allows to common-sense notions and empirical behavior about as much place in Greek, Roman, and modern European communities as Lévy-Bruhl allows them in central African, Chinese, and North American Indian communities. He admits that perhaps people are a little more reasonable than they used to be, but so little more that it is scarcely observable.

The relation of the logico-experimental field to the nonlogico-experimental field is fairly constant throughout history. Also, by his analysis of human behavior and his classification of it into residual categories Pareto establishes sociological uniformities that may serve as units of comparison. If his analysis is correct, it would seem disadvantageous to maintain studies of primitive societies and of civilized societies as separate disciplines as is the present scientific policy.

Another reason why I devote so much space to a consideration of Pareto's writings is because he emphasizes the need for a clear distinction between logico-experimental thought and behavior and other forms of thought and behavior and in doing so raises questions of terminology which, had they been earlier considered, would have prevented much confusion in social anthropology. Pareto's division of thought into two categories, the logico-experimental and the nonlogico-experimental is excellent and is necessary if we are going to investigate the part played by logico-experimental thought in society.

But it must be remembered, firstly, that our classification is never absolute since it is always relative to present-day knowledge, and, secondly, that it tells us nothing about the psychological or sociological qualities of the facts under investigation. It tells us only whether a proposition is valid, whether an inference from it is sound, and whether behavior based upon it is adapted to the end towards which it is directed. It is possible that from the logico-experimental view-point two propositions, *A* and *B,* may be placed in opposite categories, whereas from the psychological or sociological view-points they may be placed in the same category. Pareto understands that facts must be classified according to the point of view of the observer and that the classification of one observer will therefore be different from the classification of another observer. Thus he points out that the logico-experimental and the nonlogico-experimental actions of Greek sailors are psychologically the same.

But Pareto's terminology is not acceptable because his nonlogico-experimental category does not really tell us about the validity of inferences from propositions but only about the validity of the propositions themselves. Lévy-Bruhl saw that primitive thought is coherent and that savages make valid inferences from propositions even though the propositions are not in accord with experience but are dictated by culture and are contained in beliefs that are demonstrably false from a logico-experimental standpoint. It is unfortunate, therefore, that he chose to speak of primitive notions as pre-logical because we then have to talk about pre-logical logic, which is very inconvenient. Pareto, more clearly than Lévy-Bruhl, has stated that human thought and actions are in logical accord with propositions but when the propositions are invalid he calls them nonlogical. This creates an even worse terminological muddle for we have then to speak of nonlogical logic.

Lévy-Bruhl and Pareto both wanted to make the same point and both used the same cumbrous terminology. In science the validity of premises and the logical coordination of propositions are everything and the scientist aims always and above all to test his thought by observation and experiment and to avoid contradiction between his propositions. Outside the field of science a man does not trouble himself whether thought is based on observation and experiment and is not seriously inconvenienced by contradictions between his propositions. He aims only to ensure that his notions and conduct shall be in accord with sentiments, and if he can achieve that end their scientific value, and to some extent their logical value, are of little importance. A savage sees an ill-omened bird and abandons his journey to avoid misfortune. His conduct is in accord with a socially determined proposition. He does not consider whether it is experimentally sound because for him the experimental proof is contained in the proposition. A train is wrecked. Some people at once say that communists have wrecked it. That communists could not have been responsible and that it would have been entirely against their interests to have wrecked the train, are irrelevant to such people. They hate communists. A train has been wrecked. Therefore the communists are responsible.

Sentiments are superior to observation and experiment and dictate to them everywhere save in the laboratories of science. What have logico-experimental methods to do with the feelings of a lover, a patriot, a father, a devout Christian, and a communist? A lover is notoriously blind to what is evident to everyone else. What is sense to a communist is nonsense to other people. For in these realms our judgments are made to accord with sentiments and not with observations.

Feelings cannot be logical or otherwise and sentiments are outside the domain of science. But when they are expressed in words the propositions can be classed from the point of view of formal logic into logical and illogical statements, and from the point of view of science into valid and invalid statements.

Logical reasoning may be unscientific since it is based on invalid premises. It is therefore desirable to distinguish between science and logic. Science is understood in the sense given to the word by most scientific writers on the subject. Scientific notions are those which accord with objective reality both with regard to the validity of their premises and to the inferences drawn from their propositions. Unscientific notions are those which are invalid either in their premises or in the inferences drawn from them. Logical notions are those in which, according to the rules of thought, inferences would be true were the premises true, the truth of the premises being irrelevant. Illogical notions are those in which inferences would not be true even were the premises true, the truth of the premises again being irrelevant.

Much confusion that has arisen by use of such terms as nonlogical and pre-logical will be avoided by maintaining a distinction between logical and scientific. In making pots all grit must be removed from the clay or the pots will break. A pot has broken during firing. This is probably due to grit. Let us examine the pot and see if this is the cause. That is logical and scientific thought. Sickness is due to witchcraft. A man is sick. Let us consult the oracles to discover who is the witch responsible. That is logical and unscientific thought.

Pareto makes his writing unnecessarily difficult to follow by speaking of actions as well as speech as logical and nonlogical. What he means is that actions can be based on scientifically valid propositions or scientifically invalid propositions. If a man shoots another through the heart, it stops beating and dies. Acting on this proposition A shoots B through the heart. This is what Pareto calls a logical action. If a man makes magic against another he dies. Acting on this proposition, A makes lethal magic against B. This is what Pareto calls a nonlogical action. It will be more convenient to call the one an experimental, and the other a nonexperimental, action since the one is, from the viewpoint of an observer, well adapted to achieve the end aimed at whereas the other is ill-adapted.

Problems of terminology become more difficult when we leave the technological plane and begin to discuss behavior on the moral plane. In this review, however, we may use Pareto's device of contrasting experience with sentiment, science with morals, for I attempt only to expound Pareto's scheme and not to propound a scheme of my own. Like Lévy-Bruhl, he defined scientific thought and moral (mystical, nonlogico-experimental) thought in the rough and showed that there is a real sociological task to perform in unraveling and in tracing the development of their interrelations. Like Lévy-Bruhl, he left detailed analysis to others.

Pareto's reference to sentiment was dangerous. Too often we see him falling into the pit prepared for those who seek to explain behavior in psychological terms by attributing it to sentiments, needs, dispositions, and so forth. They observe a range of behavior with a common objective and say that there is a sentiment or instinct that produces the behavior. They then explain the behavior by reference to the sentiment or instinct they have hypothesized from the behavior. Men act in a certain way towards their country's flag. It is assumed from this that there is a sentiment of patriotism and the behavior is then explained by saying that it springs from a sentiment of patriotism.

Nevertheless in fairness to Pareto it must be admitted that he perceived a basic, perhaps the basic, problem in sociology, and realized that only inductive methods of research will solve it. If different societies are to be compared, it is essential to strip behavior of its variable characters and to reveal its uniformities, i.e., to reduce observed behavior to abstractions which will serve as units of comparison. And who would deny that in all societies there is a range of simple and uniform modes of behavior, call them sentiments or residues, or participations, or merely X, for else how could we, as Pareto asks, so easily understand the speech and behavior of savages and men of earlier times?

There is a great similarity between Lévy-Bruhl's collective representations and Pareto's derivations, and between Lévy-Bruhl's mystical participations and Pareto's residues. The main theoretical difference betwen them is that Lévy-Bruhl regarded the facts as socially determined and thus accounted for acceptance of belief by generality, transmission, and compulsion, whereas Pareto regarded them as psychologically determined and explained them by sentiments and other somewhat mysterious psychological drives. In any society we find a large number of collective representations (derivations) organized into a system. When we analyze them by comparison and remove what is not common to all societies, we find a residue of simple modes of behavior powerfully charged with emotions, e.g., those classified by Pareto as group-persistences: relations of family and kin, relations with places, relations between the living and the dead, and so forth. These relations are what Lévy-Bruhl calls mystical participations. Any occurrence is, as Lévy-Bruhl puts it, at once interpreted in terms of the collective representations, and as Pareto puts it, in terms of derivations. The thought of men is organized not so much by the logic of science as by the logic of collective representations or the logic of sentiments, and an action or statement must accord with the representations, or sentiments, rather than with experience. It is only in the technological field that science has gained ground from sentiment in modern societies. Hence our difficulty in understanding much of primitive magic while we readily appreciate most of their other notions since they accord with sentiments we ourselves possess, for "Derivations vary, the residue endures."

Another cardinal problem perceived by Pareto is the relation between individual psychology and culture. Indeed the treatment of this problem is perhaps the best part of his thesis. There are in all individuals certain psychological traits and in any society there are psychological types and these traits and types will manifest themselves in culture regardless of its particular forms. The sex instinct manifests itself in every society and if it is prohibited in one mode of expression it will manifest itself in another. A dominant and ambitious man will seek power by all means and at all costs whether he is born in China or Peru; whether he enters the army, the church, the law, or academic life; whether for the moment he expresses his ambitions in the idiom of socialism or conservatism. For individuals are not entirely conditioned by culture but only limited by it and always seek to exploit it in their own interests. Thus a moral ideology may be acknowledged by all men but often they twist it till it serves their interests even though it is contradicted in the process, and one man quotes as authority for his actions what another quotes as authority for condemning them. In any situation a man will select from social doctrine what is of advantage to him and will exclude the rest, or will interpret a doctrine in the manner which suits his interests best. Christian teachings are supposed to determine human behavior but what often happens in fact is that men control Christian dogma, selecting from its doctrines what pays them and excluding the rest or interpreting what conflicts with their actions so that it seems to support them.

Finally, I will draw attention to Pareto's methodology, which was sound even if his employment of it was often unsatisfactory. It may be summed up in two statements: (1) in a real situation we have to consider certain factors and neglect others if we are going to obtain scientific results. Science deals always with abstractions in this manner and allows for distortion until it can be corrected by further study of the neglected factors. Thus Pareto decided to pay no attention to environmental, historical, racial, and other factors that condition social life, but to study only the interrelations of psychological facts with one another and, to some extent, with economic changes and biological variations; (2) he tried to make a functional study of these facts by noting uniformities and interdependencies between them. He expressed contempt for people who seek to discover the origin of things both in terms of development and in terms of diffusion. Indeed one of the chief weaknesses of his book is that his exclusive interest in functional relationships of a psychological kind led him to neglect a study of cultural development and cultural variations which alone enable functional relationships to be established.

There are many points in Pareto's rambling account on which criticism might be leveled against him. Pareto's theories are pretentious. Behind a great show of impartiality and scientific method we discover plagiarist, populizer, polemicist, and metaphysician. His writings are always witty and his criticisms of philosophers are often sound, though seldom original. It cannot be said that he has contributed much to sociology. Indeed he seems to have been little acquainted with its aims and methods. However, let it be said in Pareto's favor that his treatise is so bad that it exposes, and thereby enables us to see more clearly, fallacies hidden with greater skill by other metaphysicians masquerading as scientists. Nonetheless he is a useful subject for treatment in a history of theories of primitive mentality.

Chapter 12
Lévy-Bruhl (1857-1939)

Lucien Lévy-Bruhl was a scholar whose influence has been great. His books were widely read—by philosophers, psychologists, anthropologists and historians. He was a philosopher who had already made a reputation with outstanding books on Jacobi and Comte before he turned his attention, as had his contemporary Durkheim, also a philosopher, to the study of primitive man. It was as a philosopher that he entered the field of social anthropology, the central questions in which he was interested being those of formal logic. The publication of his *La Morale et la science des moeurs* in 1903, marked the change in his interests toward the study of primitive mentality, which was to be his sole occupation till his death in 1939.

In 1912 appeared his *Les Fonctions mentales dans les sociétés inférieures* (translation, *How Natives Think*, 1926) and in 1922 *La Mentalité primitive* (translation, *Primitive Mentality*, 1923). These are his best known books and they were much criticized, some of the criticism arising from a misunderstanding of what he was saying. Other volumes followed which amplified his earlier views, and also refined them as he made use of information about ideas of primitive peoples not available to him when he wrote his earlier books. One of these is *L'Âme primitive*, 1927 (translated as *The Soul of the Primitive*, 1928). It was followed by *Le Surnaturel et le nature dans la mentalité primitive*, 1931 (translated as *Primitives and the Supernatural*, 1936), *La Mythologie primitive*, 1935, and *Expérience mystique et des symbols chez les primitifs*, 1938. A summary of his views about primitive thought is to be found in his Herbert Spencer Lecture delivered in Oxford: *La Mentalité primitive*, 1931. His last reflections on primitive mentality were published from his notebooks in 1949 after his death: *Les Carnets de Lucien Lévy-Bruhl*, 1949.

In France and Germany Lévy-Bruhl's views have been extensively examined and criticized, and it is difficult to understand why they have met with such great neglect and derision among English anthropologists. Their reception is perhaps partly due to the key expressions used by Lévy-Bruhl in his writings, such as *"prélogique," "représentations collectives," "mystique," "participations,"* and so forth. Doubtless it is also due in part to the uncritical manner in which Lévy-Bruhl handled his material which was often of a poor quality in any case. But responsibility must be shared by his critics who made little effort to grasp the ideas which lay behind the cumbrous terminology in which they were frequently expressed and who were far too easily content to pick holes in the detail of his arguments without mastering his main thesis. Too often they merely repeated his views under the impression that they were refuting them.

Though his fundamental assumptions are sociological, he always refused to identify himself with the Durkheimian group; so it is only in a formal sense that he can be called, as Webb calls him (1938, pp. 13–41), one of Durkheim's collaborators. He remained more of the philosopher pure and simple; hence his interest in primitive systems of thought rather than in primitive institutions. He held that one might as legitimately begin a study of social life by analysis of ways of thought as of ways of behavior. Perhaps one should say that he studied them primarily as a logician, for the question of logic is a crucial one in his books, as indeed it should be in a study of systems of thought.

His first two books about primitive peoples, *How Natives Think* and *Primitive Mentality,* set forth his general theory of primitive mentality and his later works were an amplification of it, though he seems in them also to have slowly modified his original views in the light of modern field reports, for he was a modest and humble man. At the end of his life he may have reversed his position, or at any rate considered doing so, if one may judge from his posthumous *Carnets.* Nevertheless, it was his views as set forth in the earlier books which constituted his distinctive theoretical contribution to anthropology, and it is therefore these I must discuss.

Like Durkheim, he condemns the English School for trying to explain social facts by processes of individual thought—their own—which are the product of different conditions from those which have molded the minds they seek to understand. They think out how they would have reached the beliefs and practices of primitive peoples, and then assume that these peoples must have reached them by those steps. In any case, it is useless to try to interpret primitive minds in terms of individual psychology. The mentality of the individual is derived from the collective representations of his society, which are obligatory for him; and these representations are functions of institutions. Consequently, certain types of representations, and therefore certain ways of thinking, belong to certain types of social structure. In other words, as social structures vary, so will the representations, and consequently the individual's thinking. Every type of society has therefore its distinctive mentality, for each has its distinctive customs and institutions, which are fundamentally only a certain aspect of collective representations; they are, so to speak, the representations considered objectively. Lévy-Bruhl did not mean by this that the representations of a people are any less real than their institutions.

Now, one can classify human societies into a number of different types, but, says Lévy-Bruhl, considered in the broadest possible way, there are two major types, the primitive and the civilized, and there are two and opposed types of thought corresponding to them, so we may speak of primitive mentality and civilized mentality, for they are different not merely in degree, but in quality. It will be observed that he wishes to emphasize the differences between civilized and primitive peoples; this is perhaps the most important single observation to be made about his theoretical standpoint, and is what gives it much of its originality. For various reasons most writers about primitive peoples had tended to lay stress on the similarities, or what they supposed to be similarities, between ourselves and them; and Lévy-Bruhl thought it might be as well, for a change, to draw attention to the differences. The criticism often brought against him, that he did not perceive how very like primitives we are in many respects, loses much of its force, once we recognize his intention: he wanted to stress the differences, and in order to bring them out more clearly, he spotlighted them and left the similarities in shadow. He knew that he was making a distortion—what some people like to call an ideal, construct—but he never pretended to be doing anything else, and his procedure is methodologically justifiable.

We in Europe, says Lévy-Bruhl, have behind us many centuries of rigorous intellectual speculation and analysis. Consequently, we are logically orientated, in the sense that we normally seek the causes of phenomena in natural processes; and even when we face a phenomenon which we cannot account for scientifically, we take it for granted that this is only because our knowledge is insufficient. Primitive thought has an altogether different character. It is orientated towards the supernatural.

> The attitude of the mind of the primitive is very different. The nature of the milieu in which he lives presents itself to him in quite a different way. Objects and beings are all involved in a network of mystical participations and exclusions. It is these which constitute its texture and order. It is then these which immediately impose themselves on his attention and which alone retain it. If a phenomenon interests him, if he is not content to perceive it, so to speak, passively and without reaction, he will think at once, as by a sort of mental reflex, of an occult and invisible power of which the phenomenon is a manifestation (Evans-Pritchard, B.F.A. 1934), (1928, pp. 17–8).

> And if it be asked why primitive peoples do not inquire, as we do, into objective causal connections, the answer is that they are prevented from doing so by their collective representations, which are pre-logical and mystical.

These assertions were rejected out of hand by British anthropologists, whose empirical tradition made them distrust anything in the nature of philosophical speculation. Lévy-Bruhl was a mere armchair theorist who, like the rest of his French colleagues, had never seen a primitive man, far less talked to one. I think I may claim to be one of the few anthropologists here or in America who spoke up for him, not because I agreed with him, but because I felt that a scholar should be criticized for what he has said, and not for what he is supposed to have said. My defense had therefore to be exegetical an attempt to explain what Lévy-Bruhl meant by his key expressions and concepts which evoked so much hostility: pre-logical mentality, collective representations, mystical, and participations. This terminology, at any rate for a British reader, makes his thought obscure, so that one is often in doubt what he wished to say.

Lévy-Bruhl calls "pre-logical" those modes of thought (magico-religious thought, as he did not distinguish between magic and religion) which appear so true to primitive man and so absurd to the European. He means by this word something quite different from what his critics said he meant by it. He does not mean that primitives are incapable of thinking coherently, but merely that most of their beliefs are incompatible with a critical and scientific view of the universe. They also contain evident contradicitons. He is not saying that primitives are unintelligent, but that their beliefs are unintelligible to us. This does not mean that we cannot follow their reasoning. We can, for they reason quite logically; but they start from different premises, and premises which are to us absurd. They are reasonable, but they reason in categories different from ours. They are logical, but the principles of their logic are not ours, not those of Aristotelian logic. Lévy-Bruhl does not hold that "logical principles are foreign to the minds of primitives; a conception of which the absurdity is evident the moment it is formulated. Pre-logical does not mean alogical or anti-logical. Pre-logical, applied to primitive mentality, means simply that it does not go out of its way, as we do, to avoid contradictions. It does not have always present the same logical requirements. What to our eyes is impossible or absurd it often accepts without seeing any difficulty involved" (1931, p. 21). Here Lévy-Bruhl was being too subtle, for he means by "pre-logical" little more than unscientific or uncritical, that primitive man is rational but unscientific or uncritical.

When he says that "primitive mentality" or the "primitive mind" is pre-logical, hopelessly uncritical, he is not speaking of an individual's ability, or inability, to reason, but of the categories in which he reasons. He is speaking, not of a biological or psychological difference between primitives and ourselves, but of a social one. It follows, therefore, that he is also not speaking of a type of mind such as some psychologists and others have delineated: intuitive, logical, romantic, classical, and so on. What he is speaking about are axioms, values, and sentiments—more or less what are sometimes called patterns of thought; and he says that among primitive peoples these tend to be mystical and therefore beyond verification, impervious to experience, and indifferent to contradiction. Taking the same stand as Durkheim on this issue, he declares that they are social, not psychological, facts, and like all such are general, traditional, and obligatory. They are present before the individual who acquires them is born and they will be present after he is dead. Even the affective states which accompany the ideas are socially determined. In this sense, therefore, a people's mentality is something objective. If it were simply an individual phenomenon, it would be a subjective one; its generality makes it an objective one.

These modes or patterns of thought which in their totality make up the mind or mentality of a people are what Lévy-Bruhl calls collective representations, an expression in common use among

French sociologists of the time, and a translation, I think, of the German *Vorstellung*. It suggests something very abstruse, whereas he means by it little more than what we call an idea, or a notion, or a belief; and when he says that a representation is collective, he means no more than that it is common to all, or most, members of a society. Every society has its collective representations. Ours tend always to be critical and scientific, those of primitive peoples to be mystical. Lévy-Bruhl would, I think, have agreed that for most people both alike are fiduciary.

If Lévy-Bruhl had wished to arouse an Englishman's worst suspicions, he could not have done better than he did by the use of the word "mystical." Yet he makes it clear that he means by this term only what English writers mean when they speak of belief in the supernatural—of magic and religion and so forth. He says, "I employ this term, for lack of a better, not with allusion to the religious mysticism of our own societies, which is something altogether different, but in the strictly defined sense where "mystical" is used for the belief in forces, in influences, and in actions imperceptible to the senses, though nonetheless real" (1912, p. 30). Now, the collective representations of primitive peoples are pre-eminently concerned with these imperceptible forces. Consequently, as soon as primitive man's sensations become conscious perceptions, they are colored by the mystical ideas they evoke. They are immediately conceptualized in a mystical category of thought. The concept dominates the sensation, and imposes its image on it. One might say that primitive man sees an object as we see it, but he perceives it differently, for as soon as he gives conscious attention to it, the mystical idea of the object comes between him and the object, and transforms its purely objective properties. We also perceive in the object the collective representation of our culture, but since that accords with its objective features, we perceive it objectively. The primitive man's collective representation of it is mystical, and consequently he perceives it mystically and in a manner entirely foreign, and indeed absurd, to us. The mystical perception is immediate. Primitive man does not, for example, perceive a shadow and apply to it the doctrine of his society, according to which it is one of his souls. When he is conscious of his shadow he is aware of his soul. We can best understand Lévy-Bruhl's view if we say that, in his way of looking at the matter, beliefs only arise late in the development of human thought, when perception and representation have already fallen apart. We can then say that a person perceives his shadow and believes it to be his soul. The question of belief does not arise among primitive peoples. The belief is contained in the shadow. The shadow is the belief. In the same way, a primitive man does not perceive a leopard and believe that it is his totem-brother. What he perceives *is* his totem-brother. The physical qualities of a leopard are fused in the mystical representation of totem, and are subordinated to it. "The reality," says Lévy-Bruhl, "in which primitives move is itself mystical. Not a being, not an object, not a natural phenomenon in their collective representations is what it appears to us. Almost all that we see in it escapes them, or they are indifferent to it. On the other hand, they see in it many things which we do not even suspect" (1912, pp. 30–1).

He goes even further than this. He says not merely that the perceptions of primitives embody mystical representations, but that it is the mystical representations which evoke the perceptions. In the stream of sensory impressions, only a few become conscious ones. Men only notice or pay attention to a little of what they see and hear. What they pay attention to is selected on account of its greater affectivity. In other words, a man's interests are the selective agents, and these are to a great extent socially determined. Primitives pay attention to phenomena on account of the mystical properties their collective representations have endowed them with. The collective representations thus both control perception and are fused with it. Primitive peoples pay great attention to their shadows precisely because, in their representations, their shadows are their souls. We do not do so, because a shadow is nothing positive for us, just a negation of light; and their and our representations in this matter are mutually exclusive. So, it is not so much that perception of a shadow causes the belief (that what is perceived is the soul) to enter into consciousness, but rather the belief that causes primitive man to pay attention to his shadow. Collective representations, by the value they give to phenomena, direct attention to them, and since representations differ widely between rude and civilized peoples, what they notice in the world around them will be different, or at least the reasons for their paying attention to phenomena will be different.

The representations of primitive peoples have a quality of their own, namely the quality of being mystical, which is quite foreign to our representations, and therefore we may speak of primitive mentality as something *sui generis*. The logical principle of these mystical representations is what Lévy-Bruhl calls the law of mystical participation. The collective representations of primitive peoples consist of a network of participations which, since the representations are mystical, are mystical also. In primitive thought, things are connected so that what affects one is believed to affect others, not objectively but as mystical action (though primitive man himself does not distinguish between objective and mystical action). Primitive peoples, indeed, are often more concerned about what we would call the supra-sensible or, to use Lévy-Bruhl's term, mystical, relations between things than about what we would call the objective relations between them. To take the example I have used before, some primitive peoples participate in their shadows, so what affects their shadows affects them. Hence it would be fatal for a man to cross an open space at midday, because he would lose his shadow. Other primitive peoples participate in their names, and they will therefore not reveal them, for were an enemy to learn a name, he would have the owner of it also in his power. Among other peoples, a man participates in his child, so when the child is sick, he, and not the child, drinks the medicine. These participations form the structure of categories in which primitive man moves and out of which his social personality is built. There are mystical participations between a man and the land on which he dwells, between a man and his chief, a man and his kin, a man and his totem, and so on, covering every side of his life.

It may here be noted that, while Lévy-Bruhl's participations resemble the associations of ideas of Tylor and Frazer, the conclusions he draws from them are very different from theirs. For Tylor and Frazer primitive man believes in magic because he reasons incorrectly from his observations. For Lévy-Bruhl he reasons incorrectly because his reasoning is determined by the mystical representations of his society. The first is an explanation in terms of individual psychology, the second a sociological explanation. Lévy-Bruhl is certainly correct in so far as any given individual is concerned, for the individual learns the patterns of thought in which, and by which, mystical connections are established. He does not deduce them from his own observations.

Lévy-Bruhl's discussion of the law of mystical participation is perhaps the most valuable, as well as being a highly original, part of his thesis. He was one of the first, if not the first, to emphasize that primitive ideas, which seem so strange to us, and indeed sometimes idiotic, when considered as isolated facts, are meaningful when seen as parts of patterns of ideas and behavior, each part having an intelligible relationship to the others. He recognized that values form systems as coherent as the logical constructions of the intellect, that there is a logic of sentiments as well as of reason, though based on a different principle. His analysis is not like the just-so stories we have earlier considered, for he does not try to explain primitive magic and religion by a theory purporting to show how they might have come about. He takes them as given, and seeks only to show their structure and the way in which they are evidence of a distinctive mentality common to all societies of a certain type.

In order to emphasize the distinctiveness of this mentality, he made out that primitive thought in general differs altogether, in quality and not just in degree, from our own (even though there may be people in our own society who think and feel like primitives, and in every person there may be a substratum of primitive mentality); and this, his main theme, cannot be sustained, and at the end of his life he himself appears to have abandoned it. If it were true, we would scarcely be able to communicate with primitives, even to learn their languages. The single fact that we can do so shows that Lévy-Bruhl was making too strong a contrast between the primitive and the civilized. His error was partly due to the poverty of the material at his disposal when he first formulated his theory, and to the double selection of the curious and the sensational at the expense of the mundane and matter-of-fact. Then, when Lévy-Bruhl contrasts us with primitives, who are we, and who are the primitives? He does not distinguish between the different sorts of us, the different social and occupational strata of our society, more pronounced fifty years ago than today; nor between us at different periods of our history. In his sense of the word, did the philosophers of the Sorbonne and the Breton peasantry, or the fishermen of Normandy, have the same mentality? And since the modern European developed from barbarism, from a type of society characterized by primitive mentality, how and when did our ancestors pass from the one to the other? Such a development could not have taken place at all unless our primitive forbears, side by side with their mystical notions, had also a body of empirical knowledge to guide them; and Lévy-Bruhl has to accept that savages sometimes wake from their dreams, that it is necessary in the performance of their technical activities that "the representations coincide in some essential points with objective reality, and that the practices are, at a certain moment, effectively adapted to the ends pursued" (1912, pp. 354–5). But he does so only as a minor concession, and without prejudice to his position. Yet it is self-evident that, far from being such children of fancy as he makes them out to be, they have less chance to be than we, for they live closer to the harsh realities of nature, which permit survival only to those who are guided in their pursuits by observation, experiment and reason.

One might further inquire into which class Plato falls, or the symbolic thought of Philo and Plotinus; and all the more so in that, among his examples of primitive mentality, we find such peoples as the Chinese included with Polynesians, Melanesians, Negroes, American Indians and Australian Blackfellows. It must also be remarked once again that, as in so many anthropological theories, negative instances are ignored. For example, many primitive peoples do not at all bother about their shadows or their names, yet typologically, on his own classification, they belong to the same class of societies as those who do.

There is no reputable anthropologist who today accepts this theory of two distinct types of mentality. All observers who have made lengthy first-hand studies of primitive peoples are agreed that they are for the most part interested in practical affairs, which they conduct in an empirical manner, either without the least reference to supra-sensible forces, influences, and actions, or in a way in which these have a subordinate and auxiliary role. It may be noted also that what Lévy-Bruhl defines as the most fundamental feature of primitive, or pre-logical, mentality, its failure to perceive, or its lack of concern at, evident contradictions, is very largely illusory. He is perhaps not entirely to blame for not seeing it to be such, for the results of intensive modern field research had not been published when he wrote his best-known works. He could not then, I think, have realized that the contradictions only appear to be glaring when the European observer sets down side by side beliefs which in reality are found in different situations and at different levels of experience. Nor perhaps could he have appreciated as well as we can today that mystical representations are not necessarily aroused by objects outside their use in ritual situations, that they are not, as it were, inevitably evoked by the objects. For example, some peoples put stones in the forks of trees to delay the setting of the sun; but the stone so used is casually picked up, and has only a mystical significance in, and for the purpose and duration of, the rite. The sight of this or any other stone in any other situation does not evoke the idea of the setting sun. The association, as I point out in discussing Frazer (see chapter 13), is brought about by the rite, and need not in other situations arise. It may be observed also that objects such as fetishes and idols are humanly constructed, and in their material selves have no significance; they only acquire that when they are endowed with supernatural power through a rite which, also by human agency, infuses in them that power, object and its virtue thus being separated in the mind. Then again, in childhood, mystical notions cannot be evoked by objects which for adults have mystical significance, for the child does not yet know them; and he may not even notice the objects—a child, at least, very often with us, one day discovers his shadow. Moreover, objects which have mystical value for some people have none at all for others—a totem sacred to one clan is eaten by members of other clans in the same community. Such considerations suggest that a more subtle interpretation is required. Again, I believe that at the time he wrote he could not have made, as we can make today, due allowance for the vast complexity and rich symbolism of primitive languages and of the thought they express. What appear to be hopeless contradictions when translated into English may not appear so in the native language. When, for instance, a native statement is translated that a man of such-and-such a clan is a leopard, it appears to us to be absurd, but the word he uses which we translate by "is" may not have the same meaning for him that the word "is" has for us. In any case, there is no inherent contradiction in saying that a man is a leopard. The leopard quality is something added in thought to the human attributes, and does not detract from them. Things may be thought of in different ways in different contexts. In one sense, it is one thing, and in another sense it is something more.

Lévy-Bruhl is also wrong in supposing that there is necessarily a contradiction between an objective causal explanation and a mystical one. It is not so. The two kinds of explanation can be, as indeed they are, held together, the one supplementing the other; and they are not therefore exclusive. For example, the dogma that death is due to witchcraft does not exclude the observation that the man was killed by a buffalo. For Lévy-Bruhl there is here a contradiction, to which natives are indifferent. But no contradiction is involved. On the contrary, the natives are making a very acute analysis of the situation. They are perfectly well aware that a buffalo killed the man, but they hold that he would not have been killed by it if he had not been bewitched. Why otherwise should he have been killed by it, why he and not someone else, why by that buffalo and not by another, why at that time and place and not at another? They are asking why, as we would put it, two independent chains of events crossed each other, bringing a certain man and a certain buffalo into a single point of time and space. You will agree that there is no contradiction here, but that on the contrary the witchcraft explanation supplements that of natural causation, accounting for what we would call the element of chance. The witchcraft cause of the accident is emphasized because, of the two causes, only the mystical one permits intervention, vengeance on a witch. The same mixture of empirical knowledge and mystical notions may be found in primitive ideas about procreation, drugs, and other matters. The objective properties of things and natural causation of events may be known, but are not socially emphasized or are denied because they conflict with some social dogma, mystical belief being in these circumstances more appropriate than empirical knowledge. Indeed, we may again assert that if this were not so it would be difficult to see how scientific thought could ever have emerged. Moreover, a social representation is not acceptable if it conflicts with individual experience, unless the conflict can be accounted for in terms of the representation itself or of some other representation, the explanation then being, however, acknowledgment of the conflict. A representation which asserts that fire does not burn the hand thrust into it would not long survive. A representation which asserts that it will not burn you if you have sufficient faith may survive. Indeed, Lévy-Bruhl, as we have seen, admits that mystical thought is conditioned by experience, that in activities such as war, hunting, fishing, treatment of ailments, and divination, means must be rationally adapted to ends.

It is now, I think, unanimously agreed among anthropologists that Lévy-Bruhl made primitive peoples far more superstitious, to use a commoner word than pre-logical, than they really are; and he made the contrast more glaring between their mentality and ours by presenting us as more positivistic than most of us are. From my talks with him I would say that in this matter he felt himself in a quandary. For him, Christianity and Judaism were also superstitions, indicative of pre-logical and mystical mentality, and on his definitions necessarily so. But, I think in order not to cause offense, he made no allusion to them. So he excluded the mystical in our own culture as rigorously as he excluded the empirical in savage cultures. This failure to take into account the beliefs and rites of the vast majority of his fellow countrymen vitiates his argument. And he himself, as Bergson naughtily observed, in constantly accusing primitive man of not attributing any event to chance, accepted chance. He thereby placed himself, on his own showing, in the pre-logical class.

However, this does not mean that, in his sense of the word, primitive thought is not more "mystical" than ours. The contrast Lévy-Bruhl makes is an exaggeration, but, all the same, primitive magic and religion confront us with a real problem, and not one imagined by the French philosopher. Men with long experience of primitive peoples have felt confounded by it; and it is true that primitives often, and especially in misfortune, attribute events to supra-sensible forces where we, with our greater knowledge, account for them by natural causation, or seek to do so. But, even so, I think that Lévy-Bruhl could have posed the problem to better advantage. It is not so much a question of primitive *versus* civilized mentality as the relation of the two types of thought to each other in any society, whether primitive or civilized, a problem of levels of thought and experience. It was because Lévy-Bruhl was dominated, as were almost all writers of the period, by notions of evolution and inevitable progress that he did not appreciate this. Had he not been so positivistic in his own representations, he might have asked himself, not what are the differences between civilized and primitive modes of thought, but what are the functions of the two kinds of thought in any society, or in human society in general—the kinds associated with what are sometimes distinguished as the "expressive" and the "instrumental" (Beattie, 1964, chapter XII). The problem would then have appeared to him in a rather different light, as it appeared in various forms to Pareto (see chapter 11), Bergson, William James, Max Weber, and others.

Contrary to the judgment of most English anthropologists, I find Lévy-Bruhl's writings a great stimulus to formulation of new problems, and I consider his influence most fruitful, not only on anthropological theory but also in directing the attention of field-workers to a new set of problems. For when in disagreement with his opinions, we must acknowledge that they are not the usual facile explanations of social anthropologists which obstruct all thought by their futility and finality and turn out to be no more than a restatement in other terms of the problems to be solved.

Chapter 13
Frazer (1854–1941)

Sir James Frazer is, I suppose, the best-known name in anthropology, and we owe much to him and to Spencer and Tylor. The whole of *The Golden Bough*, a work of immense industry and erudition, is devoted to primitive superstitions, and it rightly ranks among the great achievements of English literature and scholarship. He writes: "If we analyse the principles of thought upon which magic is based, they will probably be found to resolve themselves into two: first that like produces like, or that an effect resembles its cause; and, second, that things which have once been in contact with each other continue to act on each other at a distance after the physical contact has been severed. The former principle may be called the Law of Similarity, the latter the Law of Contact or Contagion. From the first of these principles, namely the Law of Similarity, the magician infers that he can produce any effect he desires merely by imitating it: from the second he infers that whatever he does to a material object will affect equally the person with whom the object was once in contact, whether it formed part of his body or not. Charms based on the Law of Similarity may be called Homeopathic or Imitative Magic. Charms based on the Law of Contact or Contagion may be called Contagious Magic" (p. 52).

And again he says: "If my analysis of the magician's logic is correct its two great principles turn out to be merely two different misapplications of the association of ideas. Homeopathic Magic is founded on the association of ideas by similarity. Contagious Magic is founded on the association of ideas by contiguity. Homeopathic Magic makes the mistake of assuming that things which resemble each other are the same: contagious magic commits the mistake of assuming that things which have once been in contact with each other are always in contact" (pp. 53–4).

In other words we may say that to a European observer all acts of magic rest upon one or other, or both, of two simple modes of classifying phenomena, by the similarities which exist between them and by their contiguous position in relation to each other. This is a scientific, objective, mode of classification, but the ideas of objects which are similar or contiguous are linked in the savage mind by a notion that there is real connection between them. Hence it is thought they have a sympathetic relationship between them and can act on each other. So Frazer classes the two types of association under a single heading (p. 54):

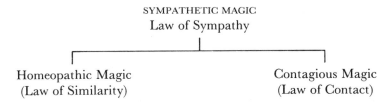

SYMPATHETIC MAGIC
Law of Sympathy

Homeopathic Magic
(Law of Similarity)

Contagious Magic
(Law of Contact)

Into this scheme of magic, Frazer has incorporated in the second edition of *The Golden Bough* the notion of taboo as negative magic and he considers that the basis of taboo is just those two laws of similarity and contact which are the invariable laws of magical thought.

The inclusion of taboos in Frazer's general theory of magic gave it a more rounded form and a fuller comprehension of the cluster of facts which are included in the performance of a magical rite. In his own words: "For it is to be observed that the system of sympathetic magic is not merely composed of positive precepts: it comprises a very large number of negative precepts, that is, prohibitions. It tells you not merely what to do, but also what to leave undone. The positive precepts are charms: the negative precepts are taboos. In fact the whole doctrine of taboo, or at all events a large part of it, would seem to be only a special application of sympathetic magic, with its two great laws of similarity and contact. Though these laws are certainly not formulated in so many words nor even conceived in the abstract by the savage, they are nevertheless implicitly believed by him to regulate the course of nature quite independently of human will. He thinks that when he acts in a certain way, certain consequences will inevitably follow by virtue of one or other of these laws; and if the consequences of a particular act appear to him likely to prove disagreeable or dangerous, he is naturally careful not to act in that way lest he should incur them. In other words, he abstains from doing that which, in accordance with his mistaken notions of cause and effect, he falsely believes would injure him; in short, he subjects himself to a taboo. Thus taboo is so far a negative application of practical magic. Positive magic or sorcery says "Do this in order that so and so may happen."; Negative magic or taboo says "Do not do this, lest so and so should happen." The aim of positive magic or sorcery is to produce a desired event; the aim of negative magic or taboo is to avoid an undesirable one. But both consequences, the desirable and the undesirable, are supposed to be brought about in accordance with the laws of similarity and contact" (pp. 111–2).

Thus with the inclusion of taboo in his analysis of magic, Frazer presents his conception of the theory and practice of magic in the following diagram:

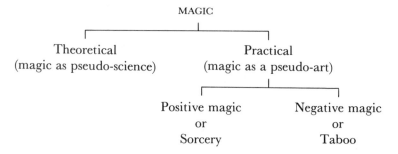

When Frazer asks himself why the beliefs and experiments of magic are not at once detected as fraud by the sensible savage, he answers by giving one of the several reasons enumerated by Tylor to account for such supineness, namely that the end aimed at in a magical rite is actually attained sooner or later by processes of nature. Hence the very failure by primitive man to detect the fallacies of magic is a tribute to his rational and inquiring mind which is able to observe that magic rites and such happenings as rain falling, wind blowing, sun rising, man dying, have a temporal sequence which may fairly be considered a causal sequence. Hence the primitive philosopher may point to the evidence of his senses as proving to any intelligent man that magic is a sensible belief. Moreover it is part of Frazer's argument that the more intelligent minds did at last perceive the futility of magic.

The analogy between the basic ideas of magic and those of science which we find merely sketched by Tylor is presented to us as a finished picture by Frazer. To him magic represents a *Weltanschauung* in every way comparable to the *Weltanschauung* of science. Both view nature as "a series of events occurring in an invariable order without the intervention of personal agency" (p. 51). In a well-known passage Frazer has stated his theory of the intellectual kinship of magic to science: "For the same principles which the magician applies in the practice of his art are implicitly believed by him to regulate the operations of inanimate nature; in other words, he tacitly assumes that the Laws of Similarity and Contact are of universal application and are not limited to human actions. In short, magic is a spurious system of natural law as well as a fallacious guide of conduct; it is a false science as well as an abortive art. Regarded as a system of natural law, that is, as a statement of the rules which determine the sequence of events throughout the world, it may be called Theoretical Magic; regarded as a set of precepts which human beings observe in order to compass their ends, it may be called Practical Magic. At the same time it is to be borne in mind that the primitive magician knows magic only on its practical side; he never analyses the mental processes on which his practice is based, never reflects on the abstract principle involved in his actions. With him, as with the vast majority of men, logic is implicit, not explicit; he reasons just as he digests his food in complete ignorance of the intellectual and physiological processes which are essential to the one operation and to the other. In short, to him magic is always an art, never a science; the very idea of science is lacking in his undeveloped mind. It is for the philosophic student to trace the train of thought which underlies the magician's practice; to draw out the few simple threads of which the tangled skein is composed; to disengage the abstract principles from their concrete applications; in short, to discern the spurious science behind the bastard art" (pp. 52-3).

And again: "Wherever sympathetic magic occurs in its pure unadulterated form, it assumes that in nature one event follows another necessarily and invariably without the intervention of any spiritual or personal agency. Thus its fundamental conception is identical with that of modern science; underlying the whole system is a faith, implicit but real and firm, in the order and uniformity of nature. The magician does not doubt that the same causes will always produce the same effects that the performance of the proper ceremony, accompanied by the appropriate spell, will inevitably be attended by the desired results, unless, indeed, his incantations should chance to be thwarted and foiled by the more potent charms of another sorcerer. He supplicates no higher power: he sues the favour of no fickle and wayward being: he abases himself before no awful deity" (p. 220). Magic assumes "a sequence of events determined by law" (p. 221). Science differs from magic not in its assumptions and approach to reality but in the validity of its concepts and the efficacy of its art.

Frazer's distinction between magic and science by the test of objective validity clearly will not hold as a means of differentiating magic from religion, between which Frazer saw "a fundamental distinction and even opposition of principle" (p. xx). Magic is to him something different in kind to religion and not merely the earliest phase in the development of its thought. He differentiates between them in much the same manner as Tylor. Tylor considered belief in spiritual beings to constitute religion and recognized that belief invariably leads to cult. Frazer stresses the cult rather more than Tylor; otherwise their theories are identical. Religion according to Frazer is "a propitiation or conciliation of powers superior to man which are believed to direct and control the course of nature and of human life. Thus defined, religion consists of two elements, a theoretical and a practical, namely, a belief in powers higher than man and an attempt to propitiate or please them" (p. 222).

Hence religion assumes that nature is under the control of spirits and that these spirits can alter its course as they please. Frazer contrasts this notion of a plastic and variable nature with the notion of nature subject to immutable laws as postulated by magic and science. "The distinction between the two conflicting views of the universe turns on their answer to the crucial question. Are the forces which govern the world conscious and personal, or unconscious and impersonal? Religion, as a conciliation of the superhuman powers, assumes the former of the alternative. For all conciliation implies that the being conciliated is a conscious or personal agent, that his conduct is in some measure uncertain, and that he can be prevailed upon to vary it in the desired direction by a judicious appeal to his interests, his appetites, or his emotions. Conciliation is never employed towards things which are regarded as inanimate, nor towards persons whose behaviour in the particular circumstances is known to be determined with absolute certainty.

Thus in so far as religion assumes the world to be directed by conscious agents who may be turned from their purpose by persuasion, it stands in fundamental antagonism to magic as well as to science, both of which take for granted that the course of nature is determined, not by the passions or caprice of personal beings, but by the operation of immutable laws acting mechanically. In magic, indeed, the assumption is only implicit, but in science it is explicit" (p. 223).

Frazer recognizes the problem of reconciling this definition with recorded knowledge of barbaric cultures in which the gods are influenced by magic or are even themselves magicians. Are not magic and religion, as Frazer defines them, in such cases an insoluble compound of ritual and belief? From his intellectualist position Frazer says that they are not insoluble, for in such cases it is easy to see whether mankind treats the gods in the same way as he treats inanimate objects, as subject to his spells which they are bound to obey through the same immutable laws as regulate all natural and magical causation, or whether mankind admits their absolute control over nature and tries to conciliate or propitiate them in consequence of his belief in their powers.

But it is not merely in their philosophies and in their modes of attempting to control nature that magic and religion are different. They belong to different strata in the history of human development, and where we find that they have amalgamated we may regard this overlapping of one stage on to the other as being in no sense primitive, and we may conclude that "there was a time when man trusted to magic alone for the satisfaction of such wants as transcended his immediate animal cravings (p. 233). For this startling conclusion, borrowed from Jevons, Frazer gives us three reasons. First, he claims that magic is logically more primitive than religion, and may therefore be fairly considered to belong to an earlier stage in the development of thought, since the simplest recognition of similarity or contiguity of ideas is not so complex as the conception of personal agents, even animals being supposed to associate the ideas of things which are like each other or which have been found together in their experiences, while no one attributes to the brutes a belief in spiritual agents. To this purely deductive argument, Frazer adds a second and inductive observation. He claims that among the aborigines of Australia, "the rudest savages as to whom we possess accurate information, magic is universally practised, whereas religion in the sense of a propitiation or conciliation of the highest powers seems to be nearly unknown; roughly speaking, all men in Australia are magicians, but not one is a priest; everybody fancies he can influence his fellows or the course of nature by sympathetic magic, but nobody dreams of propitiating gods by prayer and sacrifice" (p. 234).

It is not, therefore, unreasonable, says Frazer, to deduce from the fact that the most backward culture in the world is prolific in magic and barren in religion that all other races have advanced to their higher cultural position through the same historic stages of development from magic to religion, and he asks whether the recorded facts from Australia do not justify the query that "just as on the material side of human culture there has been everywhere an Age of Stone, so on the intellectual side there has everywhere been an Age of Magic?" (p. 235).

His third argument in favor of the priority of magic asserts that since we find everywhere an enormous variation in the forms of religious belief while the essence of magical belief is always the same, we may assume that just as magic represents a substratum of belief in civilized communities whose upper social elements are busied with some one or other of the multitude of religious creeds, so it represents as well an earlier, more primitive, phase of thought in the history of the human race in which all men held the same magical faith. "This universal faith, this truly Catholic creed, is a belief in the efficacy of magic. While religious systems differ not only in different countries, but in the same country in different ages, the system of sympathetic magic remains everywhere and at all times substantially alike in its principles and practice. Among the ignorant and superstitious classes of modern Europe it is very much what it was thousands of years ago in Egypt and India, and what is now among the lowest savages surviving in the remotest corners of the world. If the test of truth lay in a show of hands or a counting of heads, the system of magic might appeal with far more reason than the Catholic Church, to the proud motto *Quod semper, quod ubique, quod ab omnibus* as the sure and certain credential of its own infallibility" (pp. 235–6).

Frazer then proceeds to inquire about the process of mental change from an exclusive belief in magic to a belief in religion also. He thinks that he can do no more than "hazard a more or less plausible conjecture" about this change in orientation of belief. This conjecture is that the shrewder intelligences began to see that magic did not really accomplish what it set out to accomplish and fell back on the belief that there were beings, like themselves, who directed the course of nature and who must be placated and cajoled into granting man what he had hitherto believed himself able to bring about through magic on his own initiative. "The shrewder intelligences must in time have come to perceive that magical ceremonies and incantations did not really effect the results which they were designed to produce, and which the majority of their simpler fellows still believed that they did actually produce. This great discovery of the inefficacy of magic must have wrought a radical though probably slow revolution in the minds of those who had the sagacity to make it. The discovery amounted to this: that men for the first time recognised their inability to manipulate at pleasure certain natural forces which hitherto they had believed to be completely within their control. It was a confession of human ignorance and weakness. Man saw that he had taken for causes what were no causes, and that all his efforts to work by means of these imaginary causes had been vain. His painful toil had been wasted, his curious ingenuity had been squandered to no purpose. He had been pulling at strings to which nothing was attached; he had been marching, as he thought, straight to the goal, while in reality he had only been treading in a narrow circle. Not that the effects which he had striven so hard to produce did not continue to manifest themselves; they were still produced, but not by him. The rain still fell on the thirsty ground; the sun still pursued his daily, and the moon her nightly journey across the sky; the silent procession of the seasons still moved in light and shadow, in cloud and sunshine across the earth; men were still born to labour and sorrow, and still, after a brief sojourn here, were gathered to their fathers in the long home hereafter. All things indeed went on as before, yet all seemed different to him from whose eyes the old scales had fallen. For he could no longer cherish the pleasing illusion that it was he who guided the earth and the heaven in their courses, and that they would cease to perform their great revolutions were he to take his feeble hand from the wheel. In the death of his enemies and his friends he no longer saw a proof of the resistless potency of his own or of hostile enchantments; he now knew that friends and foes alike had succumbed to a force stronger than any that he could wield and in obedience to a destiny which he was powerless to control" (pp. 237–8).

In the end magic is suppressed by religion and eventually comes under the ban of the priesthood as a black art. So at a late period in the development of human thought we find a distinction drawn between religion and superstition, magic being classed as a superstition. "But when, still later, the conception of the elemental forces as personal agents is giving way to the recognition of natural law; then magic, based as it implicitly is on the idea of a necessary and invariable sequence of cause and effect, independent of personal will, reappears form the obscurity and discredit into which it had fallen, and by investigating the causal sequences in nature, directly prepares the way for science. Alchemy leads up to chemistry" (p. 374).

Finally Frazer rounds off his account of magic by showing the part it has played in the history of political development. Magic is practiced in primitive societies not only by private individuals for their own private purposes but also by public functionaries on behalf of the whole community; these men are able to gain great wealth and repute and may acquire rank and authority by their ritual functions. Moreover the profession of public magician selects the ablest, most ambitious, and most unscrupulous men in society since it sets a premium on knavish imposture. That "public magic" is often a road to political influence and social prestige and private affluence Frazer shows by many actual examples from Australia, New Guinea, Melanesia, and Africa, and he justly concludes that, "in point of fact magicians appear to have often developed into chiefs and kings. Not that magic is the only or perhaps even the main road by which men have travelled to a throne" (p. 332).

In this progress from magician to king the fear inspired by ritual power is backed by the wealth the magician is able to amass in the exercise of his profession. The profession of magician appears to be the earliest professional class in human society and the first sign of social differentiation. Frazer then brings his thesis of political development into connection with his theory of the chronological sequence of magic to religion. For he believes that the evolution of the magician-chief goes hand in hand with the breakdown of magic and the birth of religion. Hence the magician as he gains political supremacy tends at the same time to emerge as the priest. "Hence the king starting as a magician, tends gradually to exchange the practise of magic for the priestly functions of prayer and sacrifice. And while the distinction between the human and the divine is still imperfectly drawn, it is often imagined that men may themselves attain to godhead not merely after their death, but in their lifetime, through the temporary or permanent possession of their whole nature by a great and powerful spirit" (p. 372).

While Tylor traced the changes which have taken place in the form and functions of magic, religion, and science through the ages and kept his conception of their growth and decay within the limits set by knowledge derived from history and a comparative study of cultures, Frazer traced the progress of human thought through stratified grades of unilinear development, each grade representing a step on which mankind has everywhere rested awhile on his path of upward progress.

Having summarized the theories of Frazer, I shall now try to sort them out and class them as hypotheses capable of inductive proof and, in accordance with present knowledge, hypotheses which cannot be proved inductively but which have heuristic value, and hypotheses which are useless either because they are contrary to ascertained facts or being beyond proof or disproof by inductive enquiry lack also even heuristic value. Into the last class come Frazer's theories about the affective and ideational similarity between magic and science, about the development of thought through stages of magic, religion, and science, and the greater part of his analysis of magic symbolism.

Tylor and Frazer were both dominated by the evolutionary ideas of their time and tended to see different types of behavior as representative of historic stages. Frazer especially arranged his types in a temporal sequence which was hardly justified by his methods of investigation. He could have shown the historical development of magic and science, as Thorndike, for instance, has done, in a definite culture of which we have historical knowledge, or he could have carefully defined cultural types with a consensus of cultural traits and demonstrated the correlation between these types and modes of thought. He used neither of these methods, with the result that his theory of the evolutionary progress of mankind through stages of magic, religion, and science has earned Marett's title of a platonic myth. It is possible that Frazer would have been content with this description and regarded his scheme as a convenient framework on which to weave his vast assortment of facts. There is nothing in Frazer's arguments which proves a chronological priority for magic over religion and empirical knowledge. Frazer's argument that the Australians, who have the simplest material culture we know, show much magical and little religious behavior falls to the ground on the impact of critical analysis. It has been pointed out that other peoples who may be considered as low in the cultural scale as the Australians have little magic; that the Australians cannot be taken as a cultural unit since they differ widely among themselves; and that moreover many Australian tribes have pronounced animistic beliefs and cults. Frazer's plea that animals make mental associations between phenomena and that this is also the essence of magical beliefs is a very remote and superficial analogy. Magic is a system of ritual techniques and not simple mental associations between phenomena. Moreover this evolutionary theory suffers from the same drawback as others of its kind, namely that it is quite beyond proof or disproof. If anyone had been present when men performed their first rites he might have recorded their nature and we could then have classified them as religion or magic according to our several formulas. Frazer's theory of how mankind changed from a magical to a religious view of the universe is hardly presented as a serious thesis and is not treated as one here.

Nevertheless the priority in time of magic over religion, though it cannot be inductively proved might have been deductively concluded if Frazer had made an exhaustive survey of the facts by the method of correlation such as was employed by Tylor, Steinmetz, and Hobhouse, Ginsberg and Wheeler. It might be possible to show that magic is specially prominent in those societies with a low technological equipment and undeveloped political organization, and that when we examine types of society with more efficient technology and more complex social organization we find a greater absence of magical rites and a greater number of religious ones, and that finally we reach societies of greatest technical efficiency and most complex social life in which magic is almost absent and religion less prominent than in the second type, while behavior and thought are becoming more and more exclusively empirical.

An analysis of the kind suggested here, particularly of the correlation of magical and empirical thought with forms of social behavior would be well worth the labor that it would cost. There can be no doubt that magic as a dominant form of social behavior is restricted to savage and barbarous peoples. This does not mean that all uncivilized societies are magic-ridden nor does it mean that magic is totally unknown in civilized communities. It means that if we trace the changes which have taken place in those civilizations for which we possess written history we shall find that there is a slow and cumulative increase in empirical knowledge and a slowly diminishing body of magical knowledge and also that if we compare societies without the art of writing and without advanced technology with those that possess both, we shall find that on the whole the technique of magic is less prominent a mode of behavior in the latter than in the former. We may say therefore that magic is a technique characteristic of simple societies and tends to disappear with the advancement of civilization, a point of view advanced by Tylor and strikingly developed by Lévy-Bruhl in the provoking contrast he makes between Primitive Mentality and Civilized Mentality.

If we mean by science an elaborate system of knowledge, the result of experimentation in the hands of specialists, such as we think of when we speak about science today, there is little difficulty in assigning to it an historical stage in the development of human thought. But if we mean any correct knowledge of natural processes and acquaintance with technological methods, then it is clearly improper to place science at one end and magic at the other end of a series of developmental stages, as Frazer has done, since it is evident that no peoples could possibly have lived in a state of culture sufficient to engage in ritual unless they first had sufficient technological knowledge to master their environment. You cannot have agricultural or hunting magic unless you have agriculture and hunting. Moreover, the most primitive societies of today are always found to be equipped with a sound knowledge of nature. The difference between scientific knowledge used in the first sense and scientific knowledge used in the second sense is one of degree; but it may be generally stated that the first usage means that you understand that certain things do happen invariably and that the second usage means that you understand how and why they happen. In the first case you know that if you plant maize seeds in a certain type of ground at a certain time of the year maize will grow. In the second case you know why the seeds grow at all, why they grow in one soil and not in another, and why they grow at one time of the year and not at another. But even here there are many degrees of knowledge and the empirical shades into the scientific.

It is never clear what Frazer means by science, for he uses the word now in one sense now in another; but on the whole he seems to mean the conscious striving after knowledge, the systems of criticism and controls, and the use of logic and experiment, which the word implies in ordinary usage today. Used in this sense the analogy which he draws between science and magic is unintelligible. He says that science and magic both visualize a uniform nature subject to invariable laws and that the scientist and the magician have a like psychological approach to nature. It is clear from accounts of savages that they have no conception of nature as a system organized by laws and in any case the utilization of magic to influence the course of nature is surely in direct opposition to the scientist's conception of the universe. You cannot believe both in natural law and that you can delay the sun by placing a stone in the fork of a tree. If there are any regularities and uniformities of thought they are in the workings of magic and not of nature. But the whole discussion seems rather pointless, for you have to be a scientist to note regularities and uniformities and organize them into a conscious theory of the universe. Indeed Frazer himself speaks of the magical view of the universe subject to law and expressing uniformity as implicit and not explicit, and it is difficult to see any sense in theoretical magic which is not explicit. All it can mean is that if we used magic in the same way as the savage uses it we would have a theory that the world was sufficiently regular in its working for us to rely on magic to control it, since it may be expected always to react in the same manner to the performance of the same spell or rite. We should generalize our experiences in this manner because we are scientifically orientated, but since we are scientifically orientated we should at once perceive the fallacy of magic. With regard to the supposition that the man of science and the man of magic both approach their task with quiet confidence and masterful assurance and that their psychology contrasts with the nervous apprehension and humility of the man of religion, it can only be said that Frazer produces no facts in support of his contention.

The apparent futility of Frazer's analogy between science and magic is due to the fact that he sees both as modes of thinking and not as learnt modes of technical behavior with concomitant speech forms. If he had compared a magical rite in its entirety with a scientific performance in its entirety instead of comparing what he supposes to go on in the brain of a magician with what he supposes to go on in the brain of a scientist, he would have seen the essential difference between science and magic. This difference is most strikingly shown in the experimental standpoint on the two modes of behavior. Science experiments and is open to experience and ready to make adjustments in its notions of reality, whereas magic is relatively nonexperimental and the magician is impervious to experience, as science understands the term, since he employs no methods of testing or control. If moreover Frazer had not brought the scientific specialist on to the scene in order to compare him with the magical specialist, but had compared magical knowledge and behavior with scientific knowledge and behavior—that is to say had compared those forms of knowledge which accord with objective reality with those which distort objective reality and those forms of behavior which achieve their purpose with those forms of behavior which are only believed to achieve their purpose—and had compared them as types of thought and behavior in the same cultural conditions instead of in totally different cultural conditions, his investigations would have been of greater value. He might have compared empirical behavior with magical behavior among the savages of Australia and observed their interaction, their social interrelations, and their concomitant psychological states, with some chance of reaching valid conclusions about the differences which exist between them. Lévy-Bruhl who took an exactly opposite point of view, holding that magical thought and scientific thought stand to each other as black to white, made the same mistake of comparing our science with savage magic instead of comparing savage empiricism with savage magic.

Besides suffering from the influence of current psychological and evolutionary theories, Frazer's exposition also suffered from current methodological deficiencies. He used what is known as the comparative method; and this does not mean the conviction that any scientific generalization must rest on a comparative study of similar phenomena, a conviction common to all men of science and an essential part of their methodology, but a particular way of comparing phenomena which was extensively used by all anthropological writers at the end of the last century. It consisted in selecting from a vast mass of data, uneven and often poor in quality, whatever phenomena appeared to belong to the same type. This proved to be a very dangerous proceeding, because the selection of facts was made on the grounds of similarity between phenomena in virtue of a single common quality. The qualities which were different in each instance were neglected. This is a perfectly sound method of scientific analysis, so long as conclusions are restricted to the particular quality abstracted and it is not then assumed that because phenomena are alike in respect to this single quality that they are alike in other respects which have not been subject to critical comparative analysis. In a study of social facts the procedure is all the more hazardous, for these are defined by their interrelations; and if they are abstracted from their social milieu, it is essential to realize that they are only comparable in a limited number of respects and not as complete social facts. By use of the comparative method Frazer was successful in demonstrating that the ideology of magic rests upon fundamental laws of thought, for it is possible to isolate the ideological associations of a vast number of magical rites and to compare them simply as examples of evident notions which are the raw material of all human thought. But when Frazer then proceeds to find a similarity between magic and science merely because the scientist and the magician use the processes of all thought building—sensation, abstraction, and comparison—the procedure is clearly inadmissible, because it does not follow from the fact that both magic and science display in their ideologies the most elementary processes of thought that there is any real similarity between scientific and magical techniques and systems of thought. This *pars pro toto* fallacy is again shown in Frazer's argument that because magic and science both disregard spiritual beings they are similar in virtue of this absent association. This is equivalent to saying that x is not y and z is not y and that therefore x and z are the same. I conclude therefore that Frazer's theories of the similarity between magic and science and of their historic stages are unsupported by either sound evidence or logic and that they have little heuristic value. Indeed they are formulated in such a manner that it is difficult to present them in a scientific form at all and consequently they impede rather than assist us in our quest. It is useless to attempt to solve the queries which Frazer raises. We have to formulate the problems anew if we are to conduct a scientific enquiry.

Of what value is the whole Tylor–Frazer conception of magic as a mistaken association of ideas? Here we may distinguish between two propositions: (1) In the words and actions of magic we can discern the operation of certain elementary laws of thought. The associations which link the rite and its objective are so simple that they are evident to us who are far removed from the cultures in which magic flourishes. They are found to rest on perception of position and perception of similarities. (2) These associations are to us no more than memory images of qualities of things which have an ideal relationship in our minds, but the savage mistakes these ideal relations for real relations in the world around him. We and savages both think in the same way in so far as perception and comparison of sensations are concerned, but the savage then leaves us behind and goes a step further by believing that because two things are associated together in his memory image, they are objectively associated. He believes that because things are like each other, they will act on each other since they are bound by an invisible link.

We can accept the first proposition without hesitation. It was clearly enunciated by Tylor and abundantly illustrated by Frazer. We can adopt the terminology of *The Golden Bough* and speak of "homeopathic magic" and "contagious magic." But it is surprising that Frazer made no deeper analysis; for to tell us that magical thought rests on perception of position and similarities is not to tell us much, since these are the elementary processes of all thought and it follows from the fact that magic is man-made. A more comprehensive analysis could be made by listing the particular qualities of objects which are associated in the ideology of magic. For example, in the instance of the gold–jaundice association it is the quality of color. The mental associations embodied in magic can thus be resolved into even simpler elements than Frazer's laws of similarity and contagion; they can be resolved into the simplest of conscious sensations and the notions and memory images resulting from them. It can be shown upon which abstractions magic is built up, whether of sight, hearing, odor, taste, or touch. When a stone figures in magic, which of its qualities is abstracted in the magical association—its size, its color, its roughness, its temperature, or its weight? Magical associations can likewise be resolved into elementary notions of the dimensions of sensations, position in space, position in time, dimensions of size, and so on. He might also have shown us, as Thurnwald has done, how in a complicated rite a single part of a process is selected to stand for the whole. A third, but difficult, task would be to show whether it figures in a number of cultural situations, sometimes even being given a permanence and inevitability by language. Are gold and jaundice associated together only in the magical situation of therapeutic treatment, or have they an association outside this situation in the minds of Greek peasants? An example of association fixed by language is elephantiasis, for when we speak of the disease we inevitably mention this animal. The Azande of the Nile–Uelle Divide make the same comparison, and the association is embodied in the word and is therefore not restricted to situations in which elephant's foot is used to cure elephantiasis. We have to enquire also whether the abstraction of a quality in magical associations is always a culturally indicated perception, e.g., in color associations; and other lines of enquiry could be suggested.

The second proposition is most misleading and is illustrative of one of those perilous leaps backwards and forwards in the dark from observable social behavior to individual psychological processes which distinguish anthropological gymnastics. Frazer's argument runs as follows: to the Greek peasant jaundice and gold are of the same color; and since things which are alike react on one another, gold, if used according to certain rules, will cure jaundice. I would prefer to state the proposition as follows: gold and jaundice produce the same sensations of color, and this similarity is culturally indicated by their association in magical behavior. It is the middle expression in Frazer's thesis to which objection is taken. In his account he frequently informs us that in savage minds like produces like and that contiguous things remain in contact when their contiguity ceases to be objective and remains, as we would say, only a memory image. We are told that "the magician infers that he can produce any effect he desires merely by imitating it" and the "homeopathic magician makes the mistake of assuming that things which resemble each other are the same."

We may first note in criticism of this point of view that it is always uncertain what Frazer means by his statements, because the inferences he refers to are only "implicitly believed" or "tacitly assumed." But beliefs and assumptions are judgments, they are conscious processes in which the middle term between two associated images is known to the thinker. Apart from this terminological haze which hangs over the whole discussion and which alone serves to obscure all issues, there is a hopeless jumble of psychological and sociological problems in which psychological concepts are used where they are quite irrelevant. We must keep our problems distinct if we are to find our way through this labyrinth of vague generalizations. Sensations and abstractions and simple comparison of abstractions are psychological processes common to all mankind, and in a sociological study of magic they do not concern us as psychological facts. We are also not concerned with the question of why magical associations embody notions of position and resemblance. It is inconceivable that they should not. The problem which concerns us is related to the social value or social indication which is given to objects and qualities. This value may be empirical, that is to say it may attribute to a thing, and utilize, the qualities which it really possesses. For example, a stone is considered to be hard and is therefore used as a tool. Or the value may be mystical, that is to say it may attribute to a thing qualities which it does not possess and which are not subject to sensory impressions. For example, a stone may be used in magical rites or be considered the dwelling place of a spirit. The perception of similar coloring in gold and jaundice is a psychological fact which requires a psychological explanation. The embodiment of this perception in a social technique is a sociological fact and requires a sociological explanation. It is not our business to explain the sensations which the physical qualities of an object produce in men, but it is our task to explain the social qualities with which men invest the object. The tendency of Tylor and Frazer to explain social facts in terms of individual psychology has been justly criticized by Durkheim and his school. Either this means that a pattern of thought can be explained in terms of psychophysical functioning of an individual's brain, which appears to be absurd if only because the pattern existed before the individual was born and he inherited it as part of his social heritage even when it involves sensations which have to be individually experienced, or it means that a pattern of thought can be explained by an individual's mental content which is, of course, no explanation at all.

Even the simplest associations if they are to be anything more than passing images are creations of social usage, of language, of the technology of magic, and so on. This is why in experiments on association there is really so little free association and why the responses evoked in so many subjects are so often of the same type. One is not surprised that a Greek peasant can see a resemblance between the color of gold and the color of jaundice, but the problem is why he should associate these two things together in magical performances when he does not associate them together in other situations and why he associates these particular things and not other things which have the same qualities of color. It would never occur to us to associate gold and jaundice together, so why should the Greek peasant do so? The answer can hardly be avoided; he associates them together in certain situations because he learns to do so when he learns to speak and behave as other members of his society. But one presumes that the Greek peasant does not always make this association, that it is possible for him to think of and use gold without thinking of jaundice, and even that he can think of jaundice without associating it with gold. It is also pertinent to ask why he should associate gold and not something else with jaundice, and in posing this question a whole range of problems present themselves. We ask whether there are other things which in their culture fulfill the conditions of color and adaptability to the requirements of magical usage; we ask what is the social value given to gold in other situations; we ask whether there is evidence of the association in the situation of jaundice, having been borrowed as a single trait from neighboring peoples; and we may ask many other questions.

The point I wish to emphasize is that these associations are situational associations. They derive their sociological significance because they are social facts and not because they are psychological facts. It is the social situation which gives them meaning, which even gives them the possibilities of expression. Magic and gold come into cultural associations in the life of an individual because they are linked together by a magical rite. We must not say that a Greek peasant sees that gold and jaundice have the same color and that therefore he can use the one to cure the other. Rather we must say that because gold is used to cure jaundice, color associations between them become established in the mind of a Greek peasant. It may even be asked to what extent the resemblance between their colors is consciously formulated by the performer of the rite, to what extent he is aware of the color link in the association of gold and jaundice.

No savage believes that everything which has the same size, or color, or weight, or temperature, or sound, etc. are in mystical connection and can be used to operate on one another. If primitive man really mistook an ideal connection for a real one and confused subjective with objective experiences, his life would be chaos. He could not exist. It is a psychological absurdity. Why then do savages only *sometimes* make these associations between phenomena and not *always* make them? Why do *some* peoples make them, and *others* on the same cultural level not make them? Knowledge of the cultural situation in which the association is made will alone answer these questions. The association will be found to be not a general one but a particular one which is specific in a certain situation. Stones and sun are not linked in a general association, but only in the special situation in which a stone is placed in the fork of a tree to keep the sun from sinking. The association comes into being by the performance of a rite. There is no mystical relation between sun and stones, but man endows a particular stone with a ritual quality by using it in a rite and for the duration of the rite. When a savage throws water into the air he does not imagine that by doing so he produces rain. He only thinks this when he throws water into the air during the performance of a rite to produce rain. Hence, there is no mistaken association of ideas. The association between a certain quality in one thing and the same quality in another thing is a correct and universal association. It does not violate the laws of logic, for it is a psychological process altogether outside their sphere. It would certainly be a mistake were the savage to hold that because things are alike they can, in virtue of their likeness alone, act on one another at a distance or that by merely imitating an act he can produce it. But here again the savage makes no such mistake. He believes that certain rites can produce certain results and the mimetic or homeopathic elements in the rite are the manner in which the purpose of the rite is expressed. It is the rite itself, the performance of standardized movements and the uttering of standardized words and the other stereotyped conditions of ritual, which achieves the result. The savage does not say, "Whatever I imitate will happen so that if I throw water into the air rain will fall." What he says is, "There is no rain at this season of the year when there ought to be rain and if we get the rainmaker to perform a rite rain will fall and our crops will be saved." Why rites so often take a mimetic form is a psychological problem which we shall not discuss here.

If I have criticized Frazer severely, I render homage to his scholarship. *The Golden Bough* is an essential source-book for all students of human thought, and the faithful way in which he has treated his authorities is an assurance that we drink at an undiluted stream. His writings have always been, and are no less today than in the past, a stimulus to those working in the same field, and every criticism is a tribute. But we can go further than just these acknowledgments—we must take over from Frazer many sound ideas and use them in the foundations of any theory of magic which is to stand the test of criticism and research. As we are, as it were, taking these ideas away with us, they may be listed here while those ideas which we believe to be erroneous and to which we have devoted lengthy criticism are jettisoned once and for all:

1. Tylor's exposition of the variations of magic as a form of social behavior with variations in cultural development.

2. Tylor's brilliant analysis of the mechanisms which compel and maintain faith in magic among savage and barbarous peoples.

3. Frazer's observation, cautiously stated, of the oft-found identity of the public magician with the political chief.

4. The division of ritual into religion and magic on the formal basis of presence or absence of belief in spirits with attendant cult, put forward by Tylor and adopted by Frazer, is an acceptable terminological device. So much time and labor has been expended in a futile endeavor to define the respective spheres of magic and religion in the abstract that it is necessary to state that sociology studies social behavior and distinguishes between one type of behavior and another, and whether a particular type of behavior is labeled with one term or with another term is of minor interest. What is of importance is that all students in the same field should use key terms like magic and religion with the same meaning. Magic and religion are clearly what we define them to be in terms of behavior. We do not want a discussion about the relation of abstractions to one another in a cultural vacuum, but we want a discussion about the relations between magical behavior and religious behavior in specific cultures. Tylor and Frazer defined religion much more clearly than they defined magic and their division has been accepted by many scholars (e.g., Rivers, *Medicine, Man and Religion,* 1927) and may be used as a convenient starting point for more intensive research.

5. Frazer's division of magic into "homeopathic" and "contagious" likewise is a step in advance of Tylor's analysis and serves as a basis for still further analysis of the symbolism of magic.

Chapter 14
Durkheim (1858-1917)

Certainly among the most potent influences on British anthropological thought were the writings of Emile Durkheim, professor of social science at Bordeaux and later professor of sociology and education in Paris. Apart from the French heritage he received from Montesquieu and Comte, the philosophers Boutroux and Renouvier, and the historian Fustel de Coulanges, he was profoundly influenced in his earlier writings, as is especially evident in his *De la Division,* by Herbert Spencer. We must always remember too that Durkheim, like all of us, was a child of his time—a Frenchman of the Third Republic. France had passed through many vicissitudes, and patriotic Frenchmen keenly felt the need for national moral regeneration. Democracy (including a strong trend towards socialism), secularism, and positive science were the key ideas and ideals of the period. We have also to bear in mind Durkheim's rabbinical background. He played a big part in public life and was a notable propagandist in the 1914-18 war.

In this chapter I am concerned with Durkheim's theory of the origin of religion as presented in *Elementary Forms* in order to draw attention to the very serious inadequacies, from the ethnological point of view, in Durkheim's work.

Durkheim wished to discover the origin of religion; he was not prepared to accept that it was just an illusion as Tylor would have it in his animistic theory, and he found equally unacceptable the naturalistic theory of Müller and others. Religious beliefs correspond to something real; not, it is true, to what the believers think is real—gods, spirits, ghosts, souls; but to society itself or its segments or its individual members symbolized by such concepts. According to Durkheim, the Central Australian aboriginals, being the most primitive people known to us, demonstrate for us religion in its most elementary form, totemism. But though the totemic creatures are sacred, their sacredness is secondary to certain stylized emblematic designs representing them, carved on oblong pieces of wood or polished stone, called *churinga*. It is these objects which represent in symbolic form the sentiment of clan solidarity, and which give to each member of a clan a sense of dependence on that collectivity. They are a sort of clan flag. And these designs, according to Durkheim, are symbols in particular concrete representations of an impersonal force, an essence or vital principle, what he calls the totemic principle; a force which to us would be abstract but for the Australian is concrete. So religion arises out of social life itself, and we see how in Australia it is generated by periodic ceremonies in which members of a clan work themselves into hallucinatory states in which their faith is renewed in the reality of what are in fact only symbolic representations of their own social cohesion.

When Durkheim came to write the *Elementary Forms,* he was already totally committed by his earlier writings to a theory of the origin of religion. What makes one raise one's eyebrows is the fact that though in his essays on totemism and related subjects he shows that he was well conversant with much of the ethnological data on Australian aboriginals, there is no hint in them of the conclusions reached in the *Elementary Forms.* Whence came the illumination? Could it have been that the Australian data, because of its poverty, gave Durkheim a suitable illustration of a theory already propounded in his mind? I think so. Anyhow, as Van Gennep (1920, *L'État actuel du problème totémique,* p. 49) says, Durkheim more or less equates "religion" with "social," and Malinowski (1913, *Folklore,* p. 425) also complains that for Durkheim "The distinctive characters of social and religious phenomena practically coincide." So we must say a few words about his general approach to the study of social phenomena.

Very briefly, and therefore perhaps to Durkheim's disadvantage, it is as follows. Man is born an animal organism and his intellectual and moral qualities are not only the creation of society but *are* society in him; and they are traditional (transmissible), general (to all members of his community), and above all obligatory. Religion has these features and is therefore simply another aspect of society. Had Durkheim had any other theory of religion than that which he put forward in his book he would have had to go back on his whole sociological position. It follows that not only are religion and society the same but also the mental categories and society. On this point Goldenweiser (1915, p. 732) complains that in Durkheim's view these categories "are not merely instituted by society, but they are, in their origin, but different aspects of society. The category of 'genus' finds its beginning in the concept of the human group; the rhythm of social life is at the basis of the category of 'time'; the space occupied by society is the source of the category of 'space'; the first efficient 'force' is the collective force of society, bringing in its wake the category of 'causality.' The category of 'totality,' finally, can only be of social origin. Society alone completely transcends the individual, rising above all particulars. The concept of totality is but the abstract form of the concept of society: society is the whole which comprises all things, the ultimate class which embraces all other classes." It has often been said, and with some justification, that Durkheim reified society; so Malinowski (1913, p. 528) in his review of *Elementary Forms* remarks that society is written about by Durkheim as a being endowed with will, aims and desires: "an entirely metaphysical conception."

Durkheim claims that totemism is a religion on the grounds, in the first place, that it is sacred, which is for him anything protected and isolated by interdictions, and in the second place that it is a set of beliefs and practices of a social group, a collectivity, what he calls a church. Now, Durkheim can, obviously, define religion by what criteria he pleases—it is then religion to him; and he can start from premises which give him his already formulated conclusions about it, since they are already contained in the definition. But what if others do not accept his criteria? Frazer, for example, at least in his later writings, put totemism in the category of magic and not of religion. Schmidt (1931, p. 115) observes of *Elementary Forms:* "The question was asked how it was possible not merely to defend the religious character of totemism, as this book does, but actually to exalt it to the position of the source of all religion, at a time when all other researchers were more and more definitely denying any connection between totemism and religion whatsoever." And this is what Goldenweiser (1915, p. 725) has to say on the matter: "Having satisfied himself that all the elements which, according to his conception of religion, constitute a true religion, are present in totemism, Durkheim declares totemism to represent the earliest form of a religion which, while primitive, lacks none of those aspects which a true religion must have Thus is reached the culminating point of a series of misconceptions of which the first is Durkheim's initial view and definition of religion. For had he given proper weight to the emotional and individual aspects in religion, the aspect which unites religious experiences of all times and places into one psychological continuum, he could never have committed the patent blunder of "discovering" the root of religion in an institution which is relatively limited in its distribution and is, moreover, distinguished by the relatively slight intensity of the religious values comprised in it. In this latter respect totemism cannot compare with either animal worship, or ancestor worship, or idolatry, or fetishism, or any of the multifarious forms of worship of nature, spirit, ghost, and god. Several of these forms of religious belief are also more widely diffused than totemism and must be regarded as more primitive, differing from totemism in their independence from any definite form of social organization."

As is of course well known, neither Durkheim nor his colleagues and pupils had any first-hand knowledge of the primitive peoples they wrote so much about. Unfortunately in this book he was led astray in essential particulars by Robertson Smith: that religion is a clan cult; that the cult is totemic; that the god of the clan is the clan itself divinized; and that totemism is the most primitive form of religion known to us. On all these points, as has been seen, Robertson Smith's assertions could hardly be substantiated by the ethnological facts, either wholly or even in part, and, strangely enough, least of all in the Semitic field in which he was so eminent a scholar.

One of the most serious initial confusions in Durkheim's book is his ambiguous use of the word "primitive." In what sense the Central Australians can be called "primitive" will be touched on later. Here I want to suggest that Durkheim, who was too clever to fall blindly into the trap, tried to safeguard himself by saying that he did not use "primitive" in a chronological sense but only in a structural sense; this was just a trick, for he was too much under the influence of Herbert Spencer not to equate in his thought the two senses and to seek in what he regarded as the structurally most primitive the most primitive in time. But to regard the Central Australians as being more primitive in time than anybody else is meaningless. And to seek in their religion—if it can be so regarded—the origin of religion, a sort of primordium, was a pointless endeavor. In any case the origin of an institution does not explain it, especially when the origin cannot be known! And what is the evidence that religion originated in totemism, or for that matter in any one particular way rather than in many ways? Durkheim was certainly a sociologistic monist.

I think it is significant that Durkheim was a militant atheist, not just an unbeliever but a propagandist for unbelief. Religion therefore presented a challenge to him. He had to find some sort of explanation of what is a universal phenomenon in both time and space, and could only do so in terms of the sociological metaphysic to which he had irretrievably committed himself. In the light of his standpoint animistic and naturistic explanations of religion could not be accepted, both accounting for religion as one or other form of illusion (though it is difficult to see how society is any more or less objective than a dream or conceptions of the heavenly bodies).

What is totemism? This is a problem Durkheim never faces. It is usual to suppose that it is the association of an animal or plant species, occasionally a class of inanimate objects, with a social group, and typically with an exogamic group or clan. But this is a matter of definition. According to Radcliffe-Brown, totemism is a special form of a phenomenon universal in human society; it arises out of the dependence of hunting and collecting peoples on what they hunt and collect. Being a pseudo historian, he believed that clan totemism arose from some such general attitude when social segmentation took place. All this is of course speculative nonsense. Then, certainly the totem of the North American Indians, from whom, after all, the word "totem" is derived, is something very different from what Durkheim is talking about with regard to the Arunta of Central Australia. The African data—Durkheim just ignores what does not fit into his picture—are phenomena so different from what has been recorded about the Arunta that it is difficult to say more than that the same sort of label has got attached to what might appear to be the same but are in important respects quite different. The whole matter is what Van Gennep calls a bit *"touffu."* Van Gennep lists dozens of theories supposedly explaining totemism (1920, p. 341), including Durkheim's *"Emblématique-Collectiviste (sociologique)"*—he puts him (1920, p. 4) in the broad *"Nominaliste"* class with Herbert Spencer, Andrew Lang, and Max Müller.

Goldenweiser (1915, p. 725): "Nor does Durkheim's discussion of the relative priority of clan totemism carry conviction. Here his facts are strangely inaccurate, for far from it being the case that 'individual totemism' never occurs unaccompanied by clan totemism, the facts in North America, the happy hunting-ground of the guardian spirit, bespeak the contrary. Whereas that belief must be regarded as an all but universal aspect of the religion of the American Indian, it has nowhere developed more prolifically than among the tribes of the Plateau area who worship not at the totemic shrine. To regard the belief in guardian spirits, 'individual totemism,' as an outgrowth of clan totemism is, therefore, an altogether gratuitous hypothesis!"

Durkheim held that one well-controlled experiment is sufficient to establish a law. This is a very dubious assertion with regard to the natural sciences; with regard to the human sciences it cannot be sustained. Malinowski (1913, p. 530) correctly observes: "Theories concerning one of the most fundamental aspects of religion cannot be safely based on an analysis of a single tribe, as described in practically a single ethnographical work." Again (1913, p. 526): "Nevertheless, to base most far-reaching conclusions upon practically a single instance (the Arunta) seems open to very serious objections." Goldenweiser (1915, pp. 734–5) likewise comments: "The selection of Australia as the practically exclusive source of information must be regarded as unfortunate in view of the imperfection of the data. The charge is aggravated through the circumstance that the author regards the case of Australia as typical and tends to generalize from it." Again (Goldenweiser, 1915, p. 723): "While the author's rejection of the comparative method deserves hearty endorsement, the motivation of his resolve to present an intensive study of one culture arouses misgivings. For thus, he says, he might discover a law. Applicable as this concept may be in the physical sciences, the hope itself of discovering a law in the study no matter how intensive of *one* historical complex, must be regarded as hazardous."

In any case, was the experiment well controlled when the ethnographical evidences were so muddled and inadequate as to range between doubtful and unacceptable? Goldenweiser (1915, p. 723) justly says: "Also from the point of view of the available data must the selection of Australia be regarded as unfortunate, for, in point of ethnography Australia shares with South America the distinction of being our dark continent. A more instructive study in ethnographic method could be written based on the errors committed by Howitt and Spencer and Gillen, as well as Strehlow, our only modern authorities on the tribes from which Durkheim derives all his data." Durkheim relied almost entirely on what Spencer and

Gillen wrote about the Arunta, and as the matters he was discussing largely involved linguistic issues it is pertinent to remark that I can discover no evidence that either of these men were able to speak the native language of the people they wrote about. And here I must quote a statement by Mr. Strehlow the younger (1947, p. xvi), whose knowledge of the Aranda (Arunta) language is unquestionable. He writes: "I have sometimes felt that the anthropologists of the past tended to overemphasize the differences between the Australian natives and ourselves; and this, I venture to suggest, has been due largely to the language barrier between them and their informants. Too often traditions and customs were noted down in their barest outlines; and the details were later filled in by the scientists themselves according to their own conception of what the natives' ideas ought to have been on certain subjects. In other words, the parched skeletons brought back from necessarily brief field excursions were often covered with flesh and skin in the private studies of the anthropologists, and then presented to the public as living representatives of Australian natives, voicing suitably primitive sentiments. This earlier 'primitivist' attitude of scientists may be illustrated by a condensed paragraph from the introduction to the account of the well-known Horn Expedition to Central Australia in 1894. Here the scientific attitude to the aboriginals is summed up over Horn's own signature as follows: 'The Central Australian aborigine is the living representative of a stone age who still fashions his spear-heads and knives from flint and sandstone and performs the most daring surgical operations with them. His origin and history are lost in the gloomy mists of the past. He has no written records and few oral traditions. In appearance he is a naked hirsute savage, with a type of features occasionally pronouncedly Jewish. He is by nature light-hearted, merry and prone to laughter, a splendid mimic, supple-jointed, with an unerring hand that works in perfect unison with his eye, which is as keen as that of a eagle. He has never been known to wash. He has no private ownership of land, except as regards that which is not over carefully concealed about his person.... Religious belief he has none, but is excessively superstitious, living in constant dread of an Evil Spirit which is supposed to lurk round his camp at night. He has no gratitude except that of the anticipatory order, and is as treacherous as Judas. He has no traditions, and yet continues to practise with scrupulous exactness a number of hideous customs and ceremonies which have been handed from his fathers, and of the origin or reason of which he knows nothing. . . . After an experience of many years I say without hesitation that he is absolutely untamable. . . . Verily his moods are as eccentric as the flight of his own boomerang. Thanks to the untiring efforts of the missionary and the stockman, he is being rapidly 'civilized' off the face of the earth, and in another hundred years the remaining evidence of his existence will be the fragments of flint which he has fashioned so rudely.' "

I have made it clear (Evans-Pritchard, 1965, pp. 64–5) why I think the dichotomy between the "sacred" and the "profane" is a false one, and that I have never found it of the slightest value in my field research. Obviously, for dialectical purposes, Durkheim had to make a rigid opposition between the two categories, for if there is to be a "sacred" there must be a "profane"; but this is a conceptual, not empirical, antithesis. And are the concepts ours or those of the Australian aboriginals? Malinowski (1913, p. 526) very correctly asks a question: "A sharp division into things sacred and profane may hold for the Central Australians. But is it universal?" I feel by no means persuaded. In reading the detailed monograph by Dr. and Mrs. Seligman about the Veddas, no such division is suggested as existing among that extremely primitive people. Again, it would be difficult to maintain the existence of such a separation among the Melanesian peoples of whom we have very copious records. I think that Durkheim was here generalizing from his own Semitic background.

Furthermore, this black and white antithesis does not allow for the grey. This is more or less what Stanner, who claims (1967, p. 225) that Durkheim (1967, p. 229) seriously misunderstood Australian social organization, says about the aboriginals of the north: "The dichotomy is an over-simplification." It is "unusable except at the cost of undue interference with the facts of observation." Again (1967, p. 127): "I have found it impossible to make sense of aboriginal life in terms of Durkheim's well-known dichotomy 'the sacred' and 'the profane.' " Then (p. 109): "The more closely the category of 'the profane' is studied the less suitable it appears."

Also, as, according to Durkheim, almost everything among the aboriginals, both people and the natural world in which they live, is sacred in some degree, it is difficult to see what strictly can be called "profane." Nor does Durkheim deal adequately with the fact that totems are sacred only to some people and not to others of the same community.

Durkheim was an evolutionary fanatic who wished to explain social phenomena in terms of pseudohistorical origins. Hence arose one of his most serious blunders, a blunder in both logic and method. He held that since the Australian aboriginals were the least technologically developed people in the world, their religion—totemism—must be regarded as the most primitive we have knowledge of. Herein lie a whole string of unsupportable, even stupid, assumptions. In the first place, it cannot be sustained that a simple material culture and bionomic way of life necessarily mean the absence of a highly complex language, mythology, poetry, and so forth. All the evidence is to the contrary. And what then are we to say about peoples just as simple, or even simpler, in their material culture than these Central Australian aboriginals but who are not totemic at all? Why did not totemism blossom from their technologically undeveloped condition? Long ago Van Gennep (1920, p. 49) pointed out that totemism is not found among peoples even lower in the scale of civilization than the Central Australians, e.g., Bushmen, Vedda, Andamanese, the tribes in Central Brazil. I quote Goldenweiser again (1915, p. 723): "Australia is selected for the primitiveness of its social organization (it is based on the clan!) with which a primitive form of religion may be expected to occur. That at this stage of ethnological knowledge one as competent as Emile Durkheim should regard the mere presence of a clan organization as a sign of primitiveness is strange indeed."

Durkheim had to accept that beside their totem beliefs the aboriginals about whom he was writing had conceptions of the individual soul and of gods, and he tried to explain them in terms of his general theory. The idea of the soul is nothing more than the totemic principle incarnate in each individual, society individualized. There follows a splendid passage by Durkheim; but it must be soberly asked whether, even if we grant some meaning to "totemic principle," it is possible to establish any general connection between totemism and the idea of the soul. There may indeed often be some such conceptual association among peoples who have totems, but what about the peoples who do not have totems? Since, according to Durkheim, the *"principe totémique"* is the sole basis of all religion there is justification in Sidney Hartland's remark that since the idea of the soul is universal the idea of the totem must be too. But totemism is not universal.

As for the gods, or spiritual beings, Durkheim thought that they must have been totems at one time; and he explained them as idealized representations of the totality of clan totems within a tribe, a totemic synthesis corresponding to the synthesis of clans within a tribe. Durkheim adduces no evidence at all that the gods were once totems; and his structural explanation may indeed be neat, but it is little more than that. P. W. Schmidt (1935, p. 117) was right to observe that the South East Australians, whom he regarded as having an older culture than the Arunta, "have either no totemism at all to show or only fragments of it, acquired at a later date; what we do find among them is the figure of the Supreme Being, clear, definite, and quite independent of totemism." And what, we may add, about the many primitive peoples who believe in gods and have no totems?

On this matter I cite a pertinent passage from Lowie (*Primitive Religion,* 1936): "We shall content ourselves with putting the axe to the root of the theory. It is ethnographically unwarranted to deduce primeval conceptions from Australian conditions. The Australians are not so primitive as, certainly not more primitive in their culture than, the Andaman Islanders, the Semang of the Malay Peninsula, the Paviotso of Nevada. In these sociologically simplest tribes totemism does not occur. Totemism is a widespread but far from universal phenomenon, while the belief in spiritual being is universal; precisely these rudest tribes which have a decisive bearing on the question are non-totemic animists. Hence, the notion of spirit cannot be derived from totemism. Moreover, the totemic ideas of the Australians represent a highly localized product and cannot even be accepted as the earliest form of *totemism.*"

As for the "totemic principle," this is more or less equated by Durkheim with the mainly Polynesian concept of *mana* and those of *wakan* and *orenda* in North America; and this idea of what was supposed to be some sort of impersonal force analogous to ether or electricity was at the time very fashionable among anthropologists and sociologists (Marett, Hewitt, Vierkandt, Hartland, Preuss, Durkheim himself, and his collaborators Hubert and Mauss). Perhaps in this climate of theory Durkheim could scarcely have avoided some such interpretation, but, whether this be so or not, I think it would be fair to say that all those who have recently concerned themselves with the matter and in the light of what is now known about it would agree that this more or less pseudometaphysical interpretation is most misleading; and I would suggest that it is a simple logical deduction which would account for the error of the reporters—namely that any "virtue" or "quality" which is found in many persons and things must have an abstract term of reference. Moreover there is a good deal of force in a further objection (Goldenweiser, 1915, p. 727) with regard to Durkheim's identification of the "totemic principle" with *mana:* "On reading the pages devoted to this discussion the unprejudiced student soon perceives that the facts supporting Durkheim's contention are altogether wanting. There is no indication that the beliefs underlying totemic religion are generically the same as those designated by the terms *mana* or *orenda....*" All this, and much more is *aus der Luft gegriffen.*

For Durkheim totemism is a clan religion. Where there are clans there is totemism and where there is totemism there are clans. This is not correct. Van Gennep tells us that in North America we find the Kutchin, the Crow, the Hidatsa, and the Choctaw with exogamic divisions but without totems or totemic names (1920, p. 29). Then (Schmidt, 1931, p. 113): "Totemism, with which Freud begins the development of mankind, is not at the beginning. We know a whole series of peoples, ethnologically the oldest, who have neither totemism nor mother-right; the Pygmoids, the Pygmies of Asia and Africa, the South-East Australians, the Ainu, the primitive Eskimos, the Koryaks, the Samoyeds in the extreme north of the globe, the North Central Californians, the primitive Algonkins of North America, the Geztapuya tribes of South America, and the Tierra del Fuegians of the extreme south. Even if Freud's theory were right in itself it would have nothing to do with the origin of religion, morals or society, for the origins of all these lie much further back in pretotemic days, and are utterly different from Freud's phantasies." We are further informed (Van Gennep, 1920, p. 74) that although the Papuans of New Guinea have clans they are not totemic. As Van Gennep points out there are many other sorts of *unités sociales* which might be expected on Durkheim's reasoning to be totemic but have no totems or emblems or anything corresponding to them.

Apart from the fact that clans and totemism do not necessarily go together, there is the further objection to Durkheim's thesis to which I have alluded in my book (Evans-Pritchard, 1966, pp. 65–6). Among the Australian aboriginals it is the so-called horde, and then the tribe, which are the corporate groups, and not the widely dispersed (again so-called) clans; so if the function of religion is to maintain the solidarity of the groups which most require a sense of unity, then it should be the hordes and (once again, so-called) tribes, and not the clans, that should perform the rites generating effervescence. I am not the first to have raised this objection. It is implied in what Van Gennep has said about *unités sociales,* and it is explicitly stated by Lowie (1936, p. 160): "In so far as Durkheim does not identify divine society with the crowd, he rather lightly fixes on the sib as the social group that would at the same time loom as the god-like protector and curber. No doubt the individual derives sustenance and protection from his own sib, but that is equally true of his local or tribal group as a whole. Why, then, should the sib alone function as the nascent god? On the other hand, restraint is precisely what one's own sib does not usually exercise, that is left to the other sibs. If by special act of grace we follow Durkheim to his favourite Australian field, special difficulties arise. He insists that the individual acquires his culture from society. But this society from which he acquires it is only in small measure his sib. For example, in a matrilineal Australian tribe a boy belongs indeed to his mother's sib, but his training in woodcraft is derived from his father, regardless of rules of descent, and his education is completed in the camp that unites all the bachelors, irrespective of kinship. To leap from society as a whole to the individual's own sib seems to be in no way justified by Durkheim's reasoning. We are obliged to conclude that his theory neither explains how the assemblages of the ceremonial season create religious emotion, nor why the sib should be singled out for masked adoration from among all the social units, when it is only one of a series all of which jointly confer on him the blessings of culture and of protection."

With regard to the emblematic engravings on the *churinga:* the matter is very complicated—it would appear that there is some sort of hierarchy of these relics, some in stone, and some in wood—and I have been unable to find any decisive verdict about their significance in the literature, both old and new. It must suffice therefore by way of comment if I cite Radcliffe-Brown (1929) to the effect that most of the totems are not figured representationally. If this is true, it much weakens Durkheim's contentions.

This brings us to a further query, already indicated in what has gone before: If totemism is the origin of religion, what about those peoples who are not totemic and as far as we know have never been totemic, yet have religious beliefs and practices? Lowie (1936, pp. 157–9) appropriately observes, "From the ethnological point of view Dr. Goldenweiser pertinently asks whence the nontotemic peoples have derived their religion." Durkheim proceeds on the assumption, now thoroughly discredited, that the sib (clan) in the typical form of the totemic sib is a universal trait of very rude cultures. As a matter of fact, it has already been shown that the simplest tribes in both the Old World and the New World lack sibs and totems. No such institution occurs among the Andamanese of the Bay of Bengal or the Chukchi of Siberia, nor has it been reported from the Tasmanians, the Congolese Pygmies, or the Bushmen. If it be objected with some plausibility that our knowledge of the tribes just mentioned is too inadequate to permit negative data to weigh heavily, there is the wholly unobjectionable evidence from the Western Hemisphere, where the sib organization is uniformly absent from all the rudest hunting tribes and in North America is an almost regular accompaniment of horticulture. The Mackenzie River Athabaskans, the Shoshoneans of the Great Basin, the tribes of Washington and Oregon are sibless, while the sedentary Iroquois and Pueblo tribes are organized into sibs with at least totemic names, if not with full-fledged totemism; for, as we cannot resist mentioning incidentally, the sib organization is by no means uniformly linked with totemism. These simple facts had been pointed out by Dr. Swanton some years before the publication of Durkheim's book, but the French sociologist prefers to ignore them and to take for his point of departure a demonstrably false theory of primitive society. In short, then, there are many nontotemic peoples and among them are precisely those of simplest culture. But they all have some sort of religion! Shall we assume that they only obtained their beliefs and practices by contact with the borrowing from the higher totemic cultures? The assumption is not *a priori* probable, and empirically there is not the slightest proof for it except as respects specific features of religious culture, such as may be borrowed back and forth under favourable conditions. Dr. Ruth Fulton Benedict has recently examined Durkheim's thesis with reference to the North American data, selecting for discussion the relations of totemism to the most persistent of North American religious traits, the guardian-spirit complex. This feature is not only by virtue of its range far older than totemism but also turns out to be highly developed where no traces of totemism have ever been recorded. It is therefore impossible to derive the guardian-spirit belief from totemic conceptions. On the contrary, there is good evidence that in certain regions totemism, which otherwise has a very meagre religious content, "tends to take its colouring from the guardian-spirit concept, and the high-water marks of a religious attitude towards the totem, which beyond doubt are found on this continent, are intelligible from this fact." Goldenweiser, attacking Durkheim's whole theory of the origin of categories, says likewise (1915, p. 733): "The Eskimo, for example, have no clans nor phratries nor a totemic cosmogony (for they have no totems); how then did their mental categories originate, or is the concept of classification foreign to the Eskimo mind?"

Durkheim has himself laid it down that any explanation of a social fact in terms of psychology must be wrong, yet in his theory so majestic and enduring a social phenomenon as religion arises from the emotional effervescence of a crowd. I have certainly not been the first to protest. Malinowski (1913, p. 529) comments: "We feel a little suspicious of a theory which sees the origins of religion in crowd phenomena." Again (p. 530): "In his actual theory he uses throughout individual psychological explanations." Goldenweiser said (1915): "Our first objection to the derivation of the sacred from an inner sense of social pressure is a psychological one. That a crowd-psychological situation should have aroused the religious thrill in the constituent individuals, who—*nota bene*—were hitherto unacquainted with religious emotion, does not seem in the least plausible. Neither in primitive nor in modern times do such experiences, *per se,* arouse religious emotions, even though the participating individuals are no longer novices in religion. And, if on occasion such sentiments do arise, they lack the intensity and permanence required to justify Durkheim's hypothesis. If a corroborree differs from an intichiuma, or the social dances of the North American Indians from their religious dances, the difference is not in the social composition but in the presence or absence of pre-existing religious associations. A series of corroborrees does not make an intichiuma; at least, we have no evidence to that effect, and human psychology, as we know it, speaks against it. Durkheim's main error, however, seems to our mind to lie in a misconception of the relation of the individual to the social, as implied in his theory of social control. The theory errs in making the scope of the social on the one hand, too wide, on the other, too narrow. Too wide in so far as the theory permits individual factors to become altogether obscured, too narrow in so far as the society which figures in the theory is identified with a crowd, and not with a cultural historic group." Again (Goldenweiser, 1921, p. 371): "As one

reads Durkheim's picturesque description of Australian ceremonies, he realizes that the social setting with which the author
deals is one usually designated as crowd-psychological." And on
the same page: "Notwithstanding the tremendous importance
ascribed to it, society for Durkheim is but a sublimated crowd,
while the social setting is the crowd-psychological situation. Society as a cultural, historical complex, society as the carrier of tradition, as the legislator judge, as the standard of action, as public
opinion; society in all these varied and significant manifestations,
which surely are of prime concern to the individual, does not figure
in Durkheim's theory." Then Lowie (1936, p. 160): "As Goldenweiser trenchantly asks, 'Why is it that the gatherings of Indians
for secular dances are not transformed into religious occasions if
the assembly itself gives rise to sentiments of religion?' " Why indeed! And not only Indian dances but dances anywhere. According to Durkheim the dancing about in Australian ceremonies
transforms the individual, but there is no evidence for this. Radcliffe-Brown (*The Andaman Islanders*, 1922, pp. 246 *et seq*) says much
the same about Andamanese dancing, but is equally unconvinc-
ing.

As we have seen, Durkheim's whole thesis in the *Elementary Forms*
has been subjected, and not unfairly, to devastating criticism from
several points of view and by those who, for one or other reason,
were fully entitled to express an opinion. Van Gennep, Goldenweiser, and Lowie were all widely read in the literature on totemism; and Malinowski was very much at home in the literature on
the Australian aboriginals. Time has not come to Durkheim's assistance. In 1920, Van Gennep could write (p. 236): "If anything
can be said with certainty of the belief-systems which have been
studied it is that they do *not* symbolize the clan, or any other concrete social entity, or even idealizations of them, although these
elements may colour or mediate what is symbolized." In 1967,
Stanner, a recent student of Australian aboriginals (in the north of
the continent) concludes (1967, p. 256): "The sum of evidence sus-
tains three conclusions: (1) If any Australian aborigines lived, as
used to be suggested, in a stationary state of society with a static
culture, the Murinbata were certainly not among them over any
period which it is possible for inquiry to touch. (2) To identify
their religion with totemic phenomena would be a mistake. (3)
The society was not the real source and object of the religion."

Strehlow (the younger) in his book *Aranda Traditions,* about the people on whose way of life Durkheim based his entire hypothesis, does not even bother to mention him.

We have, I fear, to come down decisively against Durkheim and to conclude that he may not in any sense be regarded as a scientist—at the best a philosopher, or I would rather say, a metaphysician. He broke every cardinal rule of critical scholarship, as well as of logic; in particular in his disregard of evidence, and especially of those evidences which negated his theory. He only used the comparative method when it suited him. Since he and his colleagues of the *Année* were determined to prove their theories by appeal to what is generally regarded as ethnological data (i.e., writings about primitive peoples) they must be judged accordingly. If you appeal unto Caesar unto Caesar must you go. So, is the final verdict to be Van Gennep's (1920, p. 49), who compares Durkheim's thesis to the best constructions of the Hindu metaphysicians, the Muslim commentators and the Catholic scholastics? Yes. But to it shall be added the silent judgment of an authoritative student of the aboriginals, E. A. Worms, who completely ignores Durkheim in his article on their original religion.

And now we may ask some final questions. We have decided that though he was scornful of others for deriving religion from motor hallucination, that is precisely what he does himself. Then we may ask whether, if the Australians' belief in the existence of spiritual beings and forces is a baseless assumption, may not Durkheim's assumption that these beings do not exist be arbitrary and just as baseless? And, furthermore, I cannot understand why we should applaud Durkheim's mockery of Tylor for deriving religion from an illusion when that is what, to say it again, he does himself. Why are spiritual forms symbolizing social groups any less an illusion than those derived from dreams? We might also ask why these spiritual forms should be assumed to symbolize anything? And that question leads to a final one.

My greatest objection to Durkheim's thesis is that it is highly unscientific. In science one puts forward a hypothesis which, if it is to have any heuristic value, must be experimentally testable, and it must be shown in what way it can be so tested by observation. Now, how do we set about to prove that religious forms are only symbols of social structures, which is what Durkheim is saying? Obviously, this cannot be done for any one society or type of society, which is what Durkheim is trying to do. It can only be done indirectly by use of the comparative method, a method, as I have said before, Durkheim only used when it suited him. If it can be shown that there is some correspondence between types of social structure and types of religious belief and practice, some sort of case might be made for pursuing the inquiry further along the lines of the hypothesis. Radcliffe-Brown, who had a logical, if not an original mind, tried to show this, but his effort was neither scholarly nor convincing (Evans-Pritchard 1965, pp. 73-5). Or one might try to show from historical evidences that when there has been structural change or change in religious faith there has been uniformly some concomitant change in the other. Durkheim did not even attempt to begin to do either.

Chapter 15
Hertz (1882–1915)

We have moved a long way in thought as well as in time from the eighteenth-century philosophers, although a fundamental aim has remained the same from Montesquieu to Durkheim: to seek the general in the particular by comparing different societies and to try to understand the general in terms of the interrelationship of institutions and of certain uniform tendencies in their historical development. These comparisons and generalizations and formulations were first attempted on a universal scale, the universe being then small, and they tended to be very uncritical. The generalizations tended to be essentially deductions from philosophical and moral axioms, the facts being used merely as illustrations. Then with McLennan we get an attempt at a much more rigorous application of the comparative method to the study of primitive societies, and with Robertson Smith a stress more on the limitation of the field of comparison than on comparison itself, an insistence that the student must know his field of research thoroughly and be conversant with every fact in it before he begins to investigate even limited problems, though this is implicit rather than explicit. In their writings there is also less a desire to establish mechanical interdependencies than to show a certain consistency in ideas and values.

There is, however, a difference between the attempts of these scholars within limited fields and the essays of Robert Hertz. Like his teachers Durkheim and Mauss, he did not seek to formulate any laws of social development. The other writers whom we have so far treated to critical analysis not only considered themselves to be historians but were historians. They regarded an explanation of social phenomena to consist in showing the conditions out of which they had arisen. Durkheim and his pupils, on the contrary, regarded an explanation as an understanding of the facts; by understanding them they meant seeing them as *faits totals,* that is seeing them in relation to the total social life of which they form part. It is essentially a synthetic, a *gestalt,* an integrative approach. The basic assumptions may still have been to a large extent those of social determinism but this was not as pronounced; and Mauss and Hertz were far less rigid in this respect than Durkheim, and also less dogmatic. They did not have to fight philosophy and psychology for *Lebensraum;* that battle had been won. They were more critical and more cautious; and they had more and better ethnographic material at their disposal.

Robert Hertz was perhaps the most brilliant of the younger members of the Année Sociologique circle. Like several of its other younger members, he was killed in the first World War; he died leading his section in the attack on Marcheville on 13 April 1915, at the age of thirty-three. He had already published "Contribution à une étude sur la représéntation collective de la mort," (*Année sociologique,* X, 1907) and "La Prééminence de la main droite: étude sur la polarité religieuse," (*Revue philosophique,* LXVIII, 1909). These represent only a peripheral interest to the study on which he was engaged, an analysis of sin and expiation, and he had planned a book on these complementary ideas in primitive societies, *Le Péché et l'expiation dans les sociétés inférieures,* the almost completed introduction to which appeared posthumously "Le Péché et l'expiation dans les sociétés primitives," (*Revue de l'histoire des religions,* 1922). Mauss says (*Année sociologique,* N.S., 1, 1925, p. 24) that he hoped to publish the whole book, but it never appeared. Another work by Hertz on the myth of Athena was left in a state sufficiently completed to be published, but has not been. He has also published an article, based on a field study, of the cult of Saint Besse ("Saint Besse," *Revue de l'histoire des religions,* 1913); and the folklore notes he took down from his men at the front and sent to his wife were published in 1917 ("Contes et dictons, *Revue des traditions populaire,* 1917). He had also written a socialist brochure ("Socialisme et depopulation," *Les Cahiers du socialiste,* No. 10, 1910). In 1928 Mauss brought together in one volume (*Mélanges de sociologie religieuse et folklore,* 1928) the essays on death and the right hand, the article on the cult of Saint Besse, and a lengthy review by Hertz of a book by K. K. Grass on an ascetic and ecstatic Russian Sect, the Khluists, which was written for the *Année sociologique* but was not printed there.

Robert Hertz's widow Alice Hertz (née Bauer), who died while her husband's collected essays were in the press, tells us in her preface of his enthusiasm for his researches (largely carried out in the British Museum in 1904-6), and how, in a sense, he lived with the Dayaks of Borneo, even learning their language, so that they became for him not just figures in his notebooks but flesh and blood. However, he came to realize that such a study from books could never equal experience at first hand when in the long vacation of 1912 he began his study of the cult of Saint Besse, that curious figure garbed in the uniform of a Roman legionary, in the remote Alpine community of Cogne, near Aoste. "How much more alive than the work in the library, this direct contact with realities just as rich in possibilities as the rites of primitives at the other end of the earth."

The historical value of Hertz's writings is that they are a representative example of the culmination of two centuries of development of sociological thought in France, from Montesquieu to Durkheim and his pupils. I cannot attempt to trace even an outline of this development here. It must suffice to say that a survey of the intervening years shows how philosophical speculation, often highly didactic and illustrated with the barest information about the simpler societies—those with which Durkheim and his school mainly dealt—has grown into the systematic comparative study of primitive institutions, based on a great body of ethnographic facts collected from all over the world, which in the British Isles is called social anthropology. I regard Fustel de Coulanges's *La Cité antique* (1864) as the dividing point between the speculative and dogmatic treatises of such writers as Turgot, Condorcet, Saint-Simon, and Comte on the one side, and on the other, for example, Durkheim's detailed analyses of systems of classification, totemism, and incest prohibitions, and Hubert and Mauss's scholarly treatment of sacrifice and magic. Though I am not aware that he anywhere says so, I think that Fustel de Coulanges, and also, of course, Montesquieu, had a greater formative influence on Durkheim's thought than Saint-Simon and Comte. Would one be wrong in detecting also the influence of de Tocqueville?

The movement towards a truly scientific study of social phenomena was continuing and has continued. In Durkheim's writings facts are still sometimes subordinated to an *a priori* philosophical doctrine. This is much less so in the essays of Hubert and Mauss and in Hertz's writings, though even in them some of the formulas which clouded Durkheim's mind remain, as, for example, the ap-

peal to a collective consciousness, a vague and ill-defined conception, and to the dichotomy of sacred and profane, a polarity which
I find to be almost equally vague and ill defined. There remains
also Durkheim's irritating maneuver, when a fact contradicts his
thesis, of asserting that its character and meaning have altered,
that it is a secondary development and atypical, although there is
no evidence whatsoever that such changes have taken place.

These essays have also a methodological interest. The method
employed was that dignified in England by the name of "the comparative method," a title which means little more than that if one
wishes to make a general statement about the nature of some institution one has first to examine it in a number of different societies.
Social philosophers have been making such comparisons through
the centuries. What else was Aristotle doing in the *Politics* or Machiavelli in *The Prince*? However, among the anthropologists of the
last century and up to the present time it was claimed that a more
rigorous use of the comparative method, especially by establishing
correlations, would yield scientific formulations which might legitimately be called laws.

The method includes two different operations. In the first, what
is done is to separate out the general from the particular and the
social fact from its cultural form, thereby making a classification of
types or categories of general social phenomena. This procedure
enabled the anthropologists of the last century to note that such
institutions as marriage by capture, totemism, matrilineal descent,
taboo, exogamy, and various systems of kinship nomenclature are
widespread and everywhere have the same essential characteristics
in spite of a great variety of forms. The data for comparison were
thus classified for further study. This is what Hertz did when he
isolated two significant facts with a very wide distribution among
the simpler peoples, a second burial, or at any rate mortuary ceremony, and the association of a variety of ideas and values with the
right and left hands. In his study of second burials, he drew attention to the large number of different forms disposal of a corpse
takes in different societies but pointed out that these differences
need not be taken into account in making a sociological analysis
since the procedures have the same purpose and function.

A class of facts having been isolated for study, the second operation is to reach certain conclusions about them. How this operation
is conducted depends on what sort of conclusions are aimed at.
Encouraged by the successful use of the comparative method in

other disciplines, especially in philology, anthropologists of the last century expected that it would provide them with a means of reconstructing the past history of human societies and of defining the laws of progress revealed in it. They did not sufficiently recognize that the philologists and others who used the method to some effect were investigating divergences from a common source, whereas they, for the most part, were not. When, however, they restricted themselves to the development of institutions within a limited range of culturally related societies comparable results were produced, e.g., Maine on the development of Indo-European law, Fustel de Coulanges on the development of early Graeco-Roman religious institutions, and Robertson Smith on the development of Semitic forms of sacrifice; but even so, many of their conclusions were unverifiable. As for the general laws of social development put forward, such as those by McLennan and Morgan, they were not only totally unverifiable but they were largely based on evidences which further research showed to be unsound. Attempts at formulating laws of social progress have now been given up; but not the comparative method, for the very simple reason that it is the only method which, in one form or another, can be employed. What came now to be held by some writers, notably by Radcliffe-Brown in this country, was that, while the method was sound, it had been hitherto used for the wrong purpose. It should be used, not for reconstructing stages of social development, but for the formulation of laws of functional interdependences. However, no such laws have yet been propounded in social anthropology, and until they are it does not seem worth while discussing whether they can be, or what would be their significance if they were. Research directed to this end, at any rate on any scale, has been abandoned in this country, at least for the time being.

Durkheim and his pupils used the comparative method with as much skill and rigour as it is capable of. They were careful to concentrate on a limited range of facts in a limited region and not, like, for instance, McLennan, Frazer, and Westermarck, to take them from all over the world, lifting them in the process out of their social setting. The ethnographic data of other regions were used only to see whether the conclusions reached in the area chosen for intensive research had a more general validity or what divergences would have to be accounted for. This is what Durkheim did in his study of Australian totemism, what Hubert and Mauss did in their study of Hindu and Hebrew sacrifice, and what Hertz did in his study of mortuary rites, the core of this study being an analysis of such rites in Indonesia, mostly among the Dayak peoples. In the case of his essay on the right hand he had to cover a wider field, a more extensive survey being both feasible and required in this much less complex topic. The limitation of field is explicitly presented as a methodological principle in *"Le Péché et l'expiation dans les sociétés primitives"* (p.37). It would be an erroneous procedure to study sin and expiation by accumulating facts from all over the world and from societies of very diverse types. What is required is an intensive study of a limited and clearly defined cultural region where the f acts can be examined in their full contexts of ideas and practices. He chose the Polynesian peoples. Mauss, in an appendix to the same essay (p. 59), refers scornfully to those who make collections of facts borrowed indiscriminately from every sort of people and then interpret them superficially by an elementary psychology.

Then, though it is true that Durkheim was attempting to discover causal explanations which have a general validity and might be called laws, he did not conceive of them so naively as did some anthropologists, and his attempt seems to me to have been secondary to an endeavor to relate the facts to one another in such a way that they are intelligible to us both as a whole and singly. Causal explanation is only one kind of understanding. This is, perhaps, more evident in the writings of his pupils and collaborators. In their classical study of magic Hubert and Mauss attempt little more than to show us the fundamental setting and structure of a magic rite, and in their equally fine essay on sacrifice to show us the pattern of sacrificial acts so that we perceive how the whole rite and each part of it make sense. Hertz's essays exemplify this descriptive integration, the meaning of the facts being shown to lie not in themselves, considered as separate facts, but in their interrelation; the art of the anthropologist being to reveal this and hence their meaning. We do not understand what the double disposal of the dead in Indonesia means till we know also the beliefs held about the ghosts of the dead and also about the rules of mourning, but once we have grasped the pattern of these three sides of death—corpse, soul, and mourners—we see that each expresses the same idea of transition; and we further understand why a ruler's death cannot be announced, why widows may not be immediately inherited or remarried, why corpses of the very old and of small children are treated differently, etc. Furthermore, we can then

make a fruitful comparison between mortuary rites and other rituals of transition, e.g., initiation and marriage, as both Hertz and
Van Gennep did.

The essay on Saint Besse is an attempt by structural analysis to
relate certain prominent and puzzling features of the cult and its
attendant myths to local and politico-ecclesiastical organization,
thereby rendering them intelligible. This is what I understand by
Mauss's insistence on interpretation in terms of "total social phenomena," and he shows what he means by that in his essays on
seasonal variations of the Eskimos and on gift exchange. The purpose of the investigation does not go beyond an attempt to discover
the essential features of the phenomena studied by relating them to
other social phenomena.

These writers are mostly dealing with complexes of ideas. When
I said that we are shown the fundamental features of magical, sacrificial, or burial rites, the stress should perhaps have been placed
on these rites as expressions of conceptions and values. The world
of ideas and moral sentiments was the ambience in which these
scholars moved, and they were chiefly interested in trying to understand the world of ideas, symbols, and values of primitive men,
especially those of a religious and moral order. A study might be
made of this group of French intellectuals, not only the sociologists
but Bergson, Proust, and many others, in relation to their dual
Jewish rationalist upbringing and Catholic background. Considering that the sociologists among them were agnostics or atheists
who believed in some kind of secular non-Comteian religion of humanity or ritualized system of ethics, it might be thought that they
would have considered religious subjects not worthy of their first
attention. But they had too great an understanding of religion, and
they were rationalists too sceptical of rationalism, to take that
view. Moreover, they could not fail, given both their own high-
minded purpose and the enormous importance they attached to
ideals in collective life, to have sympathy, and even admiration, for
religious idealism, and in particular for Christian and Jewish faith
and teachings. I discuss this point no further than to draw attention to Durkheim's almost obsessive interest in religion and especially his fascination with the idea of *Ecclesia;* to the probability
that Mauss's interest in sacrifice began with a like fascination with
the drama of the Sacrifice of the Mass, and with his interest in
prayer (his unfinished essay) according to Catholic manuals; and
to the origin of Hertz's planned great study of sin and pardon

which, he makes it very clear, was his deep interest in the Sacrament of Auricular Confession. Hertz was very critical of, and, indeed, found it difficult not to express contempt for, what he called "rationalist theologians," and I think it is fairly obvious what he meant by that.

Ideas and values were not for these scholars a mere ideological reflection or superstructure of the social order. On the contrary, they rather tended to see the social order as an objective expression of systems of ideas and values. Lévy-Bruhl, an independent thinker close to the Durkheimians but whom they never persuaded to join their admittedly somewhat doctrinaire group (another brilliant contemporary writer, Van Gennep, kept, or was kept well away from it), paid lip-service to the view that primitive systems of thought are functions of institutions and vary accordingly, but he never tried to show that, in fact, this is the case. Having made this formal profession of faith, he proceeded, and grandly, to examine what really interested him, the structure of primitive thought as a virtually independent system of phenomena. Durkheim himself was also most interested in systems of moral and religious ideas as an order *sui generis*. No doubt passages, even many of them, could be cited to the contrary—that is often the case with a man who has written much and over many years—but taking Durkheim's writings as a whole, and giving particular emphasis to those of his maturity, we may agree with Lévi-Strauss that Durkheim progressively reached the conclusion that social processes "belong to the realm of ideals, and consist essentially of values." ("French Sociology" in *Twentieth Century Sociology*, 1945, pp. 508–9.) Indeed it would be difficult not to go further and agree with Dr. Peristiany when he says, "Durkheim declares that to explain the function of ideals by the contribution they make to the maintenance of the equilibrium, the solidarity or the survival of a society (as some sociologists tend to do, in the mistaken belief that they are following Durkheim's teaching) is to misconstrue the central tenet of his sociology, which assumes that, in social life, not only are all individuals subordinated to society, but that society itself is a system of ideas, a system which is neither an epiphenomenon of social morphology nor an organ devised to satisfy material needs." (Introduction to *Sociology and Philosophy*, pp. xxviii–xxix.) He eschewed mechanical explanations and appeals to inevitability, and to have done otherwise would have run counter to the personal position he took in relation to political and social affairs. Durkheim was a fervent socialist of the brand of liberal socialism of his time. So also were Lévy-Bruhl, Mauss, and others among his collaborators. I have mentioned earlier Hertz's pamphlet for the Socialist Party. In the same series, which he appears to have founded and organized, were Bianconi's brochure *L'Assistance et les communes* and Halbwachs's *La Politique foncière des municipalités*. They were also fervent patriots, and also republicans. In his brochure Hertz advocated certain social reforms which he thought might halt the depopulation of France due to premature deaths and a low birthrate. His what we would call today "welfare state" views happened to be in accord in this question with socialist propaganda, but his advocacy was in the interests of all Frenchmen, and it was objective, well balanced, and just. Nevertheless, one cannot help remarking that, in showing how weakness, stupidity, and evil are associated with the left side, he did not mention the political connotations of left and right!

It is, therefore, unfortunate that Durkheim's most quoted affirmation is to the effect that social facts are in some manner to be regarded as "things" (*des choses*), for "thing" is certainly not a scientific term but a word of common thought and speech which has the general sense of "concrete" in contrast to "abstract." Its use by Durkheim suggests that social facts are like objects, whereas what he wished to emphasize was that they are general phenomena and therefore objective. Had he used a word like "phenomena" instead of "things" much misunderstanding might have been avoided, as in this typical passage: "If it is indisputable that the social life is composed exclusively of representations, it in no way follows that an objective science cannot be made of it. The representations of the individual are phenomena equally interior; but, nevertheless, contemporary psychology treats them objectively. Why should it be otherwise with collective representations?" (In a review of Charles Seignobos's, "La Méthode historique appliquée aux sciences sociales" (1901), *Année sociologique*, V, 1902, p. 127.)

Above all, Durkheim and his collaborators of the *Année sociologique* were not economic materialists. His hostility to Marxism is well known. In his treatment of totemism he shows the total inadequacy of those who take the view that it is to be explained in terms of utility, and he shows, I think conclusively, that the regard paid to the totemic creatures is both secondary and symbolic. On to the creatures are posited conceptions and sentiments derived from elsewhere than from them. We see in Hertz's essay on the right hand the same priority given to ideas and values. The simple, the obvious explanation, that the organic asymmetry of the two hands lies at the basis of the classification of ideas and values into right and left categories, is rejected, and in its place he maintains that the hands have become the symbols, perhaps in that their slight asymmetry made them suitable for such, of polarities in thought and values because the duality in the universe of ideas must be centered in man who is the center of them; and that, if the asymmetry cannot be denied, it has been increased, often to the point of almost complete disparity, by complexes of ideas and feelings (collective representations) which the hands are made to symbolize. I am not competent to say whether or to what degree, or even in what sense, there can be said to be an organic asymmetry between the hands. The question is a very complex one, since it is partly a matter of age and situation; but it would appear that the cultural and social element is, as Hertz held, a most important, perhaps the dominant, factor in determining the degree of final disparity. Once this is understood, the asymmetry is not beyond human control. The left hands of the children of the future can be freed from guilt and inaction. Again, the easy explanation of social procedures after death is horror at the passing, the *rigor mortis,* and the onset of dissolution, but Hertz shows very clearly that in many cases there is a minimum of reaction at death, an almost entire lack of concern, so that this cannot be the right interpretation. On the contrary, the more repulsive features of dissolution, far from being shunned or secreted, are often emphasized for all to see, for they exhibit objectively the passing of the soul to its happy home. The changing condition of the body signifies changing mental states in the survivors. There is the same preoccupation with sentiments or values, though perhaps less with conceptions, in his fascinating study of the cult of Saint Besse.

Hertz's essays have also still some theoretical interest. Method and theory are not, of course, the same, but it can be said that a method of analysis is of value only if it produces some advance in theory, and that an advance in theory is as important as an exemplification of method as it is in itself. Theory in social anthropology is on a rather low level of abstraction. I consider it to be a theoretical contribution to social anthropology when something both new and significant is discovered about some important institution characteristic of primitive societies of a certain type. Even if the facts were known before as separate pieces of information, there is a theoretical advance when they are brought together and shown to be particular instances of a general fact both widespread and important, e.g., exogamy, teknonymy, rites of passage, taboo, *mana,* homeopathic, and contagious magic, etc. A theoretical advance can be, and often is, made by intensive study of a single society or social form whereby some essential features of an institution are revealed which are then found to be characteristic of a certain type of society, such as Fustel de Coulanges's analysis of the old Roman, and Robertson Smith's analysis of the old Arabian, lineage system. A theoretical contribution may be couched in terms of historical development, as was Maine's theory of movement in law from status (archaic) to contract (modern). Hertz's contribution in his essays on *Death* and *The Right Hand* was twofold. It was known, of course, that some peoples have a mortuary ceremony in addition to rites of burial, and even two disposals of the bodily remains, and also that among some peoples right and left have other senses besides those of spatial orientation, but it was not until Hertz brought together and carefully sifted a mass of information bearing on these subjects that it became evident that we are here dealing not with some sporadic and aberrant phenomena but with complexes of phenomena so widely distributed throughout the world that a common origin or borrowing are alike highly improbable, so that they invite general interpretations of a sociological kind.

His second contribution was to provide such interpretations, and they were both new and significant. Whether they are entirely correct is another matter; as everybody knows, a theory may be valuable though eventually it be shown to be inadequate. Certainly they are stimulating hypotheses which can, at least with regard to many points, be put to the test by further research.

I cannot pretend to go all the way with Hertz. It would be surprising, and not at all to the credit of our discipline, if one could do so fifty years after his essays were written. As I have said, I do not find his fundamental theoretical principle, the dichotomy of sacred and profane, of great value or even very meaningful. I consider his final attribution of secondary mortuary rites to failure of people to adjust themselves, save over a very long period of time, to the deaths of their kinsfolk an inadequate interpretation of the facts. But I have found his presentation of the problems and some of his solutions of them most useful in my own research. There are also faults in method. The main one, common to so many anthropological theorists and fatal to their constructions, was to ignore the negative instances. If a general theory is put forward as an explanation of some custom or institution of primitive peoples, it must be shown in the terms of that theory how to account for the fact that there are primitive peoples who do not have the custom or institution, or among whom it has a very different character. This is a great weakness, it seems to me, in the books and essays of the *Année* group.

To take Hertz as an example, what about peoples who do not have secondary disposals of the dead or even secondary mortuary ceremonies? What about those who do not associate opposed values with the two hands? It is true that he does mention the case of the Zuni Indians, among whom the left is regarded as far from inferior to the right, but only to dismiss this awkward case, as Durkheim used to do, as a "secondary development." Logically, it may appear to be a secondary development; but the case would have to rest on historical evidences, which are lacking. A further example is Hertz's emphasis, fortified by what Meillet (the comparative linguist of the *Année* group) told him, that in the Indo-European languages the term for right has shown great stability while the terms for left have shown considerable variability, which suggests that people avoided the word for left, using euphemisms, which in their turn had to be avoided. It is true that he instances only the Indo-European languages, but an explanation of this sort based on a single instance is no explanation at all. Other examples are necessary if it is to be more than a guess. I have investigated this point in the Nilotic languages of East Africa, spoken by peoples at least some of whom associate a duality of values with the left and the right, and I found that there the term for left has been highly stable, as has indeed also the term for right, which shows only phonetic variations in the different Nilotic tongues. The tendency Hertz mentions may be peculiar to one culture. One wonders whether it is found frequently, or even at all, among primitives.

There are also general statements which cannot be sustained. That "primitive thought attributes a sex to all beings in the universe and even to inanimate objects: all of them are divided into two immense classes according to whether they are considered as male or female" would be a most doubtful statement for many primitive peoples. Again, when he says that "collective thought is primarily concrete and incapable of conceiving a purely spiritual existence," there would be little difficulty in confuting so bald an assertion if it has the meaning it appears to have. It is much modified in *"Le Péché et l'expiation dans les sociétés primitives"* (p. 34) where he criticizes Frazer's conception of the "naturalistic positivism" of primitives and cites Lévy-Bruhl and Durkheim to show that it is not in accord with the facts. Then, would any anthropologist accept today as a general proposition about primitive peoples: "What more sacred for primitive man than war or the hunt!"

One feels sometimes in reading his essays a remoteness from the realities of primitive life. This is not to be wondered at, for, like the Master himself, Hertz had never seen a primitive people, nor, with the exception of Henri Beuchat, who died of hunger and cold on a geographical and ethnographical expedition on the Island of Wrangell in 1914, had any of the group of writers about primitive institutions among Durkheim's collaborators. This was undoubtedly a disadvantage and was seen by them to have been one; and had it not been for the holocaust of 1914–18 it would doubtless have been overcome. But we must not exaggerate the disadvantage, for it is open to question whether the wide reading a student can undertake during the many years he would have been engaged in carrying out field research and writing it up for publication does not to a considerable degree compensate him for the lack of first-hand experience of primitive peoples. I doubt whether any field anthropologist has made a more important contribution to theory than Davy's study of contract in his *La Foi jurée* or Bougle's study of caste (*Essais sur le régime des castes*), to mention only two books; and I am convinced that no field study of totemism has excelled Durkheim's analysis. I would even say that no field study of the structure of primitive thought has surpassed in depth and insight the last volumes of Lévy-Bruhl, in spite of his diffuse treatment of the subject. It is a fact, which none can deny, that the theoretical capital on which anthropologists today live is mainly the writings of people whose research was entirely literary, who brought to bear great ability, much learning, and rigorous methods of scholarship on what others had observed and recorded. When that capital is exhausted we are in danger of falling into mere empiricism, one field study after another adding to the number of known facts, but uninspired and uninspiring. If a personal note be allowed, I would, though with serious reservations, identify myself with the *Année* school if a choice had to be made and an intellectual allegiance to be declared.

Had he lived, the young Hertz might have become the equal of his teacher. One day perhaps, Mauss said in mourning his Master and his collaborators, France would replace them. *"Peut-être, la sève reviendra. Une autre graine tombera et gernera."*

Appendix
Notes and Comments

MÜLLER (1823–1900)

Max Müller was the founder in this country of comparative philology, comparative mythology, and comparative religion. He was a staunch Protestant ("the Protestants are better Christians than the Romans") and a devout one, but one of the reasons he was not elected to the Chair of Sanskrit at Oxford in 1860 was that it was said his teaching was subversive of the Christian faith—"unsettling." Furthermore he was a German. He was the most powerful representative of the nature-myth school, a predominantly German school, mostly concerned with Indo-European religions, its thesis being that the gods of antiquity, and by implication gods anywhere and at all times, were no more than personified natural phenomena: sun, moon, stars, dawn, the spring renewal, mighty rivers, etc. Müller spent most of his life at Oxford where he became professor of comparative philology and a Fellow of All Souls. He was a linguist of quite exceptional ability, one of the leading Sanskritists of his time, and in general a man of great erudition; and he has been most unjustly decried. He was not prepared to go as far as some of his more extreme German colleagues, not just because at Oxford in those days it was dangerous to be an agnostic, but from conviction, for he was a pious and sentimental Lutheran; but he got fairly near their position, and, by tacking and veering in his many books to avoid it, he rendered his thought sometimes ambiguous and opaque. In his view, as I understand it, men have always had an intuition of the divine, the idea of the Infinite—his word for God—deriving from sensory experiences; so we do not have to seek its source in primitive revelation or in a religious instinct or faculty, as some people then did. All human knowledge comes through the senses, that of touch giving the sharpest impression of reality, and all reasoning is based on them, and this is true of religion also: *nihil in fide quod non ante fuerit in sensu.* Now, things which are intangible, like the sun and the sky, gave men the idea of the infinite and also furnished the material for deities. Max Müller did not wish to be understood as suggesting that religion began by men deifying grand natural objects, but rather that these gave him a feeling of the infinite and also served as symbols for it.

Müller was chiefly interested in the gods of India and of the classical world, though he tried his hand at the interpretation of some primitive material and certainly believed that his explanations had general validity. His thesis was that the infinite, once the idea had arisen, could only be thought of in metaphor and symbol, which could only be taken from what seemed majestic in the known world, such as the heavenly bodies, or rather their attributes. But these attributes then lost their original metaphorical sense and achieved autonomy by becoming personified as deities in their own right. The *nomina* became *numina*. So religions, of this sort at any rate, might be described as a "disease of language," a pithy but unfortunate expression which later Müller tried to explain away but never quite lived down. It follows, he held, that the only way we can discover the meaning of the religion of early man is by philological and etymological research, which restores to the names of the gods and the stories told about them their original sense. Thus, Apollo loved Daphne; Daphne fled before him and was changed into a laurel tree. This legend makes no sense till we know that originally Apollo was a solar deity, and Daphne, the Greek name for the laurel, or rather the bay tree, was the name for the dawn. This tells us the original meaning of the myth: the sun chasing away the dawn.

Müller deals with belief in the human soul and its ghostly form in a similar manner. When men wished to express a distinction between the body and something they felt in them other than the body, the name that suggested itself was breath, something immaterial and obviously connected with life. The word "psyche" came to express the principle of life, and then the soul, the mind, the self. After death the psyche went into Hades, the place of the invisible. Once the opposition of body to soul had thus been established in language and thought, philosophy began its work on it, and spiritualistic and materialistic systems of philosophy arose; and all this put together again what language had severed. So language exercises a tyranny over thought, and thought is always struggling against it, but in vain. Similarly, the word for ghost originally meant breath, and the word for shades (of the departed) meant shadows. They were at first figurative expressions which eventually achieved concreteness.

Particularly in his *Introduction to the Science of Religion* (1882 edition) Max Müller is so verbose and so imprecise that it is often difficult to know what he is driving at, even what his sentences mean. He was a sententious deist of the worst possible Victorian-cum-Lutheran sort. There can be no doubt that Müller and his fellow nature-mythologists carried their theories to the point of absurdity; he claimed that the siege of Troy was no more than a solar myth: and to reduce this sort of interpretation to farce, someone, I believe, wrote a pamphlet inquiring whether Müller himself was not a solar myth! Leaving out of consideration the mistakes in classical scholarship, it is evident that, however ingenious explanations of the kind might be, they were not, and could not be, supported by historical evidence adequate to carry conviction, and could only be, at best, erudite guesswork. I need not recall the charges brought against the nature-mythologists by their contemporaries, because although Max Müller, their chief representative, for a time had some influence on anthropological thought, it did not last, and Müller outlived such influence as he had once had.

NIEBOER (1873-19)

In 1900, H. J. Nieboer published *Slavery as an Industrial System* a discussion of the part slavery has played in the social history of mankind. He was concerned with discovering the conditions favorable and unfavorable for the institution of slavery; an enquiry requiring the use of the comparative method. This method can be used for historical reconstruction, but, as Nieboer writes "It is sociological laws that we want in the first place" (p. xvi). Nieboer claimed that the field of inquiry should be that of savages, whose simple social life enables us easily to determine the factors which govern it and the effect of each of them. "We can thus, by comparing the institutions of many savage tribes, find sociological laws, several of which govern the social life of civilized nations" (p. xvi). Nieboer was well aware of the inadequacy of much of the available ethnographical information and attempted to assess the value of his sources. He followed Tylor's and Steinmetz's use of the (miscalled) statistical method in stating his findings in numbers and he protested against what many ethnologists do: "They have some theory, found by deductive reasoning, and then adduce a few facts by way of illustration" (p. xvii).

In *Slavery* Nieboer shows that the sort of slavery he is discussing is not found among hunters and fishers, except among the Indians of the northern coast of California, where special conditions, particularly an abundance of food, obtain; nor among true pastoralists, because among these people slave labor would be of no advantage and might even be a disadvantage. Likewise, it is not found where capital is required to procure subsistence, e.g., sledges and dogs among the Eskimos; or where there is no land unappropriated, as in most of the Oceanic islands, for men without capital to exploit resources (or without resources to exploit) are compelled to work for others. So in these conditions there is free labor and there is no need for personal compulsion, whereas when a sufficiency of food can be obtained by the labor of each for the support of himself and his family force has to be used to get a man to work for another. Such is Nieboer's main theme, and his conclusions seemed to him to be borne out by a study of the economic history of England and Germany. But all the old difficulties are present: the inadequacy of the sources (handled with critical caution, it is true); the difficulty of definition, as, for instance, between slavery and serfdom, and indeed of classification also, for to what degree is it meaningful to put the culturally developed Indians of California in the same class as the Aboriginals of Australia? We have to note again the complexity of the facts or the great number of factors at play, many of them not economic (as Nieboer fully accepts), which make it doubtful whether the causal correlation of slavery with economic states can be sustained. Nor, to give one negative instance, does his thesis appear to be supported by the history of Roman slavery, though there is some obscurity about the facts. Many qualifications, therefore, have to be introduced; and it must be said that, in any case, the conclusions take us little beyond what one might have expected: as a rule slaves are not kept when there is no use for them.

One of the merits of Nieboer's treatise is that he eschewed the evolutionary presuppositions which marred McLennan's and Spencer's and Tylor's treatments. He expressly stated that his classification of economic, or rather bionomic, types is for the purposes of the investigation of states and not of stages.

VAN GENNEP (1873–1957)

Arnold Van Gennep wrote several important anthropological treatises and many important books on folklore, including the volumes of *Manuel de folklore français*. Nevertheless, in spite of his erudition and excellent researches, he never received high academic recognition and was, indeed, cold-shouldered by Durkheim and his colleagues of the *Année sociologique*, whose writings he subjected to some merciless criticism, particularly in his *L'État actuel du problème totémique* (1920). This may partly be why his other books have made less impact on anthropologists, ethnologists, and sociologists, and why he is chiefly remembered for his *Les Rites de passage* (1908).

Van Gennep achieved in this book an enviable reputation by drawing attention to the widespread distribution of a common symbolic structure in transition rites celebrated to mark the passing of a person, or of a group of persons, from one social state to another—pregnancy, birth, puberty, marriage, death, and so on. Others, for example Hertz and, long before him, Fustel de Coulanges, had remarked on this symbolic structure, but it was Van Gennep who treated the subject exhaustively.

He was not speaking of physiological processes but of changes in social status. The two are, of course, connected, but social puberty, for example, often does not coincide with physical puberty, nor social death with physical death. The rites performed on such occasions, he claimed, had not been understood by writers like Tylor and Frazer because they had been considered in isolation and not taken as wholes or sequences. Only then does their meaning become apparent for only then is it seen that they consist of three related movements or phases: rites of separation (*séparation*), rites of transition (*marge*), and rites of incorporation (*aggrégation*).

The person, or group, is first cut off from earlier social attachments, then passes through a period of isolation, and finally is brought into a new social world or reintegrated into the old one. The essential character of all such ceremonies is to be found in this pattern; and furthermore ceremonies cannot be fully understood even when treated as sequences of interconnected rites; it is necessary also to consider each sequence in relation to the others, as a series which organizes the whole lives of persons and groups, passing them from one status to another from birth to death and beyond the grave. These changes of condition produce social disturbance (*perturbation sociale*), and it is the function of transition rites to reduce their harmful effects by restoring equilibrium.

Such was Van Gennep's main thesis. It may seem commonplace today but it was a revelation at the time of its publication. The thesis illustrates both the strength and the weakness of the comparative method. When used with Van Gennep's skill it reveals the general character, as distinct from particular cultural forms, of social phenomena. But the fact that they are general makes a functional explanation of them (reducing social disturbance) appear vague, inadequate and even platitudinous; and this is especially so when inconclusive instances are either ignored or are not convincingly accounted for. But the book still has theoretical value as well as historical significance.

MAUSS (1872–1950)

Marcel Mauss, Emile Durkheim's nephew and most distinguished pupil, was a man of unusual ability and learning, and also of integrity and strong convictions. After Durkheim's death he was the leading figure in French sociology. His reputation was closely bound up with the fortunes of the *Année sociologique* which he helped his uncle to found and make famous; some of the most stimulating and original contributions to its earlier numbers were written by him in collaboration with Durkheim and Hubert and Beuchat: *"Essai sur la nature et la fonction du sacrifice"* (1899), *"De quelques formes primitives de classification: contribution à l'étude des représentations collectives"* (1903), *"Esquisse d'une théorie générale de la magie"* (1904), and *"Essai sur les variations saisonnières des sociétés eskimos: essai de morphologie sociale"* (1906).

The war of 1914–18, during which Mauss was on operational service, almost wiped out the team of brilliant younger scholars whom Durkheim had taught, inspired, and gathered around him—his son André Durkheim, Robert Hertz, Antoine Bianconi, Georges Gelly, Maxime David, and Jean Reynier. The Master did not survive them (d. 1917). Had it not been for these disasters, Mauss might have given us in ampler measure the fruits of his erudition, untiring industry, and mastery of method. But he not only wrote about social solidarity and collective sentiments. He expressed them in his own life. For him the group of Durkheim and his pupils and colleagues had a kind of collective mind, the material representation of which the *Année* was its product. And if one belongs to others and not to oneself, one expresses one's attachment by subordinating one's own ambitions to the common interest. On the few occasions I met Mauss I received the impression that this was how he thought and felt, and his actions confirmed it. He took over the labors of his dead colleagues. Most unselfishly, neglecting his own researches, he undertood the heavy task of editing, completing, and publishing the manuscripts left by Durkheim, Hubert (who died in

1927), Hertz, and others. He undertook also, in 1923-4, the even heavier task of reviving his beloved *Année,* which had ceased publication after 1913. This imposed an added burden on him and further deflected him from the field of his own chief interest. Mauss became a Sanskrit scholar and a historian of religions at the same time as he became a sociologist, and his main interest throughout his life was in comparative religion or the sociology of religion. But he felt that the new series of the *Année* must, like the old one, cover the many branches of sociological research, and this could only be done if he took over those branches other than his own which would have been the special concern of those who had died. Consequently, though he published many reviews and review-articles, his only major works after 1906 were the *"Essai sur le don, forme archaique de l'échange"* (1925), *"Fragment d'un plan de sociologie générale descriptive"* (1934), and *"Une catégorie de l'esprit humain: la notion de personne, celle de 'moi' "* (1938). His projected works on prayer, on money and on the state were never completed. But he was active all the time. The second series of the *Année* had to be abandoned, but a third series was started in 1934. Then came the war of 1939-45. Paris was occupied by the Nazis, and Mauss was a Jew. He was not himself injured, but some of his closest colleagues and friends, Maurice Halbwachs and others, were killed. For a second time he saw all around him collapse, and this, combined with other and personal troubles, was too much for him and his mind gave way.

Mauss was in the line of the philosophical tradition running from Montesquieu through the philosophers of the Enlightenment—Turgot, Condorcet, Saint-Simon—to Comte and then Durkheim, a tradition in which conclusions were reached by analysis of concepts rather than of facts, the facts being used as illustrations of formulations reached by other than inductive methods. But while that is true, it is also true that Mauss was far less a philosopher than Durkheim. In all his essays he turns first to the concrete facts and examines them in their entirety and to the last detail. This was the main theme of an excellent lecture delivered at Oxford in 1952 by one of his former pupils, M. Louis Dumont. He pointed out that though Mauss, out of loyalty and affection, studiously avoided any criticism of Durkheim, such criticism is nevertheless implicit in his writings, which are so much more empirical than Durkheim's that it might be said that with Mauss sociology in France reached its experimental stage. Mauss sought only to know a limited range of facts and then to understand them, and what Mauss meant by understanding comes out very clearly in his *Essai sur le don.* It is to see social phenomena—as, indeed, Durkheim taught that they should be seen—in their totality. "Total" is the key word of the *Essai.* The exchanges of archaic societies which he examines are total social movements or activities. They are at the same time economic, juridical, moral, aesthetic, religious, mythological and sociomorphological phenomena. Their meaning can therefore only be grasped if they are viewed as a complex concrete reality, and if for convenience we make abstractions in studying some institution we must in the end replace what we have taken away if we are to understand it. And the means to be used to reach an understanding of institutions? They are those employed by the anthropological fieldworker who studies social life from both outside and inside, from the outside as anthropologist and from the inside by identifying himself with the members of the society he is studying. Mauss demonstrated that, given enough well-documented material, he could do this without leaving his flat in Paris. He soaked his mind in ethnographical material, including all available linguistic material; but he was successful only because that mind was also a master of sociological method. Mauss did in his room what an anthropologist does in the field, bringing a trained mind to bear on the social life of primitive peoples which he both observes and experiences. We social anthropologists therefore regard him as one of us.

But to understand phenomena in their totality it is necessary first to know them. One must be a scholar. It is not sufficient to read the writings of others about the thought and customs of ancient India or ancient Rome. One must be able to go straight to the sources, for scholars not trained in sociological methods will not have seen in the facts what is of sociological significance. The sociologist who sees them in their totality sees them differently. Mauss was able to go to the sources. Besides having an excellent knowledge of several modern European languages, including Russian, he was a fine Greek, Latin, Sanskrit, Celtic, and Hebrew scholar, as well as a brilliant sociologist. Perhaps to their surprise, he was able to teach Sanskritists much that they did not know was in their texts and Roman lawyers much that they did not know was in theirs. What he says about the meaning of certain forms of exchange in ancient India and in ancient Rome in the *Essai sur le don* is an illustration. This was perhaps not so remarkable as when Mauss was able to show how Malinowski had misunderstood his own account of the Trobriand Islanders. His vast knowledge, which Malinowski lacked, of Oceanic languages and of the native societies of Melanesia, Polynesia, America, and elsewhere enabled him to deduce by a comparative study of primitive institutions what the fieldworker had not himself observed.

Apart from its great value as an exercise in method the *Essai sur le don* is a precious document in itself. Of great importance for an understanding of Mauss and for an assessment of his significance as a scholar, since most of his other well-known essays were written in collaboration, it is also the first systematic and comparative study of the widespread custom of gift exchange and the first understanding of its function in the articulation of the social order. Mauss shows what is the real nature, and what is the fundamental significance, of such institutions as the *potlatch* and the *kula* which at first sight bewilder us or even seem to be pointless or unintelligible. When he shows us how to understand them, he reveals not only the meaning of certain customs of North American Indians and Melanesians but at the same time the meaning of customs in early phases of historic civilizations; and, what is more, the significance of practices in our own society at the present time. In Mauss's essays there is always implicit a comparison, or contrast, between the archaic institutions he is writing about and our own. He is asking himself not only how we can understand these archaic institutions but also how an understanding of them helps us the better to understand our own, and perhaps to improve them. Nowhere does this come out more clearly than in the *Essai sur le don,* where Mauss is telling us, quite pointedly, in case we should not reach the conclusion for ourselves, how much we have lost, whatever we may have otherwise gained, by the substitution of a rational economic system for a system in which exchange of goods was not a mechanical but a moral transaction, bringing about the maintaining human, personal, relationships between individuals and groups. We take our own social conventions for granted and we seldom think how recent many of them are and how ephemeral they will perhaps prove to be. Men at other times had, and in many parts of the world still have, different ideas, values and customs, from a study of which we may learn much that, Mauss believed, may be of value to ourselves.

Hocart (1883–1939)

Arthur M. Hocart was an industrious student, prolific writer, and in many respects an original thinker, but he does not appear to have had as much influence on the anthropology of his time as one might have expected. There may have been many reasons for this. He was shy and reserved and some found him awkward and difficult also. He did not occupy a chair till he had one at Cairo at the end of his life, and consequently was not able to influence students by personal contact as well as by his pen. A further reason is that he became identified, quite unjustly, with the University College school of Elliot Smith, Perry, and Raglan, whose theories were considered by most anthropologists of the day to be uncritical to the point of extravagance. But it was with their method rather than with their conclusions that he was in sympathy. Another reason why Hocart did not receive his due was, and still is, the antihistorical bias of most anthropologists in this country. That there is some justification for the bias can be seen from Hocart's book *Social Origins* (1954), which is a collection of essays on various ritual topics, perhaps designed for a course of lectures. Most anthropologists would regard as unduly speculative, if not purely conjectural, the theses, for example, that marriage derives from royal consecration, that human sacrifice—the killing of the king and his rebirth as a baby—is the sacrament which has given rise to all other sacraments, that all rituals began with the chief of the society (a totemic headman or king), that war was originally a ritual activity and that monasticism in Europe was copied from Buddhist monasticism.

Possibly Hocart himself did not take some of these hypotheses very seriously. He had a challenging sense of humor. But he was also a scholar, even if an erratic one, and his wide learning allowed him to draw on original, especially Sanskritic, sources not available to most of his colleagues. He was also a man of ideas who had the courage to put forward theories which most of his colleagues were likely to consider wild. Some of these ideas are most fertile, and he also makes many acute observations. Much of his criticism of theories about animism, *mana*, totemism, and idolatry, which used to be accepted, and among some writers still are accepted, hits the mark. He demolishes with ease the claim that there are primitive peoples completely ignorant of paternity. There may have been other reasons for his lack of recognition, such as a rather arid style and a slightly testy, or at least a not-suffering-fools-gladly, tone in his writings.

Whatever may have been the reasons for his seeming failure, at the time, it was Radcliffe-Brown and Malinowski who attracted more attention with their talk, which now appears naive, about functional interpretations of social phenomena. Neither, however, made any serious attempt to base their claims on anything that could be called a systematic use of the comparative method, and neither could in any case have used it as Hocart did, for neither was a scholar and Hocart was. He had a knowledge of history that they lacked and he, unlike them, could go to the original sources, for he knew Greek, Latin, Sanskrit, Pali, Tamil, and Sinhalese as well as many modern European languages.

His idea of functional interpretation was, if I understand him correctly, to compare the manner in which social activities of one sort or another are carried out in societies of different types, e.g., those of the Arunta, Winnebago, Jukun, ancient Greeks and Romans, the Hebrews, the ancient and modern Egyptians, ourselves. The same function may take widely divergent forms, though Hocart regarded it as axiomatic that there is always a tendency for function to determine structural form. So settlement of disputes by feud and in a court of law are functionally comparable; likewise are a professional man in our society earning money to buy in the market goods to maintain his family and an Australian aboriginal hunting kangaroos to maintain his. This treatment makes it interesting for students in that they learn to see a fundamental similarity beneath a diversity of institutional forms and to appreciate that the form they are familiar with in their own culture is only one of many possible modes of organizing social activities. It is evident that the conclusions derived from comparative analysis will depend on the criteria of classification. If one classes whales with fish and bats with birds one is not going to reach the same conclusions as one would if one classed both as mammals. So we have to bear in mind that Hocart's analysis is based on the sort of functional classification that zoologists use when they class whales and bats among the mammals.

I must here confess that I have not found, granted his method of functional classification, his technique of analysis, rather loaded with conjecture, to be one that I would wish to follow. His anatomical analogy is unenlightening, and his use of words like "identity" and "equivalence" and his constant use of equation signs are confusing, as are such statements as "the king is the sun." But this is a personal reaction, and it should be borne in mind that when Hocart speaks in such terms he does so in functional or symbolic senses, in the senses that in certain situations one thing can be substituted for another.

I am not saying that Hocart's analytical technique is not the right technique or one of the right techniques, but only that it does not appeal to me. It may appeal more to others. What I find more valuable than the dissection of a custom, the breaking down of it into elements, which does not for me make it more intelligible (though this procedure is perhaps more fashionable now than it was in Hocart's day), is the sense of movement imparted by his use of history, a sense so often lacking in anthropological literature; also the implicit indication that everywhere the logic of the situation imposes on the actors in it what might be said to be, at least up to a point, an inevitable structural form; and also, as in Fustel de Coulanges's *The Ancient City*, the insistence that what we today regard as institutions established for their utility have as often as not a sacred origin.

Driberg (1888–1946)

Jack Herbert Driberg was born in Assam in April 1888, of an army family. The eldest of three brothers, all of outstanding talent, he was educated at the Grange preparatory School, Crowborough, Lancing College, and Hertford College, Oxford. In 1912, he joined the Uganda administration. In 1921 he was transferred to the Sudan administration at the request of the Government of the Anglo-Egyptian Sudan, but retired from it on medical grounds in 1925. He did not always agree with these administrations about policy and methods and made no pretence of doing so. He had already published before his retirement an important ethnological monograph on the Lango tribe of Uganda and various other papers about other peoples, and on the basis of these and other unpublished studies he decided to start a new career as an anthropologist. With this end in view, he worked with Seligman and Malinowski at the London School of Economics and Political Science, where he had also the advantage of studying sociology with Wallas and Ginsberg, and prehistory with Childe. From 1927 to 1929 he gave courses of lectures at the London School of Economics and at University College, mostly on African subjects. In 1931, he began to lecture in the Department of Archaeology and Anthropology at Cambridge on the invitation of Professor Hodson and was appointed to a full-time faculty lectureship in that department in 1934, a post which he held till he relinquished it at his own wish in 1942 to do special work in connection with military operations in the Middle East. On his return to England till the time of his sudden death in February 1946 he was working in the Middle East section of the Ministry of Information. He was happy in his new post, for it continued his contact with Arab and Muslim affairs: he had accepted Islam and was buried in that faith in the Muslim cemetery near Woking.

Jack Driberg would have been the same person in any walk of life. The classical scholar, heavyweight boxer of distinction, poet, and musical critic, of Oxford; the successful administrator who won the affection of those he administered, exceptional linguist, and fighter, of Central

Africa; the inspiring tutor, stylist, and brilliant talker—at his best *splendide mendax*—of London and Cambridge; and the volunteer for desperate hazards in the years of war; all were of one piece, gay, versatile, lovable, and adventurous—an Elizabethan. His was a rare spirit and his weaknesses were consistent with the heroic in his personality and further endeared him to his friends. The gods give us faults to make us men.

Jack Driberg's romantic figure made him a great success as a teacher at Cambridge. Students felt at once that here was something outside the ordinary academic run. They admired him, and he was therefore able to influence them more than a learned anthropologist but less impressive man might have done. He had *baraka*. To him is largely due the continued development of the Cambridge Department into a flourishing school. First with Hodson, and afterwards with Hutton, he worked wholeheartedly to advance the subject of anthropology in the university, and its subsequent position is in no small measure due to his untiring efforts. He would have been an even better teacher if financial difficulties had not forced him to over-lecture, as they forced him also to overwrite. Although the Cambridge Department in his time produced no research workers, dozens of his students held administrative posts in different parts of the Empire, especially in Africa, owing their first interest in native peoples to his teaching. His work continued to bear fruit as the years went by.

As a writer, Jack Driberg was, apart from his descriptive fieldwork accounts, more a talented popularizer than an original thinker. He started academic anthropology late in life and had not the leisure afterwards, or perhaps even the bent of mind, to acquire a spacious theoretical background. He was less interested in general problems of social anthropology than in particular ethnographical problems of a special region. No one knew his theoretical limitations better than himself. For teaching purposes and in writing popular textbooks, where some theoretical approach is necessary, he made extensive use of Malinowski's lectures and writings. His own original contributions were to the ethnology of East Africa, a region about which he had unrivaled personal knowledge.

In spite of the lack of originality of his popular writings he performed an essential service to anthropology by spreading knowledge of its aims and methods. No one could have been better qualified to do this, for he wrote easily and well. His more popular books satisfied also a long-felt want for short introductions to social anthropology for students beginning the subject, whether undergraduates in the universities or in adult extra-mural classes (he was a very successful W.E.A. lecturer): such books as *The Savage as He Really Is* and *At Home with the Savage*. In *People of the Small Arrow*, he used the medium of the historical vignette to portray primitive African life to the English reader, and in *Initiation,* poetry.

However, he will not be remembered in the history of anthropology by his teaching, since it did not lead to research, or by his more popular writings, which are too much the product of a period, but by his fieldwork monograph *The Lango*. For the time it was written (1923), *The Lango* is rightly regarded as an outstanding piece of research, and it will always remain one of the few classical accounts of an African people before the lives of Africans were strongly influenced by European rule and commerce. That he wrote so good a book is due not only to his powers of observation, which were considerable, but also to his capacity for affection for the people about whom he wrote.

STEINER (1909–1952)

Franz Baermann Steiner was born in Czechoslovakia in 1909 and died at Oxford in 1952. He took a Ph.D. in Semitic languages and ethnology at the University of Prague, and later came—shortly before the Second World War—to Oxford to continue his anthropological studies at Magdalen College (Professor Radcliffe-Brown being in the Chair of Social Anthropology at the time). Czechoslovakia was overrun by Nazi forces and Steiner's family and almost all his close kin were murdered by them. Added to his misfortunes, if indeed anything can be added to so overwhelming a disaster, was not only poverty but also the loss of the fruit of many years' research. He had almost completed a doctoral thesis for Oxford University on servile institutions, when it was mislaid on a journey by train, together with the notes on which it was based, and was never recovered. It had to be entirely rewritten. It was at the time it was being rewritten that, having succeeded Professor Radcliffe-Brown in the Chair at Oxford, I first came into close contact with Franz Steiner. He was a sick man, but with great fortitude rewrote his thesis and was awarded his doctorate in 1950. His scholarship and remakable breadth of learning had long been the admiration of his colleagues, and it was much to their satisfaction that in the same year he was appointed to a University Lectureship in Social Anthropology in the University of Oxford. He was a teacher of rare ability, and he was beloved by both students and colleagues. His disappointments and disasters which might have soured another man, only made Franz Steiner more tolerant, more gentle, and more serene. His ill health continued, however, and though he seemed to be better—and at least was happier and more secure—he died very suddenly in the autumn of 1952. He was buried in the Jewish burial ground at Oxford. In the later years of his life, the faith and religious practice of his fathers were of increasing concern to him.

But in spite of his learning, or because of it, he could not publish an article that was not based upon a critical analysis of every source, in whatever language; and he had published almost nothing on anthropological subjects before his death, although since his death a number of articles have been revised and published by his Oxford friends: "Enslavement and the Early Hebrew Lineage system: An Explanation of Genesis, xlvii. 29–31, xlviii. 1–16" (*Man*, 1954, no. 102); "Notes on Comparative Economics," (*The British Journal of Sociology*, V, no. 2, 1954); "Chagga Truth: A Note on Gutmann's Account of the Chagga Concept of Truth in *Das Recht des Chagga*," (*Africa*, XXIV, 1954). The results of his field research in the Carpathian Ukraine were never published. While working on anthropological subjects he was also engaged in many other intellectual activities—philosophy, semantics, Old Testament exegesis, and also poetry. He was, I am told, a considerable poet. A number of his poems had already been published in German periodicals before his death. A volume of them, selected by his friend and literary executor, Dr. H. G. Adler, had recently appeared under the title *Unruhe ohne Uhr.*

At the time of his death Franz Steiner was engaged in preparing for publication several anthropological treatises, a sociological study of Aristotle (of which nothing except notes has been found among his papers), a book on the sociology of labor, which would have been his thesis rewritten for publication, and a critical analysis of theories of taboo. His study of taboo had reached the stage of being delivered as a course of lectures at Oxford. Though he would doubtless have revised and added to them before submitting them for publication, they were fully typed, and appeared in print, save for minor revisions, as he left them.

Taboo has often been a subject of anthropological inquiry since Captain Cook first used the word in his account of the Polynesians. It has been treated at some length by Robertson Smith, Frazer, Freud, Lévy-Bruhl, Van Gennep, Radcliffe-Brown, and others. The theories put forward by these writers were critically examined by Steiner, and he subjected the sources on which they relied to the closest scrutiny. He showed how inadequate most of these theories were and, though he did not reach any positive conclusions himself, his book is of great value to anyone interested in the idea of taboo and to those who in the future tackle once more the problems it raises.

MALINOWSKI (1884–1942)

Bronislaw Malinowski began lecturing in London in 1924. Raymond Firth (later Professor Sir) and I were his first two anthropological pupils in that year, and between 1924 and 1930 he taught most of the other social anthropologists who subsequently held chairs in Great Britain and the Dominions. The comprehensive field studies of modern anthropology can be fairly said to derive directly or indirectly from his teaching, for he insisted that the social life of a primitive people can only be understood if it is studied intensively, and that it is a necessary part of a social anthropologist's training to carry out at least one such intensive study of a primitive society.

A pupil of Hobhouse, Westermarck, and Seligman, Malinowski not only spent a longer period in fieldwork than any anthropologist before him, in a single study of a primitive people, the Trobriand Islanders of Melanesia between 1914 and 1918, but he was also the first anthropologist to conduct his research through the native language, as he was the first to live throughout his work in the center of native life. In these favorable circumstances Malinowski came to know the Trobriand Islanders well, and he was describing their social life in a number of bulky, and some shorter, monographs up to the time of his death.

His best known work is *Argonauts of the Western Pacific,* published in 1922. He starts off with a general discussion of the method and scope of his field-research, and then gives the general ethnological background to it: a general account of the country and inhabitants of the *kula* district and their way of life; then a similar picture of the natives of the Trobriand Islands. Having described in great detail the *kula* exchanges and a mass of peripheral information, Malinowski finally makes an attempt to tell us the meaning of the *kula.* The attempt is a failure, for he offers us no sociological interpretation of it of any sort. Why is this? Malinowski had no idea of abstract analysis, and consequently of structure. In so far as he had any idea of "social system" it was on a purely descriptive level. One event follows another and they are described in succession with explanatory digressions. To make *kula,* one has to have canoes, so their construction and use are described; it involves visiting foreign peoples, so their customs, crafts, and so forth are described; magical spells are used for various purposes connected with *kula,* so every aspect of magic has to be gone into in detail; there are stories of past *kula* expeditions, so there has to be a digression on myth; and so on. Having no idea of structure, there is no standard of sociological relevance. The standard is one of links between real happenings, and the so-called analysis is no more than a commentary. The book is much more concerned with magic than with *kula.* All he tells us could easily have gone into 50 pages rather than into over 500 pages. In a sense it is a piece of book making on the model of a sociological novel, for example by Zola. The failure to get away from a bare record of observation and to make analysis by a series of abstractions means that not only are we told nothing of the political interrelations of the communities concerned in the *kula* and nothing of the kinship system, but even the essential facts about the *kula* itself are omitted. He does not tell us who traded with whom; we are not told the interrelationships of the persons composing the villages which take part in the *kula;* and so forth.

The interdependencies he does cite are not those of abstractions within a theoretical framework such as we find in any natural science (which Malinowski held social anthropology to be) but between different forms of behavior—events. The Trobrianders make magic to protect their gardens and canoes or to make the one flourish and the other swift. It is an interdependence of economic and ritual activities in the sense of temporal and spatial connection—of juxtaposition. But if it was a functional interdependence, for example, would they cultivate any differently or any less without magic? This cannot be known by his method of research. It can only be known by the experimental situation provided by history or by the use of the comparative method. Certainly the use of the comparative method necessitates the idea of "system" or "structure." One does not compare a whale and a mouse as concrete, real things. One compares their anatomical and physiological systems. Likewise one cannot compare real institutions in different societies—

only features or aspects or qualities of them—i.e., abstractions. For example I compared Zande magic with Trobriand magic, but only in reference to the nature of the spell in relation to rules of inheritance. The weakness of Malinowski's approach becomes very clear when he attempts to say something general about human societies rather than about one particular society.

In a later book, *Crime and Custom in Savage Society* (1926), Malinowski writes: "We can only plead for the speedy and complete disappearance from the records of field-work of the piecemeal items of information, of customs, beliefs, and rules of conduct floating in the air, or rather leading a flat existence on paper with the third dimension, that of life completely lacking. With this the theoretical arguments of anthropology will be able to drop the lengthy litanies of threaded statement, which make anthropologists feel silly and the savage look ridiculous" (p. 126).

On the basis of this sort of information had been erected a vast edifice of anthropological theory. Since the information was largely meaningless so must be the constructions based on them. Malinowski thought it his task to free anthropology from this impasse. This book is aimed at Lévy-Bruhl's mystical savage, at the ideas of Rivers and the French School about clan solidarity, and at the hypothetical reconstructions of Rivers and others. Primitive law had received attention from Bachofen, Post, Kohler, and others in the last century, but they relied on inadequate statements; in a complex subject like law amateur observations were on the whole useless. They were also tied to the doctrine of Morgan and others: primitive promiscuity, group marriage, primitive communism, and so on. "In short," writes Malinowski, "underlying all these ideas was the assumption that in primitive societies the individual is completely dominated by the group—the horde, the clan or the tribe— that he obeys the commands of his community, its traditions, its public opinion, its decrees with a slavish, fascinated, passive obedience" (p. 3). Malinowski has no difficulty in showing that all this is nonsense, and we owe him a great debt for acting as a critical dissolvent of accepted theory, even though his contribution was negative rather than positive. But he was unscrupulous in his use of theoretical writers as strawmen and quite unconstructive theoretically—he gives no real theory of law or even an elementary definition of it or classification of its types.

Malinowski's most mature views are represented in his posthumous but almost completely revised book *A Scientific Theory of Culture and Other Essays* (1944). It is a good example of the morass of verbiage and triviality into which the effort to give an appearance of being natural–scientific can lead. Malinowski was in any case a futile thinker.

What Malinowski calls a theory is not really theory at all but is a guide to the collection and setting forth of data, a fieldworker's *vade mecum*, a wordy *Notes and Queries*. It never rises above the descriptive and operational level of analysis; and it is for the most part a verbose elaboration of the obvious and the erection of commonplaces into scientific concepts. Malinowski himself seems to have sensed this. He says (p. 175) of this book, or rather of the functional theory contained in it, that "it is meant primarily to equip the field-worker with a clear perspective and full instructions regarding what to observe and how to record." He says also, "This type of functional analysis is easily exposed to the accusation of tautology and platitude, as well as to the criticism that it implies a logical circle, for, obviously, if we define function as the satisfaction of a need, it is easy to suspect that the need to be satisfied has been introduced in order to satisfy the need of satisfying a function. Thus, for instance, clans are obviously an additional type of internal differentiation. Can we speak of a legitimate need for such differentiation especially when the need is not ever present, for not all communities have clans, and yet they go on very well without them." The book is an exercise in pragmatism and Malinowski therefore equivocates when discussing what he does not like—war. He deems that it does not satisfy a need in modern Europe. Why then do we have it?

RADCLIFFE-BROWN (1881–1955)

A. R. Radcliffe-Brown was educated at King Edward's High School, Birmingham, and at Trinity College, Cambridge, where he read the Mental and Moral Sciences Tripos. At Cambridge he came into contact with W. H. R. Rivers and A. C. Haddon, who turned his interests toward social anthropology. He was later greatly influenced by French sociology, especially by the writings of Durkheim. His own influence on the development of social anthropology was effected partly through the publication of the results of his field research in the Andaman Islands and Australia, but it was far more strongly felt in the contribution he made to theory, and especially methodology, in papers and even more by his lectures.

He wrote with great clarity both of style and of reasoning, but he wrote with difficulty and it would not be easy to know how he became so outstanding a figure in the anthropological world were one to consider his writings alone. His eminence was due rather to his power of inspiring enthusiasm among his students with whom he was always ready to discuss the problems of their science, not only in the lecture room but at any time and in any place. He numbered these students all over the world, for during his career he held chairs at Cape Town, Sydney, Chicago, Oxford, Alexandria, Yengching, Sao Paolo, Grahamstown, and Manchester. He also taught at the London School of Economics, at University College, London, and at Johannesburg. The spread of his teaching was thus very wide.

Radcliffe-Brown's main contribution to anthropological thought lies in his clear expositions, his felicity in choosing appropriate terms—he was a fashioner of conceptual tools. In this way he did not lead his students into rather slick psychological explanations, and he eschewed guesswork history (one must add, all history). He continued to advocate the establishment of laws or universals, in the sense of propositions to which there are no exceptions, by comparative analysis, though he did not use statistics, and his version of the comparative method was in practice mainly a return to the illustrative method. Indeed, I have to say, with regret, that Steinmetz would have stigmatized much of what he wrote as idle speculation, and Nieboer would have regarded it as an example of what he strongly protested against, the capricious practice of some writers of thinking up some plausible explanation of some social phenomenon and then searching around for illustrations which seem to support it and neglecting the rest of the related material. I cite briefly a few examples. In his early paper "The Mother's Brother in South Africa," he may have been right in challenging the concept of survivals, but his positive contribution does not seem to me to be, as it has been claimed to be, a model of scientific procedure: quite the contrary. He tries to show that, according to what he calls the principle of equivalence of siblings, the sentiment of tenderness towards the mother is extended to her brother and that of respect for the father to his sister, but he makes no attempt in that paper to relate this supposed extension to the kinship system as a whole (for instance, the mother's brother is also the father's wife's brother), to property rights, to political authority, and so forth. The evidences are selected and are furthermore restricted to five illustrations (the sources for two of the societies not being given), every other people in the world being ignored, though they all have sister's sons and mother's brothers. The argument is no more than circular redescription and is, anyway, invalidated by the evidence from other societies, particularly by Malinowski's later and detailed information about the Trobriand Islanders. In another essay Radcliffe-Brown (whose views about the relation of sociology to history, it may be borne in mind, were those of Comte and of the Marxist theorists), tells us that the form taken by religion is determined by the form of social structure, so we may expect to find, for example, ancestor cult where there is a lineage system, as in China or ancient Rome; but there are many societies with ancestor cults without a trace of a lineage system, and the most perfect example of a lineage system is perhaps that of the Bedouin Arabs, who are Muslims. In yet another essay he asserts that where man depends largely on hunting and collecting for the means of subsistence, animals and plants are made objects of "ritual attitude," this being a particular instance of a general law: that any object or event which has important effects on the material or spiritual well-being of a society tends to become an object of "the ritual attitude." But this is simply just not the case, unless we are to understand by "ritual attitude" attention of any sort, thereby depriving the expression of any precise meaning. The general law ignores in its application to totemic phenomena a vast mass of ethnographic evidence, particularly in Africa, which runs counter to the thesis put forward. Nor does the evidence from pastoral and agricultural peoples support it. A final example: he says that where societies are divided into moieties, these are in a state of balanced opposition, opposition being defined as "a combination of agreement and disagreement, of solidarity and difference." How, we may ask, could it be otherwise? The statement is a truism contained in the definition of moieties, and much the same could be said of any social group. Such generalizations supported by a few selected illustrations, are either so general as to be devoid of significance or, where more precisely formulated, rest on too slender a base of evidence and fail to take into account negative evidences. Kroeber's comment on the old dilemma of the sociologist is relevant: "by the time he finds a formula that no one can cite exceptions to, it has become so essentially logical, so remote from phenomena, that no one knows precisely what to do with it."

WHITE (1900–1975)

Leslie A. White is an extreme determinist and historical materialist. He is a Marxist, though he does not emphasize his dependence on Marx, but rather on the more rigid expositions of Durkheim. In fact, he does little more than substitute for Durkheim's "social," "society" and "sociological" the words "cultural," "culture," and "culturological." However, the distinction he draws between the sciences of sociology and culturology is not at all a clear one, especially with regard to Durkheim. What White regards as culture—artifacts and symbols—are for Durkheim social things, the material or ideational links between members of a society or community of one kind or another. In *The Science of Culture* (1949), White tries to establish a separate science of culture, culturology, by arbitrarily reducing the scope of sociology to an ill-defined social psychology, which is little more than the psychology of individuals acting as members of social groups, and since they act in no other way this is as much as to say that there is no science of sociology, only sciences of psychology and culturology. His discussion of the matter is little more than terminological. Durkheim never distinguished between society and culture, e.g., language was for him the medium of communication between members of a society, not something *sui generis,* which can be studied without regard to its social function. It follows that the criteria Durkheim used in the definition of a social fact are those used by White to define a cultural fact: generality, transmissibility, and the quality of being both external and obligatory. A man is born into a society (culture) which existed before he did, he puts it on as he would a suit of clothes, and it is equally there when he is no more. Consequently social (cultural) facts are super-organic or extra-somatic and therefore cannot be understood in biological or psychological terms, but only in terms of other social (cultural) facts.

White adopts the Comteian classification of the sciences, particularly his three stages, the animistic, the metaphysical, and the positive. He adopts also the Marxian thesis that the history of man is a history of technological changes, each producing other cultural changes and causing also changes in productive relations and consequently in every kind of social institution. All this happens quite regardless of human will, which is an illusion. "But the fallacy of assuming that we can increase and perfect our control over civilization through social science is even more egregious than we have indicated. To call upon science, the essence of which is acceptance of the principles of cause and effect and determinism, to support a philosophy of Free Will, is fairly close to the height of absurdity. Verily, science has become the modern magic! The belief that man can work his will upon nature and man alike *if only he had the right formulas* once flourished in primitive society as *magic*. It is still with us today, but we now call it science" (p. 343).

Man, then, is a creature of culture, which obeys its own laws. What these laws are is not clear, beyond the unquestionable fact that culture tends to be cumulative. But this can hardly be called a law, especially as White admits that the whole thing may be destroyed by hydrogen bombs. If there is to be a natural science of culture there must be laws of culture, but White tells us no more about them than did Tylor, the first culturologist (in White's opinion) in that he set out to explain cultural traits in terms of their association, historic, geographic, and functional, with other cultural traits. He was concerned with that, not with human beings (social interaction). "The next noteworthy attempt to establish a science of culture was that of Emile Durkheim" (p. 88); but White thinks that by "collective representations" he really refers to cultural traits, as when he says, for example, "We need to investigate, by comparison of mythical themes, popular legends, traditions, and languages, the manner in which social representations (i.e. culture traits) adhere to and repel one another, how they fuse or separate from one another" (p. 89).

On the negative side, White is right. Human behavior is to be explained in terms of human behavior and not by appeal to psychological tendencies. But what has he to offer on the positive side? Nothing. Once again, we are told at length how one must proceed in a scientific study of cultures, but there is little to show of the kind of testable general statements which it is held can be derived from a comparative study. He really makes only one attempt at an explanatory analysis of one item of culture, the incest taboo.

White's general thesis is that "Nowhere is culture a mere aggregation or agglomeration of traits; culture elements are always organized into systems. Every culture has a certain degree of integration, of unity; it rests upon a certain basis, and is organized along certain lines or principles. Thus, a culture may be organized around the hunting of seal, reindeer breeding, the cultivation of rice, or manufacturing and trade. Military activity also may be an important factor in the organization and life of a culture. Within any given cultural system a number of sub-systems, which we may call patterns, can be distinguished. Painting, music, mythology, philosophy, or science, mechanics, industrial crafts, the medical arts, and so on are such patterns" (p. 215). In chapter XI, he wishes to prove this general thesis in his treatment of the topic of incest taboos. His explanation of the prohibition is that put forward by Tylor, but is as old as St. Augustine: by compelling members of a group to marry out the group has to make many alliances outside itself and consequently is integrated through these links into a wider society, thereby greatly increasing its strength and security. He states this conclusion as follows: "But when we turn to the cultures that determine the relations between members of a group and regulate their social intercourse we readily find the reason for the definition of incest and the origin of exogamy. The struggle for existence is as vigorous in the human species as elsewhere. Life is made more secure, for group as well as individual, by co-operation. Articulate speech makes co-operation possible, extensive, and varied in human society. Incest was defined and exogamous rules were forumulated in order to make co-operation compulsory and extensive, to the end that life be made more secure. These institutions were created by *social* systems, not by *neuro-sensory-muscular-glandular systems*. They were syntheses of culture elements formed within the interactive stream of culture traits. Variations of definition and prohibition of incest are due to the great variety of situations. In one organization of culture traits—technological, social, philosophic, etc.—we will find one type of definition of incest and one set of rules of exogamy; in a different situation we find another definition and other rules. Incest and exogamy are thus defined in terms of the mode of life of a people—by the mode of subsistence, the means and circumstances of offense and defense, the means of communication and transportation, customs of residence, knowledge, techniques of thought, etc. And the mode of life, in all its aspects, technological, sociological, and philosophical, is culturally determined" (pp. 328-9).

Now, a blanket explanation of this sort is of very little value in itself and certainly does not constitute a law. To achieve this significance it would have to be shown how the many different definitions and extensions of the incest prohibition and rules of exogamy do in fact vary with other social institutions. It is no use blandly asserting that they will be found to do so. We are at once brought up against negative instances which have to be explained in terms of the theory, or the theory has to be abandoned. It is the same old story: 415 pages telling us that cultures are natural systems subject to rigorous laws, both functional and historical, but there is nothing in them about any actual cultures as exemplifications of these laws. What are these interdependencies and how do they vary concomitantly? It is a curious but highly significant fact that not the slightest attempt is made by White in his writings about American Indians, the record of his considerable field research, to demonstrate the validity of his theoretical standpoint by appeal to ethnographic fact.

Bibliography

A full bibliography of Evans-Pritchard's work, edited by T. O. Beidelman, has been published by Tavistock Publications, 1974. The only subsequent addition to that is the republication of the 1936 article, "Science and Sentiment: An Exposition and Criticism of the Writings of Pareto," in *J.A.S.O.* V, no. 1. 1974.

Many of Professor Sir Edward Evans-Pritchard's notes and unpublished articles contained quotes and book references but no page, edition, or volume details. In most cases it has been possible to locate these and include them both in the text and in the bibliography.

ABBREVIATIONS

B.F.A.   *Bulletin of the Faculty of Arts* (Faud I University; now Egyptian University, Cairo)
J.A.S.O.   *Journal of the Anthropology Society of Oxford*
J.R.A.I.   *Journal of the Royal Anthropological Institute*
T.L.S.   *The Times Literary Supplement*, London

SOURCES USED FOR COMPILATION

1933   "The Intellectualist (English) Interpretation of Magic," *B.F.A.* I, pt. 2
1934   "Lévy-Bruhl's Theory of Primitive Mentality," *B.F.A.* II, pt. 2; republished in *J.A.S.O.* I, no. 2, 1970
1936   Review of *Pareto* by Franz Borkenau, *Man* XXXVI, 172
1936   "Science and Sentiment: an Exposition and Criticism of the Writings of Pareto," B.F.A. III, pt. 2; republished in *J.A.S.O.* V, no. 1, 1974
1940   Obituary of Lucien Lévy-Bruhl, *Man* XL, 27
1947   Obituary of Jack Herbert Driberg, *Man* XLVII, 4
1951   *Social Anthropology*, Cohen & West

1952 Obituary of Franz Baermann Steiner, *Man* LII, 264
1954 Introduction to *The Gift* by Marcel Mauss, Cohen & West
1955 "Ritual Topics," review of *Social Origins* by A. M. Hocart, *T.L.S.*, 591
1955 Obituary of A. R. Radcliffe-Brown, *The Times*, Oct. 27
1956 Preface to *Taboo* by Franz Steiner, Cohen & West
1960 "Ritual Reintegration," review of *The Rites of Passage* by Arnold Van Gennep, *T.L.S.*, 236
1960 Introduction to *Death and the Right Hand* by Robert Hertz, Cohen & West
1962 *Essays in Social Anthropology*, Faber & Faber
1963 *The Comparative Method in Social Anthropology*, Athlone Press
1964 Foreword to *Sacrifice* by H. Hubert and M. Mauss, Cohen & West
1965 *Theories of Primitive Religion*, Clarendon Press, Oxford
1965 Foreword to *The "Soul" of the Primitive* by Lucien Lévy-Bruhl, Allen & Unwin
1970 Foreword to *Kings and Councillors* by A. M. Hocart, edited by R. Needham, University of Chicago Press
1970 Review of *Frazer and the Golden Bough* by R. Angus Downie, *T.L.S.*, 28
1971 "John Millar," *J.A.S.O.* II, no. 3
1972 "Adam Ferguson," *J.A.S.O.* III, no. 1
1972 "Henry Home, Lord Kames," *J.A.S.O.* III, no. 2
1972 "Condorcet," *J.A.S.O.* III, no. 3
1973 "Montesquieu," *J.A.S.O.* IV, no. 2

WORKS CITED IN THE TEXT

ARON, R., *Les étapes de la pensée sociologique*, Paris, 1967.
BEATTIE, J. H., *Other Cultures*, 1964.
BLACK, J. S., and CHRYSTAL, G., *The Life of William Robertson Smith*, 1912
BORKENAU, F., *Pareto*, 1936.
BOUSQUET, G. H., *Précis de sociologie d'après Vilfredo Pareto*, 1925.
CHARLTON, DONALD G., *Positivist Thought in France during the Second Empire, 1852–70*, Oxford, 1959.
COMTE, A., *Cours de philosophie positive*, 6 vols., 1830–42.
    Système de politique positive, ou traite de sociologie, instituant la religion de l'humanité, 4 vols., Paris, 1851–4.
    Catéchisme positiviste, Paris, 1852 (1966 edition with introduction by Pierre Arnaud).
    Testament d'August Comte, 1884.
CONDORCET, MARQUIS DE, *Esquisse d'un tableau historique des progrès de l'esprit humain*, ed. O. H. Prior, Paris, 1933 (The *Esquisse* was first published in Paris in 1795).
    Sketch for a Historical Picture of the Progress of the Human Mind, translated by June Barraclough, with an introduction by Stuart Hampshire, 1955.

Bibliography

Choix de textes, ed. J. B. Severac (*Les grands philosophes français et étrangers*)

COULANGES, F. DE, *La Cité antique*, Paris, 1864.

DICEY, A. V., *Lectures on the Relation Between Law & Public Opinion in England*, London, 1920.

DRIBERG, J., *The Lango*, London, 1923.

DURKHEIM, E., "La prohibition de l'inceste et ses origines," *Année sociologique*, 1, 1898.
  "De la définition des phénomènes religieux," *Année sociologique*, 2, 1899.
  "Sur le totémisme," *Année sociologique*, 5, 1902.
  Les Règles de la méthode sociologique, Paris, 1895.
  Les Formes élémentaires de la vie religieuse, Paris, 1912.

FERGUSON, ADAM, *An Essay on the History of Civil Society*, 1766. Page numbers cited come from 1967 edition edited by Duncan Forbes.
  Institutes of Moral Philosophy, 1772.
  The History of the Progress and Termination of the Roman Republic, 1783.
  Principles of Moral and Political Science, 2 vols., 1969.

FRAZER, SIR, J. G., *Condorcet on the Progress of the Human Mind*, Zaharoff Lecture, 1933.
  The Gorgon's Head, 1927, pp. 369–83. See also in the same book "The Road to the Scaffold," pp. 384–92.
  The Golden Bough, 1900.

GOLDENWEISER, ALEXANDER A., "Review of *Les Formes*," *American Anthropologist*, 1915.

HERTZ, R., "Contribution à une étude sur la représentation collective de la mort," *Année sociologique*, vol. x, 1907.
  "La prééminence de la main droite: étude sur la polarité religieuse," *Revue philosophique*, LXVIII, 1909.
  "Saint Besse," *Revue de l'histoire des religions*," 1913.
  "Contes et dictons," *Revue des traditions populaire*, 1917.
  "Le Péché et l'expiation dans les sociétés primitives," *Revue de l'histoire des religions*, 1922.

HOCART, A.. M., *Social Origins*, London, 1954.

HOMANS, G. C., and CURTIS, C. P., *An Introduction to Pareto, his Sociology*, 1934.

HOME, HENRY (LORD KAMES), *Essays on the Principles of Morality and Natural Religion*, 1751.
  Elements of Criticism, 1762.
  Sketches of the History of Man 1774.

JOGLAND, HERTA HELENA, *Ursprünge and Grandlagen der Soziologie bei Adam Ferguson*, Berlin, 1954.

KANEKO, UMAJI, *Moralphilosophic Adam Ferguson's* (sic), Lucka, 1903.

KETTLER, DAVID, *The Social and Political Thought of Adam Ferguson*, Ohio, 1965.

LEHMANN, WILLIAM C., "Adam Ferguson and The Beginnings of Modern Sociology," Ph.D. dissertation, Columbia University, 1930.

LEVI-STRAUSS, C., "French Sociology" in *Twentieth Century Sociology*, 1945.

LÉVY-BRUHL, D., *La Philosophie d'Auguste Comte*, 1900, fourth edition, 1921.

 La Morale et la science des moers, 1903.

 Les Fonctions mentales dans les sociétés inférieurs, 1912 (trans. *How Nations Think*, 1926).

 La Mentalité Primitive, 1922 (trans. *Primitive Mentality*, 1923).

 L'Âme primitive, 1927 (trans. *The 'Soul' of the Primitive*, 1928).

 Le Surnaturel et le nature dans la mentalité primitive, 1931 (trans. *Primitives and the Supernatural*, 1936.)

 La Mythologie primitive, 1935.

 L'Expérience mystique et des symbols chez les primitifs, 1938.

 Les Carnets de Lucien Lévy-Bruhl, 1949.

LOWIE, ROBERT H., *Primitive Religion*, 1936.

LUBBOCK, J., *The Origin of Civilisation*, 1870.

LUKES, STEVEN, *Emile Durkheim. His Life and Work*, 1973.

MAINE, H., *Ancient Law*, 1861.

MALINOWSKI, B., "Review of *Les Formes*," *Folk-Lore*, 1913.

 Argonauts of the Western Pacific, 1922.

 Crime and Custom in Savage Society, 1926.

 A Scientific Theory of Culture and Other Essays, 1944.

MARX, KARL, *The Poverty of Philosophy*, 1910.

MAUSS, M., *Essai sur le don, forme archaique l'échange*, 1925.

 Fragment d'un plan de sociologie générale descriptive, 1934.

 Une categorie de l'esprit humain: la notion de personne, celle de 'moi,' 1938.

MCLENNAN, J. F., *Primitive Marriage*, 1865.

 Studies in Ancient History, 1876. 2nd series edited by his widow and Arthur Platt, 1896.

 Patriarchal Theory, 1885.

MILL, J. S., *Auguste Comte and Positivism*, 1865 (Michigan, 1961).

MILLAR, JOHN A., *A Historical view of the English Government from the Settlement of the Saxons in Britain to the Revolution in 1688*, 1786, 1803.

 The Origin of the Distinction of Ranks or an Inquiry into the Circumstances which give rise to Influence and Authority in the different Members of Society, 1771. Page numbers cited come from 4th edition, Edinburgh, 1806.

MONTESQUIEU, CHARLES-LOUIS DE SECONDAT, BARON DE, *Oeuvres complètes*, 3 vols; 1950–5.

 Considerations on the Cause of the Greatness of the Romans and their Decline, translation by David Lowenthal, 1965 (first published anonymously in French in Holland in 1734).

 L'Esprit des lois, 4 vols, 1950–61. (I have used a French edition of 2 vols. (Editions Garniers Frères), n.d. But page numbers cited come from an English translation, *The Spirit of Laws*, 1750.)

MORGAN, H., *The Systems of Consanguinity and Affinity*, 1871.

MÜLLER, M., *Introduction to the Science of Religion*, 1882.

Bibliography

MYREŞ, J. L., "The Method of Magic and of Science," *Forklore*, 36, 1925.

NIEBOER, H. J., *Slavery as an Industrial System*, The Hague, 1900, 2nd edition, 1910.

PARETO, V., *Trattato di Sociologia Generale*, 2 vols. 1916.
The Mind and Society, 4 vols., 1935.

PETERS, E. L., "Proliferation of Segments in the Lineage of the Bedouin of Cyrenaira," *J.R.A.I.*, 90, 1960.

POLLOCK, F., *Principles of Contract*, 1876.

RADCLIFFE-BROWN, A. R., *The Andaman Islanders*, 1922.
Structure and Function in Primitive Society, 1952.

RIVERS, W. H. R., *Medicine, Magic and Religion*, 1927.

ROBERTSON, SMITH, W., *The Old Testament in the Jewish Church*, 1881.
The Prophets of Israel, 1882.
Kinship and Marriage in Early Arabia, 1885.
Lectures on the Religion of the Semites, 1889, 3rd edition, with additional notes by Stanley A. Lock, 1927.
Lectures and Essays of William Robertson Smith, 1912.

SCHMIDT, R. W., *The Origin and Growth of Religion*, 1931 (German edition, 1912).

SEIGNOBES, C., *La méthode historique appliquée aux sciences sociales*, 1901.

SOROKIN, P., *Contemporary Sociological Theories*, 1928.

STANNER, W. E. H., *On Aboriginal Religion* (The Oceania Monograph No. 11), 1963.
"Reflections on Durkheim and Aboriginal Religion," *Social Organization, Essays presented to Raymond Firth*, 1967.

STEINER, F., "Enslavement and the Early Hebrew Lineage system: An explanation of Genesis," *Man*, 1954.
"Notes on Comparative Economics," *British Journal of Sociology*, V, 1954.
"Chagga Truth," *Africa*, XXIV, 1954.

STEWART, DUGALD, *Collected Works of Dugald Stewart*, 10 vols., Edinburgh, 1854–8.

STREHLOW, T. G. H., *Aranda Traditions*, 1947.

TYLOR, E., *Anuhuac*, 1861.
Researches into the Early History of Mankind, 1865.
Primitive Culture, 1871.
"On a Method of Investigating The Development of Institutions; applied to Laws of Marriage and Descent," *J.R.A.I.* XVIII, 1889.

VAN GENNEP, A., *Les Rites de passage*, 1908.
L'État actuel du problème totémique, 1920.

WEBB, C. C., *Group Theories and Religion and the Individual*, 1938.

WHITE, L. A., *The Science of Culture*, 1949.

Index

Index

Index